LINCOLN CHRISTIAN COLLEGE AND SEMINARY

D1288379

Helping Others
Help Children

Helping Others Help Children

Clinical Supervision of Child Psychotherapy

EDITED BY

T. Kerby Neill

AMERICAN PSYCHOLOGICAL ASSOCIATION

Washington, DC

Copyright © 2006 by the American Psychological Association. All rights reserved. Except as permitted under the United States Copyright Act of 1976, no part of this publication may be reproduced or distributed in any form or by any means, including, but not limited to, the process of scanning and digitization, or stored in a database or retrieval system, without the prior written permission of the publisher.

Published by
American Psychological Association
750 First Street, NE
Washington, DC 20002
www.apa.org

To order
APA Order Department
P.O. Box 92984
Washington, DC 20090-2984
Tel: (800) 374-2721
Direct: (202) 336-5510
Fax: (202) 336-5502
TDD/TTY: (202) 336-6123
Online: www.apa.org/books/
E-mail: order@apa.org

In the U.K., Europe, Africa, and the Middle East, copies may be ordered from
American Psychological Association
3 Henrietta Street
Covent Garden, London
WC2E 8LU England

Typeset in Goudy by World Composition Services, Inc., Sterling, VA

Printer: Data Reproductions, Auburn Hills, MI
Cover Designer: Minker Design, Bethesda, MD
Technical/Production Editor: Genevieve Gill

The opinions and statements published are the responsibility of the authors, and such opinions and statements do not necessarily represent the policies of the American Psychological Association.

Library of Congress Cataloging-in-Publication Data

Helping others help children : clinical supervision of child psychotherapy / edited by T. Kerby Neill.— 1st ed.
    p. cm.
   Includes bibliographical references and index.
   ISBN 1-59147-404-3
   1. Child psychotherapy—Study and teaching. 2. Psychotherapists—Supervision of. I. Neill, T. Kerby.

RJ504.H42 2005
618.92'8914—dc22
                                       2005032542

British Library Cataloguing-in-Publication Data
A CIP record is available from the British Library.

Printed in the United States of America
First Edition

CONTENTS

115299

CONTRIBUTORS

Ignacio David Acevedo-Polakovich, MS, Department of Psychology, University of Kentucky, Lexington

Tamara L. Brown, PhD, Department of Psychology, University of Kentucky, Lexington

Patricia Callan Burke, LCSW, Division of Child and Adolescent Psychiatry, Center for School Mental Health Analysis and Action, University of Maryland School of Medicine, Baltimore

Kathleen M. Chard, PhD, PTSD Division, Cincinnati Veteran's Administration Medical Center, Cincinnati, OH

Christina C. Clark, PsyD, Independent Practice, University Psychological Services Association, Inc., Dayton, OH

James J. Clark, PhD, LCSW, College of Social Work and College of Medicine, Department of Psychiatry, University of Kentucky, Lexington

Elizabeth L. Croney, LCSW, Croney & Clark, Inc., Lexington, KY

Phillippe B. Cunningham, PhD, Family Services Research Center, Department of Psychiatry and Behavioral Sciences, Medical University of South Carolina, Charleston

Eleanor T. Davis, LCSW-C, Division of Child and Adolescent Psychiatry, Center for School Mental Health Analysis and Action, University of Maryland School of Medicine, Baltimore

Robert D. Friedberg, PhD, ABPP, Department of Psychiatry, Pennsylvania State Milton S. Hershey Medical Center, Pennsylvania State College of Medicine, Hershey

Joseph E. Hansel, EDS, University of Kentucky, Lexington

Jennifer L. Hartstein, PsyD, Adolescent Depression and Suicide Program, Montefiore Medical Center, Albert Einstein College of Medicine, Bronx, NY

Scott W. Henggeler, PhD, Family Services Research Center, Department of Psychiatry and Behavioral Sciences, Medical University of South Carolina, Charleston

Elizabeth L. Holloway, PhD, Leadership and Organizational Change Program, Antioch University, Yellow Springs, OH

Hans Otto Kaak, MD, Professor of Psychiatry and Pediatrics, University of Kentucky Medical Center, Lexington

Philip C. Kendall, PhD, ABPP, Department of Psychology, Temple University, Philadelphia, PA

Alec L. Miller, PsyD, Department of Child and Adolescent Psychology, Montefiore Medical Center, Albert Einstein College of Medicine, Bronx, NY

T. Kerby Neill, PhD, Department of Psychiatry, University of Kentucky, Lexington

Jeff Randall, PhD, Family Services Research Center, Department of Psychiatry and Behavioral Sciences, Medical University of South Carolina, Charleston

Dee C. Ray, PhD, LPC, NCC, RPT–S, Child and Family Resource Clinic, Counseling Program, University of North Texas, Denton

Sonja K. Schoenwald, PhD, Family Services Research Center, Department of Psychiatry and Behavioral Sciences, Medical University of South Carolina, Charleston

Andrea M. Smith, MS, Department of Psychology, University of Kentucky, Lexington

Michael A. Southam-Gerow, PhD, Department of Psychology, Virginia Commonwealth University, Richmond

Sharon H. Stephan, PhD, Division of Child and Adolescent Psychiatry, Center for School Mental Health Analysis and Action, University of Maryland School of Medicine, Baltimore

Carolyn Webster-Stratton, RN, PhD, Director, Parenting Clinic, University of Washington School of Nursing, University of Washington, Seattle

Mark D. Weist, PhD, Division of Child and Adolescent Psychiatry, Center for School Mental Health Analysis and Action, University of Maryland School of Medicine, Baltimore

ACKNOWLEDGMENTS

This work reflects the authors' own professional journeys—a sharing of the professional traditions of which we are a part—and our new vision. We have gathered our thoughts afresh to look to the futures of children and the role that the therapists we train may play in their lives.

Like most professionals of my time, I became an instant supervisor. I was prepared by a solid internship at the VA's Perry Point Medical Center and the Menninger Foundation's postdoctoral program in clinical child psychology, where I received superb, cross-disciplinary supervision but no training in supervision. In 1970, I began work in an inner-city clinic in New Haven, Connecticut, and received an immediate baptism of fire—supervising fellows in Yale's postdoctoral psychology program, psychiatric residents, social workers, and African American paraprofessionals who, in the militant 1970s, were suspect of any White man, especially if he was green. I have continued to supervise in Kentucky, making efforts along the way to build my supervisory capacity through reading, workshops, and the wisdom of colleagues. In preparing this book, I have virtually drowned in readings on supervision and child psychotherapy. As 30 years of supervisory life passed before my eyes, I realized I would do much differently now.

The impetus for this book came in 2000 when my wife and I returned from 18 months of work in a Guatemalan barrio. I was asked to conduct a supervision workshop for the Kentucky Board of Psychology. In preparing for the workshop, I was struck by the paucity of writing on supervision with children. I mused about writing on supervision of child psychotherapy, and my family reacted so enthusiastically that they turned musing to action. Their encouragement sustained this effort.

I quickly realized this work would require collaborators. I thank all those who contributed chapters and acknowledge many who were extremely gracious in their tolerance of editorial harassment. I encouraged contributors to be practical. Though our work would be grounded in professional research and literature, we were writing for supervisors in the trenches. I hope that the ideas we present will help child supervisors and will encourage others, in emulation or frustration, to add to the supervision literature in child psychotherapy.

Thomas Pittman, whose skilled neurosurgery saved my life during the revision phase of this book, bears major responsibility for the finished product, but none for any deficiencies in the content. Kathy King and Tag Heister of the Department of Psychiatry at the University of Kentucky were gracious and efficient in obtaining reference material for my chapters. I am grateful to the American Psychological Association (APA) for its support of this effort and to Lansing Hays, Emily Welsh, Emily Leonard, and Genevieve Gill for practical and encouraging editorial support. I owe a debt of gratitude to those who reviewed chapters, both APA's anonymous reviewers whose critiques have greatly enhanced this work, and Ronita Giberson, David Hanna, Kimberly Hoagwood, and especially Paul Stratton, who not only critiqued chapters but also regularly called my attention to articles relevant to this project. My son, Sean Neill, unleashed his considerable editorial talents on several chapters. Brendan Neill's gift of a copier/scanner/printer was an unexpected blessing in this effort. Mary Ellen Garry Neill deserves not only the profound gratitude due a partner whose spouse dares to withdraw and prepare a book but also kudos for reading and reacting to much of the text. She deserves credit for making my and others' writing more readable. I thank her for her love, her unflinching honesty, and her crusade against the use of the passive voice.

Helping Others
Help Children

INTRODUCTION

T. KERBY NEILL

This is a work for supervisors of child psychotherapy: professionals who monitor, train, and care for those who serve children and families. Supervisors influence the clinical culture of the settings where they work. They can be in the vanguard of effective innovation or follow minimally effective fads. They can champion valuable lessons of the past or cling to traditions with no merit. Supervisors will forge the future of child mental health.

Furthermore, this is a book for aspiring child clinicians for it is rich in ideas to help them define goals for professional growth. It should also help them engage in supervision constructively, preparing them to distinguish good supervision from poor supervision. Supervisors are fallible. Although I am fortunate some former supervisees claim me as a valued mentor, I have been guilty of giving poor advice and even of nodding off in supervisory sessions. There is a time to listen and a time to confront.

Psychotherapy supervision is a formal, extended relationship between a credentialed practitioner and a therapist in training to monitor the quality of client care, develop the therapist's abilities, and evaluate the supervisee's readiness to function more independently. Supervision is an integral element in some child and adolescent therapies. Supervisory support is critical to all trainees. Bernstein, Campbell, and Akers (2001) see "caring for caregivers" as essential to sustain clinicians in the nurturing roles they must take with families.

Among the challenges psychotherapists face as supervisors of those who work with children are ballooning service demands, serious financial constraints, urgency to measure treatment outcomes, debates over the effectiveness of treatments, and questions about where our energies are most usefully spent. Today, supervisors support the work of child clinicians in demanding settings. John Weisz (2000), endeavoring to transfer laboratory successes with children to community settings, found it difficult for dedicated therapists in the community to fit new procedures into

> their clinic routines, into their demanding workloads, and into the complex array of . . . life circumstances their clients present. My colleagues and I were wrong, some years ago when we wrote about differences between lab and clinic . . . we underestimated the differences. (p. 1)

In spite of these demands, supervision of child psychotherapy receives little attention. In a recent professional newsletter, an experienced child psychiatrist lamented, "I cannot recall any meetings regionally or nationally for child psychiatry supervisors" (Ritvo, 2003, p. 339). I think her concern can be echoed across the mental health professions.

The first four chapters in this volume consider issues of general relevance to supervising therapy with children: supervision models, the context and current state of child psychotherapy, ethics in child work, and cross-cultural supervision. The next two chapters address supervision of play, filial, and cognitive therapies. The play chapter offers an approach to teaching measurable and meaningful play skills. Play is a basic skill used when engaging and working with children, and many other therapies include elements of play. Cognitive therapies are well established, and cognitive–behavioral elements are strongly represented in many therapies with the best research support.

Chapter 7 describes the struggle to introduce a well-researched, manualized, cognitive–behavioral treatment for anxious children into busy, multidisciplinary, urban mental health centers. While the specific treatment addressed problems less typical of the clinicians' caseloads, the project armed the clinicians with cognitive approaches they found valuable. The chapter offers important lessons for clinical innovators. Multisystemic therapy (MST; chap. 8) is a sophisticated process that incorporates a range of other therapies (e.g., behavioral, interpersonal, cognitive, family, etc.) into an overarching structure. In a tight system of quality assurance, supervision supports clinicians, tackles treatment barriers, and ensures fidelity in a treatment that targets adolescents with serious drug or conduct problems.

The Incredible Years group curriculum for parents and teachers of young aggressive children (chap. 9) offers a well-researched and creatively organized intervention using manuals, compelling videos, and pertinent homework. Group leaders need not be clinicians (often they are teachers), but receive intensive training and continuing supervision to enhance their skills.

Chapters 10 and 11 address therapy with two demanding and highly vulnerable groups: suicidal, self-harming teens and traumatized children. Supervisors of such work must be keenly alert to the therapy process and the emotional toll therapy can exact on clinicians.

Mental health services are profoundly affected by the settings in which they occur. The growing emphasis on offering mental health services, either in schools or in collaboration with schools, makes attention to supervision in school settings of special relevance. Chapter 12 offers supervisors a guide to fostering mental health services in the structure and culture of schools.

This work considers supervision issues across disciplines and supports collaboration rather than competition. The authors reflect different disciplines, cultural experiences, and approaches. They were encouraged to be both scholarly and practical. It is hoped that this work will support supervisors in their efforts to help others help children and families.

REFERENCES

Bernstein, V. J., Campbell, S., & Akers, A. (2001). Caring for the caregivers: Supporting the well-being of at-risk parents and children through supporting the well-being of the programs that serve them. In J. N. Hughes, A. M. La Greca, & J. C. Conoley (Eds.), *Handbook of psychological services for children and adolescents* (pp. 107–131). New York: Oxford University Press.

Ritvo, R. Z. (2003). Clinical scholarship. *AACAP News, 34,* 339.

Weisz, J. (2000). Lab-clinic differences and what we can do about them: 1. The clinic-based treatment development model. *Clinical Child Psychology Newsletter, 15,* 1–3, 10.

1

A SYSTEMS APPROACH TO SUPERVISION OF CHILD PSYCHOTHERAPY

T. KERBY NEILL, ELIZABETH L. HOLLOWAY, AND HANS OTTO KAAK

Supervision of psychotherapy with children, from infancy to age 18, is strikingly distinct from supervision of therapy with adults. Child therapy demands different knowledge, evokes intense emotions in supervisees, and requires engagement with many social systems. It is also more likely to draw supervisors into confronting those systems (Kadushin & Harkness, 2002).

A CASE EXAMPLE IN CHILD PSYCHOTHERAPY SUPERVISION

Sue, a new social worker with a community mental health center (CMHC), has seen 6-year-old Mary twice a week for the 6 months that Mary has been in her fourth foster care placement. Mary, diagnosed with reactive attachment disorder, inhibited type, and her older brother, Jack, an angry boy who often lashes out at others, were placed in state care after being seriously neglected and abandoned. Mary's earlier foster placements ended in 1 to 3 months because the families could not tolerate Jack's

7

behavior. Eric, Sue's supervisor at the CMHC, provides weekly supervision for Sue as required by the state board of social work.

When therapy began, Mary was withdrawn and uncommunicative, but Sue patiently drew Mary out through affirming play. Incrementally, Sue included Mary's current foster mother in therapy. Under Eric's guidance, she designed experiences with Mary and her foster mother to reduce Mary's fearfulness. Mary began to show hopeful signs of bonding with her highly nurturing foster mother and of participating in school.

On a Thursday, Mary's state foster care worker brought her to therapy. He asked to speak to Sue alone at the end of the session and told her that Mary had just completed her last session. Mary and Jack were going to a new foster home in another community on Monday, although Mary was not told about the move to avoid any crisis. The state foster care worker said that Jack had blown the placement by frequently running away and that Jack was currently in an emergency shelter. Sue was stunned but was quickly angered. She insisted that there was no need to move Mary; that Mary's progress could be lost; that therapy requires a termination process; and "that you don't play with kids' attachments or teach them to trust by deceiving them."

Too agitated to see her next client, Sue cancelled and called Eric. Eric called back within the hour, and Sue told her story. Eric tried to calm Sue and promised to call the foster agency. The state supervisor, already informed of the incident by her social worker, immediately questioned Sue's maturity and professionalism. When Eric raised the importance of attachment issues, he was cut off by the state supervisor who said it was policy to place siblings together and the children were going to a therapeutic foster home that could surely handle any upset experienced by Mary.

Challenges the Case Presents for the Supervisor

As a supervisor, Eric has an immediate responsibility to Mary. If he is convinced that this move is harmful and that the current foster mother wishes to continue with Mary, Eric must become Mary's advocate. Often supervisors, not supervisees, have the clout and experience to advocate for clients when it is critical. Eric would be wise to seek professional and legal consultation with Sue observing. He might ask the state foster care agency for extra time to ensure the move is in Mary's best interest. This could allow him to mobilize a measured response and reduce the risk of interagency polarization. Eric must be able to articulate the risks to Mary's future and the therapeutic reasons for staying with her current foster family. He also might need to plead Mary's case up the steps of the state supervisory ladder. If the state persists in the move, Eric may need to ask a court to stay Mary's move and appoint a guardian ad litem to represent her interests.

Less immediately, Eric must support Sue and help her understand that her reaction was valid but expressed unproductively. With Sue, he needs to explore how this crisis may have been prevented—with Sue's mistakes as well as his own on the table. If Eric had insisted on close collaboration with the foster care agency, might their staff have acted differently? Should Eric have ensured teamwork between Sue and Jack's therapist? Was Sue clinically and emotionally prepared for this case? Did she receive adequate supervisory time? What steps might Sue, Eric, and the CMHC take to improve future collaboration between mental health care and foster care?

MODELS OF SUPERVISION

Many supervision theories, models, and approaches enrich the literature, yet writing on supervision of child therapy is sparse. Enzer (1987) noted the special emotions, evident in the opening example, that are often evoked in therapists working with children. Two recent works on supervision in child therapy (Knaus, 2002; Kratochwill, Lepage, & McGivern, 1997) discuss a range of important supervision issues while touching only lightly on what makes supervision of child psychotherapy different. Supervision does not need to be reinvented for child therapy, but the content and emphases of supervision change when working with children. We have chosen to organize our presentation around Holloway's systems approach to supervision (SAS; 1995). As critiqued by Bradley, Gould, and Parr (2001), Holloway's model is comprehensive and friendly to a range of theoretical orientations but is weaker on specific techniques. In weaving the unique fabric of child therapy supervision on Holloway's loom, we have sought to include other supervision models when their colors could illuminate our work.

Particular therapies also have their own supervision emphases. Psychodynamic supervision (Ekstein & Wallerstein, 1958) focuses heavily on the emotional reactions of the supervisee, supervision of client-centered therapy is supervisee-centered (Rogers, 1951), and supervision of behavior therapists reinforces supervisees to implement behavioral therapies (Boyd, 1978). Family therapy offers strong systems perspectives, and the supervisor may engage the therapist and family system through live supervision (Campbell, 2000). Strong parallels between specific therapies and preferred supervision practices are also evident in chapters 6 and 8 of this volume. While acknowledging that one's theory of human nature is not likely to change in transition from therapist to supervisor, Bernard and Goodyear (2004, p. 76) warned that supervision clearly differs from therapy, and a "single lens can lead supervisors to think in 'therapeutic' rather than educational ways about their supervisees." In the 1970s, supervision models forged for graduate training began to more explicitly reflect that difference (Bernard, 1997).

THE SUPERVISORY RELATIONSHIP

The supervisory relationship is central to Holloway's SAS (1995) model. This centrality is echoed in major works on supervision (Bernard & Goodyear, 2004; Falender & Shafranske, 2004; Muse-Burke, Ladany, & Deck, 2001). Holloway understands that the supervisory relationship is fluid, citing Bordin's (1983) perspective that mistakes will occur in supervision but that the weakening and repair of the supervisory alliance are at the heart of its growth and effectiveness. Supervisory relationships that go well tend at first to be didactic and supportive, with a focus on supervisee competencies. As the relationship matures, the focus may shift to the supervisee's personal concerns as they relate to performance. In the end, the therapist requires less direction, and the relationship becomes more consultative. The developmental supervision approach of Stoltenberg, McNeill, and Delworth (1998) proposed a richly detailed view of this process, emphasizing trainees with unique learning styles whose understanding, anxieties, and needs change in the course of becoming therapists and whose supervision must change as well.

ORIENTATION AND THE SUPERVISION CONTRACT

Good supervisory relationships begin with a solid orientation and a detailed contract. There are a few general orientations for supervisees in the literature (Berger & Buchholz, 1993; McCann, 1999), but orientations must also be program specific. Trainees and supervisors are introduced to multisystemic therapy (chap. 8) in intense 5-day workshops. Whitman (2001) described a 90-minute workshop that begins a training cycle for psychiatrists, psychologists, and social workers. Participants begin by sharing past experiences of supervision. Then the trainer discusses contracts and the qualities of good supervisees and supervisors. Trainees are encouraged to confront supervision problems and are given guidance for doing so. Whitman reported that trainees viewed the workshop as a positive commitment of the agency to their training.

It is important that orientations include critical risk issues, such as threats to self and others and domestic violence. In working with children, issues of abuse, confidentiality, boundaries, and limit setting, especially the use of physical limits, need to be clarified. Later review of the orientation information, particularly relating to risk management, is advisable. One therapist described his first day of training as an "exhausting day of newness," noting, "I expect we were told essential information, but I have no recollection of that" (Alred, 1999, p. 254).

Good contracts clarify relationships and expectancies (Hewson, 1999). Contracts specify the time and duration of supervision, means and criteria for evaluation, types of clients and caseload, learning goals, basis for canceling supervision or scheduling additional time, preparation for supervision, treatment approaches, agency expectancies, and expectancies about observation. They emphasize that therapy and supervision occur in an ethical realm. Because gender, culture, and values can significantly affect supervision, supervisory participants should share some of their background and open a discourse on cultural influences on both therapy relationships and their supervisory relationship. This is the time for supervisors to address some of their own limitations and struggles, past and current, that can affect their clinical or supervisory performance. Doing so helps therapists realize that their emotional reactions are integral to clinical practice and relevant to supervision. Supervisors can also share how their own colleagues and supervisors were sources of feedback and growth. Supervisees must be comfortable contacting their supervisors or backups when in doubt. They should know to whom they can turn if supervision is going poorly.

Preparation for supervision must be clarified. Are there forms to be completed? Will an agenda for the session be mutually developed? Is the supervisee expected to bring tapes or clinical records?

THE CONTEXT OF SUPERVISION

According to Holloway (1995), four contextual factors shape the supervisory relationship: the supervisor, the supervisee, the client, and the setting where supervision occurs. The relationship is also shaped by supervision tasks (i.e., growth goals for trainees) and functions (i.e., growth promoting actions by supervisors).

The Supervisor

The Supervisor's Role

Supervisors act in roles of power—they can reward, coerce, or unduly influence trainees (Kadushin & Harkness, 2002). Holloway (1995) explored the concept of "power with" rather than "power over," where the intent is to empower rather than to control the trainee. A balance is most likely achieved when both parties can talk comfortably about their relationship. Failure to achieve such a balance can be harmful to both parties, as exemplified in the following:

A trainee, assigned to a renowned, recently widowed supervisor, received unalloyed praise in every session but did not feel that the supervisor truly engaged him or his work. Insecure and too intimidated by the differences in age, power, and reputation to constructively confront his wounded supervisor as he might a peer, the trainee was happy to accept an "easy A." In a wasted semester, the trainee did not grow, and the supervisor did not receive any invitation to move from grief back to competence.

Power disparities are greatest when the supervisor has both clinical and administrative roles. Problems with a supervisor over nonclinical, administrative issues, or internal agency disputes can complicate supervision. Such concerns prompted Page and Wosket (2001) to recommend clinical supervision by consultants outside of a supervisee's agency. But separate supervisors can also be at odds, as when administrators fail to understand the demands of working with children and families or the requirements of a particular therapy. For this reason, some child treatment approaches insist that the roles be joined (see chap. 8). As combined roles are common, supervisors in dual roles must be alert to the power discrepancies in such supervisory relationships and must model a constructive balance of their roles for the trainee.

The Supervisor's Theoretical Orientation

There is usually a strong tie between a supervisor's theoretical orientation and his or her approach to supervision (Putney, Worthington, & McCulloughy, 1992). Haley (1987) contrasted differences in orientation and their implications for supervision. In Orientation A, responsibility for change is with the client whose spontaneity, growth, and understanding are the keys to change. In Orientation Z, the therapist bears responsibility for change so that planning, problem solving, and action are the keys to intervention. Haley preferred Orientation Z and suggested a highly directive supervisory approach: "the supervisor's task is not only to make the therapy go well . . . but also to protect the family from a beginner's incompetence" (Haley, 1987, p. 216). Carl Rogers, who represents Orientation A, even lamented the term *supervision* and speaks of the need for a person who "will serve as an interested but noncoercive and nonjudgmental source of stimulation and clarification" (Rogers, 1951, p. 475). There are lots of options between Orientations A and Z, and research on styles of supervision suggests that trainees object to approaches that are either too directive or too easygoing (Cherniss & Egnatios, 1977). Ultimately, the supervisor's approach should be governed by the requirements of the therapy and the needs of the supervisee and client. Page and Wosket (2001) stressed the need for clear direction in cases of serious misjudgment, as in the following example.

A supervisee revealed he had taken a 12-year-old, male client for a motorcycle ride during therapy. The supervisor responded angrily, offering several reasons why this was inappropriate. He then explored the supervisee's motives for the ride. Through this exploration, the supervisee became aware of his desire to impress the child, to prove he was manly, and to avoid some of the work of therapy. In this case, a mistake that was confronted became an opportunity for growth.

The Supervisor's Competence and Experience

Munson (2002) suggested that good supervisors read and keep abreast of the literature; write well and guide the writing of supervisees; and become keen observers, listeners, and communicators. Supervisors are expected to be competent in the application of psychological science, in assessment and therapy, and in the development of trainees through supervision (Holloway & Wolleat, 1994). Campbell (2000, p. 4) offered a self-evaluation checklist encouraging prospective supervisors to assess their work as counselors; their supervisory training; their awareness of multicultural, ethical, and legal issues; their ability to conceptualize and manage multiple tasks; and their capacity to support and challenge and to be sensitively present with a supervisee. Though supervision is demanding, few supervisors receive specific training in supervision (Bradley & Kottler, 2001). Because of the strong demand for services to children, clinicians are often prematurely pressed into working with children, and practitioners experienced with children are prematurely pressed into supervising them. Such circumstances are risky. Misguided work can cause harm "so severe as to dwarf the client's original problem" (Caplan & Caplan, 2001, p. 1).

Supervisors who are teaching clinicians to work with children in community settings need to be prepared for a struggle. Supervision on the job is quite different from that in sites dedicated to training (see chap. 7, this volume). In the community, workers have full caseloads, time and facilities for supervision are at a premium, and audio or video review or live supervision may be viewed as luxuries. Because serious learning does not occur "on the fly," the supervisor and trainee should have a powerful interest in more systematic learning. In clinical settings with good learning environments, supervisors often devote as much time to motivating administrators regarding the need for training as they do to motivating trainees.

Universities usually train their students in newer therapies and experienced therapists may want advanced training. In both situations, supervisors may encounter supervisees who are competent in therapies or are experienced with clients who are unfamiliar to the supervisor. The guidelines of the Association of State and Provincial Psychology Boards (ASPPB; 1998, p. 4) have recommended that supervisors should not allow supervisees to engage in practice "they cannot perform competently themselves." This recommendation is designed to protect the client, but the client may also profit from the trainee's skills. Supervisors balance potential gains for the client against risks. "As the supervisor continues to consolidate his or her experience and identity, a greater sense of security is manifested in the supervisor's openness and eagerness to learn and receive input from supervisees" (Falender & Shafranske, 2004, p. 15).

Challenges for which the therapist and the supervisor may be unprepared are common in rural areas. Rural practitioners are generalists by necessity (Kersting, 2003) because their clients lack other options (Wagenfeld, Murray, Mohatt, & DeBruyn, 1994). Rural clinicians counsel or supervise in areas that are specialties in urban areas. Rather than abandon challenging clients, dedicated clinicians usually have to rely on consultation. Sharing and mutually solving clinical dilemmas with trainees can even be a strength in rural supervision as exemplified in the following example.

> A rural clinician saw a 16-year-old boy whose parents were distraught over his request for a sex-change operation. The boy, who did not appear psychotic and functioned well in most settings, insisted that he was a girl in a boy's body. Both clinician and supervisor were perplexed. In the presence of the clinician, the supervisor called an out-of-state center specializing in gender issues. The center provided references, consultation, and access to staff as an ongoing resource. With such resources, the therapist and supervisor could proceed more responsibly and confidently.

Remote supervision (i.e., via phone, video, or Internet) can be a powerful supplement when supervisors approach the limits of their competence (Kanz, 2001; chaps. 8 and 9, this volume). Electronic networks also offer creative opportunities for enhancing children's systems of care (Ouellette, 2002) or providing clinical services to widely dispersed children, as exemplified in the following example (Ritterband et al., 2003).

> In a rural state, an adult psychiatrist, puzzled by a 7-year-old boy's dramatic shift from being compliant and happy to being angry and defiant, asked that his interview of the child be observed on a university, telemedicine link. A consultant suggested the child draw pictures. One of the child's pictures was of his neighbor with a large penis. Sensitive inquiry revealed the boy's symptoms followed sexual abuse by the neighbor, a revelation that guided meaningful protection and therapy.

Personal Characteristics of the Supervisor

Borders (cited in Muse-Burke et al., 2001) suggested that good supervisors are comfortable with authority and evaluation; provide clear, frequent feedback; enjoy supervision; understand their strengths and limitations; are open to self-exploration; and have a sense of humor. Nelson has summarized from research a list of ways to be a "lousy supervisor" (cited in Bernard & Goodyear, 2004, p. 151). Most of these ways reflect failures of respect, interest, or honesty with supervisees. Honesty means supervisors wisely share relevant doubts and errors, otherwise supervisees are less likely to disclose their fears and mistakes (Falender & Shafranske, 2004).

Munson (2002) suggested certain supervisory styles may be more helpful in confronting particular supervisee reactions, offering technical help to a supervisee who feels overwhelmed by a client's problems may help more than discussing human resilience. It is hoped that in their own training and years as therapists, supervisors will map their personal styles. They will know with what personalities and problems they work best and what issues pose difficulties for them. An easygoing supervisor may need to work against the grain to evaluate a weak trainee or to guide a therapist in situations where fidelity to a highly structured approach is critical.

The Supervisee

Supervisees come in glorious variety. They may have little life experience outside of school, or they may be mothers entering a career after raising a family. They may be new to the field or seasoned professionals seeking to upgrade their skills.

The Supervisee's Professional Experience and Competence

A competent child clinician will be grounded in child development, in an understanding of family, and in a range of therapy skills depending on his or her theoretical orientation. Because of their variety, some trainees will come with skills or acquire competencies more quickly than others. In their competence-based model of supervision, Falender and Shafranske (2004) recommended that competencies be "evaluated on the basis of readiness rather than on a predetermined schedule" (p. 22).

Stoltenberg et al. (1998) proposed an individual developmental model (IDM) of supervision that seems most relevant to trainees new to the field of psychotherapy. They consider domains of competence in which therapists grow, and they posit three levels of development that they analyze along three dimensions: motivation, autonomy, and awareness. Level 1 supervisees may be hard working, anxious, and focused on acquiring basic skills (i.e., motivation); they may require more structure and reassurance (i.e., autonomy); and they may be too self-conscious about their performances to truly hear their clients or to sense their own strengths and weaknesses (i.e., awareness). At Level 2, trainees vacillate between confidence and confusion, wrestle with dependence and greater autonomy, and become more aware of themselves and their clients. On reaching Level 3, trainees are predicted to be more stable in motivation, to be able to manage doubt constructively, to be comfortable seeking consultation, to be able to focus on the therapeutic interaction, and to be able to use their self-awareness therapeutically.

The Supervisee's Personal Characteristics

As therapists, most of us in the mental health field prefer working with certain presenting problems or diagnoses. Working outside our comfort zone requires us to wrestle more with our feelings and to look for more support and direction. Our histories enrich or hinder our work. For this reason, it is important for a supervisor to be aware of past powerful experiences, such as trauma, addiction, or growing up in a troubled or highly protected home that may shape a trainee's practice. Memories of our own childhood and our experiences of family underlie values we often feel viscerally. Enzer (1987) spoke of the regularity with which one's personal history emerges in child therapy training. It is hard not to takes sides when families are warring. Hence, learning to remain effective, by not blaming but by cultivating an empathic understanding of all parties, is a basic rite of passage for child and family therapists. There are also times when a child is at such risk that other family alliances are secondary. Supervision is the forge where such difficult distinctions are hammered out.

In research by Nelson and Holloway (1990), both male and female supervisors were less likely to accept efforts by female supervisees to be more assertive in supervision. Noting the growing feminization of the helping professions, Munson (2002) proposed a conscious partnership model to meet gender concerns in supervision, but, as Nelson and Hollaway warned, gender issues are not always cross-gender problems.

Supervisees in a Group

Group supervision offers an economy of teaching, opens clinicians to more clinical situations and feedback, empowers clinicians who join in supervising their peers, and helps supervisees realize their emotional reactions are part of learning to do therapy. Group supervision is also constructively applied to the training and development of supervisors. Process issues, which may be evaded in individual supervision, may be virtually unavoidable in groups. Group supervision is integral to the implementation of several therapies in this volume. Groups can be intense. They can turn sour with negative results for trainees. Group supervision requires constructive group empowerment and deft management of group process. Each group will have its own dynamics and development. Bernard and Goodyear (2004) and Hayes, Blackman, and Brennan (2001) provided thoughtful discussions of group supervision. The unique elements of supervising child therapy continue in groups.

The Client

Holloway (1995) reminded us that "the client is always present in supervision" (p. 92). She identified three relevant areas for understanding client factors: the client's characteristics, the client's problem and diagnosis, and the therapy relationship.

Client Characteristics

The qualities of children ultimately determine what makes child psychotherapy and its supervision different from adult psychotherapy. Each stage of child development presents its own challenges. Challenges unmet at one stage extend into the next. Life events, such as abuse, injury, or loss of a parent, have different significance at different levels of maturity. Children are so unique that working with them is a specialty, and there are increasing subspecialties that focus on particular ages or on life events at given ages (e.g., neglected infants or teens with chronic illness; Roberts, 2003; Sameroff, McDonough, & Rosenblum, 2004).

No one likes being introduced by their most personal faults, but that may be the first experience a child has on entering therapy if the intake process is not structured to avoid it (e.g., seeing parents or teens alone first). The late Leo Kanner used to joke that he got three types of referrals, "Make him over, rake him over, and take him over" (M. E. Neill, personal communication, March 12, 1966). Clarifying expectations is often the first step in the dance between the therapist and the parties involved in the child's referral. Parents often seek therapy for their children under duress from family, schools, or courts and often come, like the children, with considerable apprehension.

A therapist was taken aback when a mother, holding her child protectively, began the first meeting by asking, "Have you been saved?" After an awkward silence, the therapist said she was sure that she would be respectful of the family's religious faith. This was a sufficient response for the mother to relax and describe her concerns to the therapist.

In working with children, supervisors must help trainees answer the question, "Who is the client?" Is the child the client? If so, what are your responsibilities to the child's legal guardians? Is the family the client? What does it mean if the child, siblings, mother, and father have competing agendas? How do you respond to each person? Are schools or courts involved or are they paying and seeking to dictate treatment? Does this also make them clients? Is the client yours and also the referring specialist's? In child therapy, there are typically multiple clients with differing claims at different times and intervention sites. The answers to these questions are rarely simple and may depend on the child's age, the custody arrangements, the nature of the problem, or the understandings with payers, as exemplified in the following case example.

> A master's-level psychologist was contracted to provide special educa-
> tion evaluations to a school system. After testing, he met the parents to
> share a draft report, to elicit feedback, and to review recommendations.
> School administrators opposed such meetings, noting that parents could
> get final reports from the school if they wished. Unsure this would meet
> his ethical duty to the parents, the psychologist consulted his supervisor
> who affirmed the need for the parent meetings. When the schools
> remained adamant, the psychologist terminated the contract.

Client Problem and Diagnosis

A behavior that is a problem at one age may not be a problem at another. The *Diagnostic and Statistical Manual of Mental Disorders* (4th ed., text rev.; American Psychiatric Association, 2000) provides diagnoses that are applicable to children. Some are diagnoses that can be used with adults, and some are diagnoses that can be applied only to children or children of certain ages. Different professions may also classify the same behaviors differently, and the diagnoses may often help define the work of therapy.

The nature of the presenting problem may also change the dynamics of the therapist's relationship with the client and the supervisor. Client traits may provoke therapists to distance themselves or to become enmeshed with the client. A boy who is persistently depressed may engender feelings of frustration and incompetence in his therapist. An aggressive girl who also lies and sulks may lead her therapist to feel rejected and resentful. Therapists bring these feelings into supervision either in mood and attitude or, more constructively, as concerns they are ready to share.

Presenting problems also determine where, how, by whom, or whether a child is seen. Knitzer's (1982) analysis of the plight of "unclaimed children" made a compelling case that our most troubled children, often in state custody, are more likely to be unserved or served erratically—though continuity is critical for them. Particular services may also pose barriers to some ethnic groups. In the past, few university-based supervisors or researchers saw the challenging clients seen in the community. If the researcher–practitioner training gap is too narrow, community, academic, and research supervisors need to seek each other out and collaborate around the service needs of the most challenging children (Marsh & Fristad, 2002).

The Therapy Relationship

A good therapeutic relationship is vital for successful therapy. Sometimes difficulties in the therapy relationship are mirrored in the supervisory relationship; a therapist at a standstill with a child may come to a standstill in supervision. Knauss (2002) cited other examples of such parallel processes—therapists who challenge their supervisors when working with limit-testing youth or who seek magical solutions when working with highly dependent children.

It is worth trying to match the client to a supervisee's skills and background, though clients and therapists who initially seem incompatible may work surprisingly well together. When a therapist seems a poor match for a client, alert supervision is in order. When therapists become embroiled in conflicts with clients or consistently respond to clients poorly, they may need to be removed from the case. Although trainees need to be extricated when they are in too deep, they may differ from their supervisors in defining "too deep." A supervisee may feel overwhelmed and despairing of his or her skills, whereas the supervisor may feel therapy is in a testing phase, which can lead to a strong therapeutic alliance. Severely abused children may aggressively test their therapists, as exemplified in the following case.

> A counselor in a treatment center saw a young boy whose extreme behaviors had resulted in numerous foster home placements. Early in therapy, the counselor had surgery on her toe and needed to use a special shoe. In a session following the surgery, the boy became angry and stomped the counselor's injured foot, inflicting acute pain and ending the session. In a meeting with her supervisor, the counselor expressed serious doubt about continuing with the boy, viewing his attack as a personal statement of her value to him. The supervisor helped her see the boy's behavior in terms of his past abuse and limited self-control. The counselor agreed to continue treating the boy. Two years later, the child was flourishing in foster care and expressing warmth for the counselor. She thanked her supervisor for helping her stick it out.

The Institutional or Community Setting

All institutions are embedded in a culture, and their services are shaped by that larger culture. O'Donoghue (2003) advocated that all supervisors "restory" their supervision by engaging in careful reflection on the cultural, local, and personal influences on their work and by assessing these influences in light of basic practice principles, such as a need to respect and empower others. In the United States, managed care has changed many aspects of counseling and supervision; it can affect the shape, duration, and content of child therapy (Chambliss, 2000). Reimbursement policies may restrict child psychiatric services to medication, require therapists with a particular degree, insist on the presence of the supervisor in the session, or deny payment for meetings with a child's teacher. Managed care and financial pressures in organizations can move therapy from a service model to a production model. When policies adversely affect children, supervisors should confront offending agencies or inform their professional associations whose collective action may be required to confront managed care excesses.

Agency Clientele

Agencies that primarily serve adults often fail to recognize the demands of serving families and children. The importance of off-site meetings in schools or homes or in other agencies may not be appreciated. Agency goals for productivity, expressed as financial targets or as numbers of billable services, may be unrealistic for persons working with children. Supervisors must be in a position to negotiate reasonable caseloads for their supervisees. For some children, commitments above and beyond normal clinic practice will be necessary. To assume such commitments, therapists need agency and supervisory support. The maxim, "It takes a village to raise a child," is recognition of the extensive support children require. The twist on the maxim, "It takes just one child to raze a village," warns of the potential consequences of improperly doing child therapy. Multisystemic therapy programs, which report uncommon success with challenging youth (Henggeler, Schoenwald, Borduin, Rowland, & Cunningham, 1998), have much smaller caseloads and much greater levels of supervision than most agencies can afford.

Organizational Structure and Climate

Therapists-in-training are often affiliated with a university while being trained in a service agency. The relationship between the two institutions and their differing missions can be problematic. The ASPPB recommends that supervised experiences occur where the "major focus of the setting is on training rather than on generating funds" (1998, p. 3). Supervisors who carve out a haven for trainees within a service agency should be alert to ethical dilemmas that can occur, such as pressuring clinicians to change diagnoses or to change the identified client in a family for billing rather than for clinical purposes.

Scaife (2001) spoke of establishing a "learning culture" within agencies. The supervisory staff's own interest in learning is the first measure of a learning culture. Resources, such as one-way mirrors, a capacity to videotape, time allotted to training, and a professional library, can mark an organization's commitment to teaching. In chapter 9 of this volume, Webster-Stratton speaks of the need for administrative champions when innovating programs. There is longstanding encouragement in child mental health for enriching the skills of practitioners through interdisciplinary training (Hobbs, 1975; Neill, 1997). Some sites favor the training of one discipline over another, but helpful cross training may suffer from the collective egos of the individual disciplines. Supervision by a professional outside one's discipline also may not be accepted by one's own accrediting or licensing organization.

Nontraditional Service Settings

Increasingly, children are served in community settings or in homes. Such arrangements may create complexities. Therapists located in schools may clash with school staff over approaches to limit setting. Intensive, wraparound services may be provided in homes, but issues of confidentiality may arise as neighbors wander into a chaotic household or are turned away. Special permission to release confidential information and consultation with coaches may be required to ensure that a troubled child can experience much-needed success on a sports team. Supervisors need to give special thought to the demands of intervention in novel settings.

THE TASKS AND FUNCTIONS OF SUPERVISION

To help understand what happens in supervisory sessions, Holloway (1995) offered five tasks and five functions of supervision. These tasks and functions constitute a matrix as seen in Table 1.1. The tasks of supervision summarize domains in which a trainee is expected to grow and the supervisor uses the functions to facilitate that growth. A supervisor might help a trainee grow in a particular counseling skill by performing several functions: evaluating, instructing, or modeling. Holloway's matrix is similar to the one developed by Bernard (1997) in her earlier discrimination model. What Bernard described as supervisory roles, Holloway expanded and expressed as functions (Bernard & Goodyear, 2004). Ladany, Friedlander, and Nelson (2005) proposed a somewhat different paradigm for the supervisory task environment. They consider common sequences of critical events in supervision, such as confronting skill deficits, role conflicts, or countertransference.

TABLE 1.1
Holloway's Tasks and Functions of Supervision

Tasks (Growth goals for trainees)	Functions (Growth promoting actions by supervisors)
Counseling skill	Monitoring and evaluating
Case conceptualization	Instructing and advising
Professional role	Modeling
Emotional awareness	Consulting
Self-evaluation	Supporting and sharing

Note. Each function may support any task of supervisee growth.

They offered compelling examples of how such events may be resolved or unresolved to the betterment or detriment of the supervisory alliance.

Tasks of Supervision

Counseling or Therapy Skills

Skill development is a primary focus for new therapists. Chapters 5 through 11 abound in skills primarily related to child therapy. Other skills used with adults may have a different emphasis when used with children, such as case coordination, limit setting, or self-disclosure.

Case Coordination. Sometimes called case management, case coordination is a skill with deep roots in social work. It involves communicating and planning with persons and agencies whose involvement is needed to achieve a positive outcome for the child. Case coordination is particularly critical for children in state custody or for those with serious emotional problems (Neill, 1997). The crisis with Mary, illustrated in the example that opened this chapter, represented the therapist's failure to carefully communicate and plan with her foster care agency. Case coordination means not only getting all the current players on the same page with respect to planning but also mobilizing a range of resources to help the child and family. Coordination should also promote a true culture of interagency collaboration in the community.

Limit Setting. Children can wildly and dangerously tantrum or can calculatingly violate rules. Setting meaningful limits is an essential skill for child therapists. Ideally, therapy occurs in a setting (e.g., a designated play or therapy room) where children cannot do great damage. However, when children are seen in an office or borrowed space in an agency, the rules for limits may change. Supervisors need to help therapists acquire de-escalation skills so therapists can avoid using physical limits. Therapists must also know how to get help or to properly use physical control if safety is an issue. It helps to calmly express the need for limits in terms of one's concern for the child, "It wouldn't be fair to you if I let you learn to hurt people!" Greene's (1998) guidelines for anticipating the needs of explosive children can serve therapists well. Greene particularly warned against pushing behavioral consequences when evidence suggests they are not working.

Boundaries and Self-Disclosure. Boundary concerns are always grist for supervision. Neediness, intimidation, manipulation, or sexiness can tempt a therapist to violate boundaries. Boundaries with children are not as readily defined as those with adults. It may be appropriate for a therapist to send a child a birthday card. A therapist at the family's invitation may attend a child's school performance, especially if the child is fearful, and the performance represents a triumph of the child's work in therapy. A therapist may accept a hug from an 8-year-old Hispanic girl at the end of therapy, as rejecting the hug might violate cultural expectancies. However, a hug's significance can be different if the girl is 13-years-old or has a history of sexual abuse.

Self-Disclosure. Hill and Knox (2002) sifted the wisdom regarding self-disclosure in work with adults and offer principles to guide therapists (e.g., avoiding disclosure that meets the therapist's needs). In child work, personal questions can come with disarming immediacy. A candid answer may build trust and facilitate collaboration, but many questions have a broader purpose. Parents, concerned about a therapist's maturity or empathy for the stresses of parenting, may ask whether the therapist has children of his or her own. A teen in an intake session with her parents may challenge, "Didn't you ever get drunk?" Nondefensive questions often help therapists keep a purposeful focus on the therapy. Replying to a teen's question about his favorite band, the therapist may ask, "How will listening to Metallica or Willie Nelson affect our work together?" A trainee, barraged with personal questions by a young boy he was seeing in therapy, approached his supervisor who suggested that he encourage the boy to answer his own questions with his "best guesses" about the therapist. The boy's guesses described a perfect match for his recently divorced mother.

Case Conceptualization

Schroeder and Gordon (2002) provided a helpful description of the role of assessment in case conceptualization. Beginning with a careful clarification of the issues in the referral, they consider the social context of the referral; the child's development; the family issues; the environmental factors including culture; the medical status; the child and family strengths; and the frequency, seriousness, and impact of the child's behaviors. Part of the assessment is determining whether other specialized assessments need to occur and whether parents, peers, or teachers must be involved in effective intervention. Viable theory underpins case conceptualization. A weak grasp of theory diminishes a therapist's ability to move from problem definition to intervention. Schroeder and Gordon emphasized the ongoing, hypothesis-testing nature of assessment. The following vignette illustrates the importance of thorough assessment for case conceptualization.

> A social worker saw a 9-year-old boy who suffered chronic headaches. His repeated evaluations included elaborate neurological procedures. Viewing a video of the initial session, the supervisor sensed hesitancy as the mother gave a social history. She encouraged the social worker to gently and empathically press for clarification. In the subsequent session, the mother confessed that the boy's father was a convicted drug dealer. When the father was imprisoned, she discovered his ample cash, divorced him, and moved away. Since then, the family had lived in constant fear that he might find and harm them.

Hypervigilance was the family lifestyle. These revelations overturned prior case conceptualizations. A few sessions in which the boy openly shared and discussed these family secrets, resulted in alleviation of his headaches.

Professional Role

Many expectancies accompany the therapist's role. The therapist is expected to be grounded in a professional body of knowledge and to remain current in that knowledge. He or she is expected to master new skills as the field develops. He or she is also expected to seek supervision or consultation when puzzled or unsure. A professional therapist creates and maintains clinical records, works with professional networks, and acts on principles of ethical practice.

Ethics and Advocacy. Ethical concerns are pervasive in child psychotherapy and are crucial to professional development. As Falender and Shafranske (2004) observed, even "the acts of encouraging hope in the face of despair or challenging a client to further self-responsibility are moral acts. . . ." (p. 31). Ethics can take passive forms, such as avoiding harmful practices, or more positive forms, such as modeling. Modeling may be the best way to teach ethical behavior. Some psychiatrists, for example, do not accept any gifts, or perks, from pharmaceutical sales representatives and make that known to their supervisees.

Advocacy is ethics in action that flows naturally from a systems perspective in supervision (Montgomery, Hendricks, & Bradley, 2001). It is simply inescapable in working with children who are vulnerable by definition. The mental health system is prone to hurting children. For example, the number of children removed from parental custody to access intensive, long-term mental health services is a national tragedy (Gilberti & Schulzinger, 2000). Sometimes, basic professional communication serves an important role in advocacy, as exemplified in the following case.

> A therapist reported that she had seen a generally shy 13-year-old girl who was in constant conflict with her mother. The girl had been in state custody because of sexual abuse by her mother's boyfriend. In joint sessions, the mother was extremely critical of her daughter whom she described as a sexual competitor. When an argument at home escalated to blows, the mother called the police and insisted the girl be taken to a psychiatric hospital where she was admitted and diagnosed with a bipolar disorder. The therapist, distressed at both the hospitalization and the diagnosis, called her supervisor. She observed that the girl was routinely provoked and saw no signs of a serious disorder. The supervisor suggested that the admitting psychiatrist may have based the diagnosis on the mother's account and might greatly appreciate the therapist's

perspective. The supervisor also asked the therapist to contact protective services to notify them of the discrepancy.

Supervisors must decide when to advise and consult with the supervisee or when to model advocacy. By addressing a situation in writing, one can describe an issue clearly and frame it in appropriate legal, ethical, or clinical terms. There is a written record if the party concerned fails to respond. Letters allow the supervisee to take a major role in confronting the problem and allow the supervisor to guide and to cosign lending his or her professional standing to the issue.

Emotional Awareness

Therapists who seem to be making unwarranted assumptions about clients may be acting on unexplored emotions or on implicit assumptions about change and human nature, which need to be examined through supervision (Auger, 2004). The transformation of one's personal reactions to a client from an embarrassing disruption to a potentially revealing, clinical ally is one of the most satisfying areas of personal growth in supervision. Emotionally aware clinicians distinguish between annoyance related to realities in their own lives and annoyance that stems from the client's presentation. Insights into the evocative qualities of a child or parent can guide constructive interventions. This is what Stoltenberg et al. (1998) meant when they spoke of advanced clinicians therapeutically using their self-awareness.

The use of process notes (i.e., recollections of the therapist's decision process and feelings written immediately after the session) can help increase a trainee's self-awareness. The interpersonal process recall approach to supervision immediately reviews videotape after a session and encourages recall of thoughts and feelings, as well as self-evaluation of the therapist's actions (Kagan & Kagan, 1997).

Self-Evaluation

Clinicians need to learn the limits of their competence and when to refer or seek help. They need to know when their emotional reactions are warning signs of overinvolvement or of work stress. Ultimately, the supervisee should be the best judge of her or his needs. In today's pressured clinics, supervisors need to model and encourage opportunities to slow down and to take stock of one's clinical work, one's progress in supervision, and one's professional growth. When trainees analyze their videotaped sessions or develop drafts of their performance evaluations, they can increase their capacity for self-evaluation.

The Functions of Supervision

Monitoring and Evaluating

Monitoring. The supervisor is responsible for the well-being of the supervisee's clients. This means supervisors speak to issues of safety, risk management, and treatment fidelity. New therapists must be well prepared and closely observed in therapy. New skills can be practiced and monitored in role-play before use in therapy. Observing via a one-way mirror or a video monitor and communicating with the therapist offers protection for everyone. Review of videotaped sessions is a core supervisory tool. Because of the prominence of nonverbal activity, audiotape is of less value with younger children. Though some trainees fear and resist videotaping, videotape review, along with live supervision, was the most highly valued supervisory activity rated by supervisees and supervisors in research by Goodyear and Nelson (1997). Checklists are sometimes used to aid the monitoring skills used in sessions (see chaps. 5 and 9, this volume).

Evaluating. Three types of evaluation pertain to supervision: evaluation of therapeutic progress, evaluation of the supervisee, and evaluation of the supervisory process, including the supervisor. The major works on supervision suggest that all three are often slighted in practice.

EVALUATING THERAPEUTIC PROGRESS. Ellis and Ladany (1997) asserted that client outcomes are the acid test of clinical supervision. Research on the effect of supervision on child outcomes is vague. Freitas (2002) noted that such research has all the complexities of therapy outcome research with the "layer of the supervisor–supervisee relationship added" (p. 364). A case can be made that supervision improves outcomes when it assures fidelity to an empirically supported treatment (Gresham, 1997; Henggeler, Schoenwald, Liao, Letorneau, & Edwards, 2002). Evaluation of outcomes involves (a) a good assessment of the child's problems, (b) the faithful application of an intervention that is theoretically or empirically sound (e.g., using a protocol when available), and (c) the choice and use of measurable indices of child or family progress. The growing movement to evaluate treatment progress by integrating serious measurement into treatment plans or by using case study designs is discussed in chapter 2.

EVALUATING THE SUPERVISEE. The evaluation of the supervisee is central to the power differential between supervisee and supervisor. Sometimes neither is comfortable with this aspect of the relationship. "Many participants report their greatest levels of confusion related to the dual characteristics of supervision as both benevolent and critical" (Bradley & Kottler, 2001, p. 19). Bernard and Goodyear (2004) believe "establishing criteria for evaluation may be the most challenging and conceivably the most labor-intensive aspect of the evaluation process" (p. 23). Adult or standardized, agency-evaluation formats may miss key elements of child work, and supervisors should be wary of using them for child therapists. Recent works on supervision emphasize the importance of clarity in the evaluation process, the need for ongoing evaluation throughout supervision, and the periodic completion of formal evaluations (Bernard & Goodyear, 2004; Falender & Shafranske, 2004; Gould & Bradley, 2001; Kadushin & Harkness, 2002). Even if an agency orientation explains the evaluation process, supervisees still need a sense of how their individual supervisor evaluates. Criteria of the evaluation can be shared with examples of how the supervisor uses any forms. It may also help to review Bernard and Goodyear's (2004, p. 310) "Supervisee's Bill of Rights."

Uncritical evaluations, lathered with praise, are of little value to trainees, their clients, or future training and employment sites. When ongoing evaluation has been good, the written evaluation is no surprise. If it is a surprise, a frank discussion of the issue may be critical to the future of the supervisory relationship (Benson & Holloway, 2005). Supervisees need access to due process if they disagree with their evaluation or supervisor.

If clients are identified in supervisory records, the supervisory records must be maintained with the same security as patient records. Supervisory recommendations or information of a critical nature (e.g., a referral of the child to protective services or a supervisor's consultation with a child's prescribing physician) should be in the client's record.

EVALUATING THE SUPERVISORY PROCESS AND THE SUPERVISOR. Quality supervision includes an opportunity for mutual evaluation. The supervisee should be able to evaluate the overall supervisory process, including the agency policies and supports and the supervisor's performance. Examples of supervisory evaluation are found in the works of Bernard and Goodyear (2004) and Falender and Shafranske (2004). Supervisees need help when supervision seems to be going nowhere, as exemplified in the following case example.

> When an aggressive 10-year-old boy entered therapy with a new trainee, he resisted involvement by insisting on playing chess or checkers and by sullenly matching the therapist's moves. Over 3 months, the supervisor repeatedly suggested that the trainee wait the boy out. Unable to resolve his differences with his supervisor, the trainee approached the training director who suggested he work with a new supervisor. The new supervisor recommended behavioral management with the entire family, which yielded excellent results.

Instructing and Advising

Many professionals are generically trained and acquire the expertise to work with children and families in practice sites. Those who supervise child work must be ready to teach in the areas of case coordination, child development, developmental psychopathology, and child and family

intervention. In the authors' experience, knowledge of developmental disa-
bilities is almost a standard gap in the training of mental health professionals.
For issues they frequently encounter, supervisors should have materials to
share and bibliographies to recommend. Whereas instructing is important,
supervisors must also be cautious about turning supervision into class instruction. The classroom model leaves the supervisor in an expert role and allows
the supervisee to leave his fears and self-doubts at the door.

Modeling

Supervisees need to see their mentors work. Conducting play therapy
and juggling the competing interests in a family session are best seen before
they are practiced. Respect for demanding clients is more readily demonstrated than explained. Videos of expert therapists can be both helpful and
intimidating. They should be followed by discussion and consideration of
alternative approaches. Vast developmental differences in children under-
score the value of opportunities to observe children at different ages, as
well as to observe good work with such children, as exemplified in the
following example.

> An experienced psychologist arranged for psychiatric residents to ob-
> serve her providing developmental evaluations of young children at
> increasing ages, beginning at 3 months, over a period of 8 weeks. After
> each session, she explained how and why she varied the evaluation
> tasks. She explained the variations in her language for the older children.
> The residents evaluated the experience as the most helpful presentation
> of their training year.

Consulting

Consultation involves great mutuality and is a sign that the supervisee
and the supervisory relationship are growing. Supervisors can empower a
trainee by shifting into a more consultative role. After collaborating with
a supervisee in the conceptualization of a case, the supervisor may want to
ask, "If we are right about this situation, what do you want to do when you
see this boy next time?" Professionals will seek and provide consultation
throughout their career. When supervisors are perplexed, it is advantageous
to seek consultation in the presence of the trainee, as in the earlier example
of the boy who wanted to change his gender.

Supporting and Sharing

Therapists who work with troubled children and families should not
work in isolation. Bound by confidentiality, trainees cannot share their
frustrations with friends and family, their natural support systems. Supervisors
who do not create a safe haven for sharing feelings and are unwilling to

share their own growth pains and struggles can leave supervisees in an emotional limbo. The Level 1 therapists in the model of Stoltenberg et al. (1998) may fear that confronting negative reactions will call both their competence and career choice into question. The supervisor must create an atmosphere in which the supervisee can explore doubts, painful reactions, and growing self-awareness. Well-run supervision groups can also be powerful sources of trainee support. Because some supervisees evade problems, Holloway (1995) includes constructive confrontation in her description of support and sharing.

CONCLUSION

Using Holloway's (1995) Systems Approach to Supervision, this chapter addresses key supervisory themes with an emphasis on the supervision of child psychotherapy. Though Holloway's matrix may capture much of the supervisory interaction, it does not capture some of the structural issues of supervision—determining how much time to give to a supervisee, setting priorities within the supervisory session, or guaranteeing sufficient scope and depth in covering the supervisee's caseload. It is clear that these are important matters. They are reflected in discussions of preparation, format, agenda setting, and availability of the supervisor in subsequent chapters. The next chapter looks at the current state of child psychotherapy. Later chapters flesh out many issues introduced in this chapter, offering a broad range of approaches to supervision for different child therapies, for highly challenging youth and families, and for the changing settings of child psychotherapy.

REFERENCES

Alred, G. (1999). A trainee's perspective. In R. Bor & M. Watts (Eds.), *The trainee handbook: A guide for counseling and psychotherapy trainees* (pp. 253–267). London: Sage.

American Psychiatric Association. (2000). *Diagnostic and statistical manual of mental disorders* (4th ed., text rev.). Washington, DC: Author.

Association of State and Provincial Psychology Boards. (1998). *Supervision guidelines: From the final report of the ASPPB Task Force on Supervision Guidelines*. Montgomery, AL: Author.

Auger, R. W. (2004). What we don't know can hurt us: Mental health counselors' implicit assumptions about human nature. *Journal of Mental Health Counseling, 26*, 13–24.

Benson, K. P., & Holloway, E. L. (2005). Achieving influence: A grounded theory of how clinical supervisors evaluate trainees. *Journal of Qualitative Research in Psychology, 2*, 117–140.

Berger, S. S., & Buchholz, E. S. (1993). On becoming a supervisee: Preparation for learning in a supervisory relationship. *Psychotherapy, 30*, 86–91.

Bernard, J. M. (1997). The discrimination model. In C. E. Watkins Jr. (Ed.), *Handbook of psychotherapy supervision* (pp. 310–327). New York: Wiley.

Bernard, J. M., & Goodyear, R. K. (2004). *Fundamentals of clinical supervision* (3rd ed.). New York: Pearson Education.

Bordin, E. S. (1983). A working alliance based model of supervision. *The Counseling Psychologist, 11*, 35–41.

Boyd, J. (1978). *Counselor development: Approaches, preparation, practice.* Muncie, IN: Accelerated Development.

Bradley, L. J., Gould, L. J., & Parr, G. D. (2001). Supervision-based integrative models of counselor supervision. In L. J. Bradley & N. Ladany (Eds.), *Counselor supervision: Principles, process, and practice* (3rd ed., pp. 93–124). Philadelphia: Brunner-Routledge.

Bradley, L. J., & Kottler, J. A. (2001). Supervision training: A model. In L. J. Bradley & N. Ladany (Eds.), *Counselor supervision: Principles, process, and practice* (3rd ed., pp. 3–27). Philadelphia: Brunner-Routledge.

Campbell, J. M. (2000). *Becoming an effective supervisor: A workbook for counselors and psychotherapists.* Philadelphia: Accelerated Development.

Caplan, R. B., & Caplan, G. (2001). *Helping the helpers not to harm: Iatrogenic damage and community mental health.* New York: Brunner-Routledge.

Chambliss, C. H. (2000). *Psychotherapy and managed care: Reconciling research and reality.* Needham Heights, MA: Allyn & Bacon.

Cherniss, C., & Egnatios, E. (1977). Styles of clinical supervision in community mental health programs. *Journal of Consulting and Clinical Psychology, 45*, 1195–1196.

Ekstein, R., & Wallerstein, R. S. (1958). *The teaching and learning of psychotherapy.* New York: Basic Books.

Ellis, M. V., & Ladany, N. (1997) Inference concerning supervisees and clients in clinical supervision: An integrative review. In C. E. Watkins Jr. (Ed.), *Handbook of psychotherapy supervision* (pp. 447–507). New York: Wiley.

Enzer, N. B. (1987). Supervision. In R. L. Cohen & M. K. Dulcan (Eds.), *Basic handbook of training in child and adolescent psychiatry* (pp. 225–246). Springfield, IL: Charles C Thomas.

Falender, C. A., & Shafranske, E. B. (2004). *Clinical supervision: A competency-based approach.* Washington, DC: American Psychological Association.

Freitas, G. F. (2002). The impact of psychotherapy supervision on client outcome: A critical examination of 2 decades of research. *Psychotherapy: Theory, Research, Practice, Training, 39*, 354–367.

Gilberti, M., & Schulzinger, R. (2000). *Relinquishing custody: The tragic results of failure to meet childrens' mental health needs*. Washington, DC: Bazelon Center for Mental Health Law.

Goodyear, R. K., & Nelson, M. L. (1997). The major formats of psychotherapy supervision. In C. E. Watkins Jr. (Ed.), *Handbook of psychotherapy supervision* (pp. 328–344). New York: Wiley.

Gould, L. J., & Bradley, L. J. (2001). Evaluation in supervision. In L. J. Bradley & N. Ladany (Eds.), *Counselor supervision: Principles, process, and practice* (pp. 147–180). Philadelphia: Brunner-Routledge.

Greene, R. W. (1998). *The explosive child*. New York: HarperCollins.

Gresham, E. M. (1997). Treatment integrity in single-subject research. In R. D. Franklin, D. B. Allison, & B. S. Gorman (Eds.), *Design and analysis of single case research* (pp. 93–117). Mahwah, NJ: Erlbaum.

Haley, J. (1987). *Problem-solving therapy* (2nd ed.). San Francisco: Jossey-Bass.

Hayes, R. L., Blackman, L. S., & Brennan, C. (2001). Group supervision. In L. J. Bradley & N. Ladany (Eds.), *Counselor supervision: Principles, process, and practice* (pp. 183–206). Philadelphia: Brunner-Routledge.

Henggeler, S. W., Schoenwald, S. K., Borduin, C. M., Rowland, M. D., & Cunningham, P. B. (1998). *Multisystemic treatment of antisocial behavior in children and adolescents*. New York: Guilford Press.

Henggeler, S. W., Schoenwald, S. K., Liao, J. G., Letorneau, E. J., & Edwards, D. J. (2002). Transporting efficacious treatments to field settings: The link between supervisory practices and therapist fidelity in MST programs. *Journal of Clinical Child and Adolescent Psychology, 31*, 155–167.

Hewson, J. (1999). *Training supervisors to contract in supervision*. In E. Holloway & M. Carroll (Eds.), *Training counselling supervisors* (pp. 67–91). London: Sage.

Hill, C. E., & Knox, S. (2002). Self-disclosure. In J. C. Norcross (Ed.), *Psychotherapy relationships that work: Therapist contributions and responsiveness to patients* (pp. 233–265). London: Oxford University Press.

Hobbs, N. (1975). *The futures of children*. San Francisco: Jossey-Bass.

Holloway, E. L. (1995). *Clinical supervision: A systems approach*. Thousand Oaks, CA: Sage.

Holloway, E. L., & Wolleat, P. (1994). Supervision: The pragmatics of empowerment. *Journal of Educational and Psychological Consultation, 5*, 23–43.

Kadushin, A., & Harkness, D. (2002). *Supervision in social work*. New York: Columbia University Press.

Kagan, H., & Kagan, N. I. (1997). Interpersonal process recall: Influencing human interaction. In C. E. Watkins Jr. (Ed.), *Psychotherapy supervision: Theory, research, and practice* (pp. 262–283). New York: Wiley.

Kanz, J. E. (2001). Clinical-supervision.com: Issues in the provision of on-line supervision. *Professional Psychology Research and Practice, 32*, 415–420.

Kersting, K. (2003). Teaching self-sufficiency in rural practice. *Monitor on Psychology, 34*, 60–62.

Knaus, L. K. (2002). Supervisory issues related to treating children with serious emotional disturbance. In D. T. Marsh & M. A. Fristad (Eds.), *Handbook of serious emotional disturbance in children and adolescence* (pp. 112–127). New York: Wiley.

Knitzer, J. (1982). *Unclaimed children: The failure of public responsibility to children and adolescents in need of mental health services.* Washington, DC: Children's Defense Fund.

Kratochwill, T. R., Lepage, K. M., & McGivern, J. (1997). Child and adolescent psychotherapy supervision. In C. E. Watkins Jr. (Ed.), *Handbook of psychotherapy supervision* (pp. 347–365). New York: Wiley.

Ladany, N., Friedlander, M. L., & Nelson, M. L. (2005). *Critical events in psychotherapy supervision: An interpersonal approach.* Washington, DC: American Psychological Association.

Marsh, D. T., & Fristad, M. A. (2002). Introduction. In D. T. Marsh & M. A. Fristad (Eds.), *Handbook of serious emotional disturbance in children and adolescence* (pp. 3–5). New York: Wiley.

McCann, D. (1999). Supervision. In R. Bor & M. Watts (Eds.), *The trainee handbook: A guide for counseling and psychotherapy trainees* (pp. 114–129). London: Sage.

Montgomery, M. J., Hendricks, C. B., & Bradley, L. J. (2001). Using systems perspectives in supervision. *Family Journal: Counseling and Therapy for Couples and Families, 9,* 305–313.

Munson, C. E. (2002). *Handbook of clinical social work supervision.* New York: Haworth Press.

Muse-Burke, J. L., Ladany, N., & Deck, M. D. (2001). The supervisory relationship. In L. J. Bradley & N. Ladany (Eds.), *Counselor supervision: Principles, process, and practice* (pp. 28–62). Philadelphia: Brunner-Routledge.

Neill, T. K. (1997). Service coordination: A guide to systematic services for children with severe emotional disturbances. In R. J. Illback, C. Cobb, & H. Joseph Jr. (Eds.), *Integrated services for children and families: Opportunities for psychological practice* (pp. 157–190). Washington, DC: American Psychological Association.

Nelson, M. L., & Holloway, E. L. (1990). Relation of gender to power and involvement in supervision. *Journal of Counseling Psychology, 37,* 473–481.

O'Donoghue, K. (2003). *Restorying social work supervision.* Palmerstown North, New Zealand: Dunsmore Press.

Ouellette, P. M. (2002). Community telenetworking: 21st century solutions for strengthening parent–school–community partnerships in children's mental health field. *Electronic Journal of Social Work, 1,* 1.

Page, S., & Wosket, V. (2001). *Supervising the counselor: A cyclical model* (2nd ed.). East Sussex, England: Brunner-Routledge.

Putney, M. W., Worthington, E. L., Jr., & McCullough, M. E. (1992). Effects of supervisor and supervisee theoretical orientation and supervisor and supervisee matching on intern's perception of supervision. *Journal of Counseling Psychology, 39,* 258–265.

Ritterband, L. M., Cox, D. J., Walker, L. S., Kovatchev, B., McKnight, L., & Kushal, P. (2003). An Internet intervention as adjunctive therapy for pediatric encopresis. *Journal of Consulting and Clinical Psychology, 71,* 910–917.

Roberts, M. C. (Ed.). (2003). *Handbook of pediatric psychology.* New York: Guilford Press.

Rogers, C. R. (1951). *Client-centered therapy.* Boston: Houghton Mifflin.

Sameroff, A. J., McDonough, S. C., & Rosenblum, K. L. (Eds.). (2004). *Treating parent–infant relationship problems: Strategies for intervention.* New York: Guilford Press.

Scaife, J. (2001). *Supervision in the mental health professions: A practitioner's guide.* Philadelphia: Taylor & Francis.

Schroeder, C. S., & Gordon, B. N. (2002). *Assessment and treatment of childhood problems: A clinician's guide.* New York: Guilford Press.

Stoltenberg, C. D., McNeill, B., & Delworth, U. (1998). *IDM supervision: An integrated developmental model of supervising counselors and therapists.* San Francisco: Jossey-Bass.

Wagenfeld, M. O., Murray, J. D., Mohatt, D. F., & DeBruyn, J. C. (1994). *Mental health and rural America: 1980–1993.* Washington, DC: Health Resources and Services Administration.

Whitman, S. M. (2001). Teaching residents to use supervision effectively. *Academic Psychiatry, 23,* 143–147.

2

THE CHANGING CONTEXT OF CHILD PSYCHOTHERAPY AND IMPLICATIONS FOR SUPERVISORS

T. KERBY NEILL

Child psychotherapy is like playing street ball in a changing neighborhood. The new kids on the block and the ones who grew up there argue about the rules. Various authorities may intervene. How the game is played, where it is played, who can play, and how many can play all hang in the balance. This chapter considers the changing neighborhood of child psychotherapy, the current debates over child psychotherapy, the promise these changes may offer, and the role supervisory leadership must play in achieving that promise.

THE CHANGING NEIGHBORHOOD OF CHILD PSYCHOTHERAPY

Today, children receiving psychotherapy come from families that are culturally and economically diverse. Child diagnoses are changing, and medication is revolutionizing practice. There are new roles for providers and new providers. Intervention is no longer confined to clinics. Insurers and government are major payers who want to control services. Professional disputes rage over what constitutes good child psychotherapy. In spite of a continued high rate of psychiatric disorders in children, there is a shortage of child-trained professionals, the service system is fragmented, and too few child clinicians avail themselves of the interventions that have strong research support (Hoagwood & Olin, 2002).

Service Demand Is High and the Population Is Changing

Using data from three large national samples, Kataoka, Zhang, and Wells (2002) estimated that over 75% of children in need of mental health care are simply not served and that Latino and uninsured youths were even less likely to be served. Even children identified as abused and neglected or seriously disturbed are severely underserved (Cicchetti & Toth, 2003; Marsh, 2004). Friedman (2001) summarized smaller surveys that showed that few children (i.e., less than 10%) who are served attend specialty mental health services and that most were seen in schools where services vary enormously in intensity and quality (see chap. 12, this volume). Professions lack the numbers and resources to meet this challenge, and the existing workforce "does not reflect the ethnic characteristics of the population" in need of services (Torralba-Romero, 1998, p. 81). But the problem is also one of competence. Recent innovations have "not been followed by equally rapid advances in the clinical preparation of the workforce" (Hansen, 2002, p. 93), nor in the upgrading of skills in older professionals. The raw demographics and the range of children's problems cry out for more professionally and culturally competent professionals. They call, still louder, for preventive approaches (see chap. 9, this volume). We need professionals who can develop, disseminate, and supervise effective therapeutic and preventive initiatives.

Diagnoses Proliferate but Offer Partial Understanding

Contrasting the American Psychiatric Association's current *Diagnostic and Statistical Manual of Mental Disorders* (4th ed., text rev.; *DSM–IV–TR*; 2000) with the 1952 version reveals a revolution in the number and specificity of childhood psychiatric diagnoses. Epidemiological studies also suggest that one diagnosis increases a child's likelihood of additional diagnoses (Angold, Costello, & Erkanli, 1999). Although there are diagnostic approaches other than the *DSM–TR–IV*, such as Achenbach's (1998) dimensional measures or the diagnostic classifications of the Zero to Three: National Center for Infants, Toddlers, and Families (1994), *DSM–IV–TR* diagnoses are powerfully established in medicine, in organizing research on childhood disorders and therapies, and in managed care systems in which diagnoses can become a dangerous shortcut to describing children. In spite of *DSM–IV–TR* emphases on assessing a larger picture, one can find clinical records that list symptoms, *DSM–IV–TR* diagnoses (i.e., Axis I and II), and interventions with no mention of a child's history or social situation. Diagnosis is best when it is a continuing process in an ecological context, as exemplified in developmental psychopathology that gives attention to family, community, health, culture, vulnerabilities, strengths, critical events, and mediating influences as the child grows (Toth & Cicchetti, 1999).

The *DSM–IV–TR* is a work in progress and has a number of weaknesses. Peterson and Seligman (2004), who sought to classify and understand strengths, faulted the *DSM–IV–TR* on a number of counts, including its emphasis on deficits; its use of complex, overly heterogeneous categories; and its failure to capture gradations of a problem behavior. Prilleltensky (1994) also warned that a diagnostic system that places illness in the individual distracts from larger social ills such as experiences of poverty, maltreatment, or discrimination that can promote mental health symptoms.

Supervisors face the challenge of ensuring that assessments are comprehensive and that diagnoses are made carefully and communicated in ways that are helpful, recognizing a child's strengths, history, culture, and total environment. Hobbs's (1975) discussion of the advantages and risks of children's diagnoses, which is still relevant, noted that they can aid and inform or frighten families, guide and facilitate treatment or limit service, evoke empathy and support, or prompt rejection.

Medication May Help or Hurt

Psychotropic medications, the fruit of modern research which are supported by intense marketing and often encouraged by managed care, are transforming child treatment. Many children benefit from medication, although long-term effects are unknown, and the extent of its use is controversial (Jellinek, 1999; Safer, Zito, & dosReis, 2003). When is medication safe, justified, or best paired with therapy? When is it simply social control? Phelps, Brown, and Power (2002) described promising marriages of medication and psychotherapy for many childhood conditions. Conscientious supervisors inform themselves about medications used with children and ensure that supervisees are aware of the rationale for medications, note any behavioral changes, and are alert to potential side effects. They recognize the need to foster collaboration between therapists and prescribing professionals so medication can be used wisely.

Professional Roles Are Changing

The classic roles of the child mental health trinity—psychiatry, psychology, and social work—are no more. Psychiatry's focus is now diagnosis and medication (Eisenberg, 2001), a role shared with primary care physicians, nurse practitioners, and, in some states, psychologists. Specialists in families and various counseling disciplines have entered the therapy arena. Each claims some priority by virtue of training, costs, or focus, especially now that the rules of reimbursement are often paired with particular disciplines. Diagnoses also vary with discipline or the setting in which a professional works—a social worker may view learning problems differently than a school psychologist, an occupational therapist, or a probation officer. Because supervisors must guide supervisees, who in turn guide families, through the complexities of a multidisciplinary, often fragmented, service world, supervisors should take a lead in interdisciplinary cooperation and understanding.

Therapy Takes Place in a Changing Workplace

What happens in therapy is often dictated by where it takes place. Today, psychiatric hospitals rarely provide more than assessment, stabilization, and medication. Most long-term, out-of-home treatment occurs in residential treatment centers or in forms of therapeutic foster care (Chamberlin & Smith, 2003). Although private practitioners usually use traditional outpatient therapies, therapists or supervised paraprofessionals in clinics increasingly visit home, school, and community centers and provide a range of intensive services (Burns, Schoenwald, Burchard, Faw, & Santos, 2000). Sparked by federal and foundation initiatives, a few regions offer a spectrum of children's services in a multiagency, collaborative, system of care (Holden & Brannan, 2002). Collaborative models may also be fostered by managed care carve outs, when providers commit to meet all the mental health needs of a given population for a targeted sum. Local agency practices may pressure therapists to adhere to fixed or fragmented service models or to restrict the sites in which services are offered. Good supervisors help trainees determine which models and service locations are most appropriate and help support their use and development.

Funding Impacts the Shape of Child Psychotherapy

When families pay directly for services, the arrangement is part of the therapeutic alliance. When grants fund services, the parameters of service are often specified by the grant. Today, however, most payments are part of large agency contracts. Third-party payers manage expenditures by determining who can do what kind of therapy, under what conditions, and for what length of time. It is not unreasonable for payers to seek cost-containment, particularly in response to provider excesses. As noted in a recent review of children's treatments (Fonagy, Target, Cottrell, Phillips, & Kurtz, 2002), much hospitalization of children "may have been driven more by the perverse incentives of providers than by the known benefits of inpatient care" (p. 3). Still, managed care staff may make treatment decisions that would be unethical for supervisors with similar, sparse information. Managed care organizations tend to encourage a narrowing of practice. Supervisors must often juxtapose their clinical and ethical judgment against pressure to conform to payer guidelines or to structure treatment with a view to an agency's fiscal bottom line.

If the rules of street ball are evolving in the changing neighborhood of child mental health treatment, supervisors have a special role to play in evaluating the new rules and in affirming or challenging them for the well-being of children and families.

THE DEBATE: WHAT IS EFFECTIVE CHILD PSYCHOTHERAPY?

For much of the 20th century, psychotherapists were divided into competing camps. Psychodynamic therapists traced child problems to inner conflicts, which they hoped to elicit and alleviate through feedback and interpretation in a sensitive therapeutic relationship. Behaviorists rejected the world of subjective experience and emphasized learning through reward, no reward, or punishment. Family therapists emphasized the child as part of a larger system and contended that the family, not the individual, should be the unit of treatment. As therapies multiplied, more therapists acknowledged the positive contributions of different therapies. Therapists increasingly described themselves as eclectic or integrative (Norcross, Hedges, & Castle, 2002), choosing from different approaches to meet the needs of their client. The work of Reisman and Ribordy (1993) represented an effort to integrate dynamic, behavioral, cognitive, and family approaches to therapy with children.

Choosing therapeutic strategies for a child and family is critical to helping the child, but it is no easy task. In 1988, Kazdin counted at least 230 forms of child psychotherapy. His latest count stands at 550 (Kazdin, 2000). In the welter of therapies, the challenge is to discover what works for whom, by whom, with which problems, and under what circumstances (Paul, 1967). In 1975, Haley, who was convinced of the superiority of family therapy, issued a provocative challenge:

> Mental health clinics are not primarily concerned with treatment out-come. If they were, every clinic would have a research unit which examines results and changes therapy procedures on the basis of the findings. Mental health clinics have never changed a therapeutic approach or discharged a psychiatrist, psychologist, or social worker on the basis of follow-up results of therapy. (p. 3)

One might expect research to play a key role in settling the claims of competing therapies, but outcome research requires special rigor, ample funds, and time. Research methodologies and funding have lagged, and the promise of research has been slow to shape practice. Within the last 2 decades, however, research has assumed a major role in shaping the therapy debates.

The Current Psychotherapy Debates

Present child psychotherapy debates can be organized around four themes: (a) laboratory research versus practice research, (b) common factors versus specific therapy effects, (c) mechanisms of change versus generic therapies, and (d) "whom do we treat?" Each issue carries consequences for supervision.

Laboratory Research Versus Practice Research

Clinicians currently confront two striking sets of research: one shows many child therapies work in well-conducted laboratory studies; the other fails to find such encouraging results in typical clinical practice (Weisz, Donenberg, Han, & Kauneckis, 1995). Bickman (1999) and his colleagues have conducted extensive outcome studies of large innovative, community-based services for children. Although many children improved, and although Bickman did not monitor the actual therapy, he found that outcomes were unrelated to the service coordination, the amount of therapy, the therapist's qualifications, or the presence of supervision. Armed with his and others' data, Bickman has become a serial killer of psychotherapy's sacred cows, questioning whether clinical experience, advanced degrees, continuing education, licensing, accreditation, or supervision influence clinical outcomes.

What do we do to improve outcomes in clinical settings? Major professional groups and a number of clinical leaders are addressing this question. The American Academy of Child and Adolescent Psychiatry convenes experts to develop practice parameters for many diagnoses. These are published and updated in its journal and posted on its Web site (http://www.aacap.org). Mental health guidelines for children developed by other groups are available or referenced on a Web site hosted by the National Institutes of Health (http://www.guidelines.gov/), and the Substance Abuse and Mental Health Services Administration is developing its National Registry of Effective Programs and Practices. Experienced clinicians also offer guidelines, handouts, and worksheets in their areas of expertise (e.g., Barkley, 1998). There is a growing emphasis on the use of evidence-based or empirically supported treatments (ESTs), the Division of Clinical Psychology of the American Psychological Association sought treatments with defined levels of research support for designation as ESTs. Its Work Group on Clinical

Child Psychology judged a number of treatments to be *well established* or *probably efficacious* (Lonigan, Elbert, & Johnson, 1998). The Work Group emphasized that its work was limited—it was descriptive of ESTs, but not prescriptive. The supervision of several ESTs is described in this volume.

Kazdin and Kendall (1998) asserted that failure to use ESTs where they are available requires "a very strong justification" (p. 218). However, the rush to ESTs must be tempered by three realities: (a) there are many diagnoses, or combinations of diagnoses, with no established ESTs; (b) many potentially effective therapies lack the test of quality research with relevant comparison groups; and (c) much research supporting ESTs is conducted under laboratory conditions that differ from community realities. This final point garners much attention in the EST debate. Some therapists argue that community conditions are too different to make laboratory findings relevant. Weisz and Hawley (1998) noted that in the community children and parents may have weak motivation for treatment, children may have several diagnoses (i.e., 3.5 on average), families may have multiple problems, clinicians may be stressed, and few situations may be prone to solutions with a neatly tailored EST manual. Still, some ESTs show good results with challenging community samples (Brestan & Eyberg, 1998; Pelham, Wheeler, & Chronis, 1998). The bulk of existing evidence supports particular approaches with some problems. Kazdin (2005), for example, made a powerful case for training parents in child management when children present with oppositional, aggressive, and antisocial behavior.

Although community realities may complicate efforts to apply standardized treatments, supervisors need to be aware that both clinical guidelines and ESTs are rich resources for the craft. Even for seriously troubled children whose problems seem to exceed the sum of their diagnoses and the collective resources of our care-taking system, guidelines and ESTs may address particular problems within a longer, larger plan of care or systemic therapy (chap. 8, this volume).

Many advocates of ESTs support the idea that good outcomes depend on the specific effects of specific treatments. This is sometimes equated with a medical model of treatment in which the diagnosis guides the course of a specific intervention.

Common Factors in Therapy Versus Effects of Specific Treatments

Do different therapies really have different effects? Frank and Frank (1991) emphasized the common elements across all psychotherapies. They suggested that most positive results of psychotherapy were due to common factors shared by most therapies. On the basis of statistical meta-analysis of hundreds of studies (i.e., mostly adult), Wampold (2001) affirmed a common factors view of psychotherapy. He suggested major effects were due to four common factors: (a) a working alliance between client and therapist, (b) the therapist's allegiance to the intervention, (c) the placebo effects due to the healing setting and client's hopes and expectancies, and (d) the therapist's competence. Because outcome effects between therapists are larger than between therapies, Wampold attributed the difference to therapist competence. Wampold warned that a common-factors theory does not mean *anything goes*. Effective therapy requires "the active participation of the client and the therapist and that each believes that the procedure chosen will be beneficial to the client" (Wampold, 2001, p. 217). Shirk and Russell (1996) suggested that early meta-analyses of psychotherapy with children and adolescents can support a common-factors interpretation— "The data are just not fine grained enough to confidently conclude otherwise" (p. 69).

Ultimately, specificity is likely to work in tandem with common factors but not likely to eliminate them. Both advocates and opponents of specific ESTs cite the importance of therapist variables and a therapeutic alliance, even in treatment with manuals (Weisz & Kazdin, 2003). Work by Jensen, Weersing, Hoagwood, and Goldman (2005) suggested that little of the research supporting ESTs evaluated the degree to which common or nonspecific factors determined actual outcomes.

The common factors debate reminds supervisors that a positive therapeutic alliance is essential and that therapists must be confident in their skills. Therapists must also help families understand what therapy is about and how it works—a step easily neglected with children. The common factors model requires attention to cultural differences, particularly between the client's and the therapist's belief systems. In a stark example, an 8-year-old girl of immigrant parents presented at a clinic as tense and sad with deteriorating schoolwork. Her parents claimed she was the victim of an angry relative who had subjected her to the evil eye. After several weeks of therapy with no change, she arrived at the clinic skipping and smiling. Her drawings were no longer tiny, rigid figures tucked in a corner but were expansive and colorful. Over the weekend, a neighbor had conducted an elaborate costumed ritual to free her from the evil eye.

Mechanisms of Change

Considering the mechanisms of change within a therapy is like determining the active ingredients in an effective herbal medicine. There is little research demonstrating actual mechanisms of change in children (Weersing & Weisz, 2002). This is a core concern for Shirk and Russell (1996), who deplored the gap between theories of child therapy and research in child development, particularly work on the causes of pathology. Similar symptoms can have different causes, but this is not addressed when diagnoses are simply matched with brand name therapies that fail to specify either the cause of the symptoms or the process of change. Consider the following vignette:

> A boy from an extremely strict family was placed in residential treatment because of his defiance and aggression. For several months in therapy, he enacted sadistic scenarios in which an alien tortured and killed women and children. The therapist, out of his own discomfort, looked for ways to redirect the play and empathized, "Bad things must have happened to the alien to make him want to hurt people so much." Finally, in client-centered therapy's spirit of radical acceptance, the therapist entered the play mirroring the behavior of the alien. Sadism disappeared from the boy's play. He began relating to the therapist in a positive manner, and his conduct outside of therapy began improving.

What does this vignette tell us? Was radical acceptance of the boy's thoughts and feelings, demonstrated by the therapist's willingness to enter his play, effective? Was the therapist's earlier mode of response reinforcing the sadism? Was the boy so scared by the therapist's behavior that he decided to shapeup? Should the therapist have joined the boy's sadism right away? Was joining in the sadism more effective because it was a clear reach for the therapist? Could change occur if the child was not safe in a supportive milieu? Do these gains have a prayer of continuing without major changes in the boy's family before the boy leaves residential care?

Mechanisms of change are elusive. They can be very hard to define in the dynamic therapies. For example, the descriptions of the processes of *interpretation* and *working through* in Coppolillo's (1987) work on therapy with children were quite fuzzy. Although change mechanisms seem more evident in behavioral interventions, even behavioral techniques can be poorly specified, misapplied, mistimed, or negated by confounding circumstances (Peterson, Homer, & Wonderlich, 1982). In one study, cognitive behavior therapy for depressed children produced positive effects without evidence of change in the cognitive processes presumed to underlie such improvement (Kolko, Brent, Baugher, Bridge, & Birmaher, 2000). The thinking of Shirk and Russell (1996) and the gaps in our research cited by Hoagwood (2005) should temper the current debates by reminding us how much we have yet to learn.

Such awareness only increases the need for supervisees to identify their hypotheses regarding means of change and to continuously assess them against measures of client response to intervention. Chorpita, Daleiden, and Weisz (2005) suggest thoughtful mining of the research literature for the most promising techniques and approaches to the situation of a particular child. Some supervisees try to escape such rigor by proclaiming therapy an art. There is art in therapy, but it is no basis for elevating "what is done to the level of the intangible. . . ." (Munson, 2002, p. 484).

Whom Do We Treat?

The question, "whom do we treat?" is as old as child psychotherapy. Different therapies focus on the child, the parents, or the family, but, it is hoped that a careful assessment of the child's situation guides the intervention. With younger children, the focus will be on the caretakers and the parent–child relationship (Brinkmeyer & Eyberg, 2003; Sameroff, McDonough, & Rosenblum, 2004; chaps. 5 and 8, this volume). As children get older, certain types of aggressive behaviors may dictate a primary focus on the parents (Kazdin, 2005). Jacobs and Wachs (2002) insisted on working with parents for two strategic reasons: (a) having the child see an expert can undermine the parent's role and (b) improved parenting is a continuing resource for the child. Maximizing caretakers' functioning should always be a consideration, but there are many times when it is appropriate to see the child or teen alone, such as when a child is in temporary care because of abuse, an extremely alienated teen, or, more commonly, a child whose parents can provide only part of what is needed. Mufson and Moreau (1999) flexibly involved parents at different stages of their empirically supported, interpersonal work with depressed teens. Children can also be seen in groups to great effect when learning social skills or when peer support is critical. Supervisors guide therapists through the whom-to-treat decision with each new referral.

THE BEST WE HAVE TO OFFER

Quality efforts to integrate the growing child therapy research are now published regularly. Recent examples range from practical guides to evidence-based therapy (Ammerman, Hersen, & Last, 1999; Christophersen & Mortweet, 2001; Hibbs & Jensen, 2005; Schroder & Gordon, 2002) to critical reviews of the research (Evans et al., 2005; Fonagy et al., 2002; Kazdin & Weisz, 2003; Russ & Ollendick, 1999). Several of these works end with chapters assessing the state of the field. In their concluding chapter, Fonagy et al. (2002) suggested that a general model in child mental health was emerging from multiple streams of theory and research. I have taken the liberty of rephrasing themes from Fonagy et al. as a set of principles, noting similar conclusions from Weisz and Kazdin (2003), Hoagwood's (2005) summary in Evans et al. (2005), or Russ and Ollendick (1999). These principles are as follows:

1. Children's behavior must be understood within a *wide perspective*, including biological and social systems that mutually influence each other. Therefore, change requires system-level

interventions and measurements. Weisz and Kazdin stressed a similar need for breadth and duration of outcome measures.

2. Children's behavior is only *a marker on a developmental trajectory*. Therefore, intervention must consider both treatment and prevention (also Russ & Ollendick, 1999).

3. As therapy expands to include parents, families, and social systems, intervention sites will include home, school, and community. Weisz and Kazdin reported that research has "pushed the boundaries" of the traditional weekly office visit (2003, p. 441). Hoagwood urges therapies to encompass the perspectives of families and of all key stakeholders.

4. In many cases, treatment goals must provide relief, adaptation, or supports rather than cures. Weisz and Kazdin suggested that chronic conditions, such as attention-deficit/hyperactivity disorder and developmental disorders, require a continuing-care model or, at least, a regular monitoring with treatment as needed.

5. A child with complex problems requires specific multicomponent and multidisciplinary interventions and less generic therapy. Russ and Ollendick referred to the integration of approaches to cover multidetermined conditions. Weisz and Kazdin cited a similar approach to address co-occurring disorders. Hoagwood stressed the need to more rapidly and effectively deploy empirically supported practices.

6. There must be a clear sensitivity to gender and cultural issues. The "contextual framework for considering interventions will become more essential as we become a more diverse society" (Russ & Ollendick, 1999, p. 555). Weisz and Kazdin noted that cultural issues may define the effective boundaries of some treatments.

7. The focus of therapy must shift from the mental health expert toward the collaboration and empowerment of children and parents.

TOWARD SUPERVISION THAT IMPACTS OUTCOMES

If it is too early to foreclose on therapies that are not specified in guidelines or that lack EST status, it is too late to practice without attention to research, rigor in assessment, detailed planning, fidelity in implementation, and outcome measurement. Woody, Detweiler-Bedell, Teachman, and O'Hearn (2003), with supervisees in diverse settings, needed an exportable format for evidence-based supervision. They developed planning and assessment in clinical care (PACC) that guides practice and requires measurements of progress using instruments that clinicians choose or develop with their supervisors. Supervisors in learning organizations can evaluate themselves and staff against measures of treatment process and outcomes (Lyons, Howard, O'Mahoney, & Lish, 1997). Several of the therapies described in this volume advocate informal or formal feedback from clients after each session (see chaps. 6 and 9, this volume). Help with individualized measurement and evaluation is also found in the literature on single case research and on evidence-based evaluation (Edwards, 1996; Franklin, Allison, & Gorman, 1997; Hodges, 2004; Mash & Hunsley, 2005).

Respecting the common factors data, supervisors must teach the skills that build and sustain a therapeutic alliance. In work with children, multiple alliances are needed, often with conflicting parties. With a thoughtful, open-minded grasp of how therapy might create change, supervisors can help supervisees continuously evaluate their hypotheses. Supervisors guide therapists in deciding who, both in the family and in the community, must be involved in intervention. If attitudes, clinic hours, location, or policies are barriers to involvement of the necessary parties, supervisors are often in the best position to tackle such barriers.

Supervisors often hear proposals for intervention, which supervisees couch in general mental health terminology, that simply lack the scope or the traction to produce change. Supervisors who keep abreast of our growing body of research and theory and who closely attend to outcomes are positioned to increase the clinical leverage of their supervisees. As the therapeutic neighborhood changes, it is the experience, dedication, and continued learning of supervisors that will ensure therapists are well prepared to help children and families.

REFERENCES

Achenbach, T. M. (1998). Diagnosis, assessment, taxonomy, and case formulation. In T. H. Ollendick & M. Hersen (Eds.), *Handbook of child psychopathology* (3rd ed., pp. 63–87) New York: Plenum Press.

American Psychiatric Association. (1952). *Diagnostic and statistical manual of mental disorders*. Washington, DC: Author.

American Psychiatric Association. (2000). *Diagnostic and statistical manual of mental disorders* (4th ed., text rev.). Washington, DC: Author.

Ammerman, R. T., Hersen, M., & Last, C. G. (1999). *Handbook of prescriptive treatments for children and adolescents* (2nd ed.). Boston: Allyn & Bacon.

Angold, A., Costello, E. J., & Erkanli, A. (1999). Comorbidity. *Journal of Child Psychology and Psychiatry, 40*, 57–87.

Barkley, R. A. (1998). *Attention deficit hyperactivity disorder: A handbook for diagnosis and treatment* (2nd ed.). New York: Guilford Press.

Bickman, L. (1999). Practice makes perfect and other myths about mental health services. *American Psychologist, 54,* 965–978.

Brestan, E. V., & Eyberg, S. M. (1998). Effective psychosocial treatments of conduct disordered children and adolescents: 29 years, 82 studies, and 5,272 kids. *Journal of Clinical Child Psychology, 2,* 180–189.

Brinkmeyer, M. Y., & Eyberg, S. M. (2003). Parent–child interaction therapy for oppositional children. In A. E. Kazdin & J. R. Weisz (Eds.), *Evidence-based psychotherapies for children and adolescents* (pp. 204–223). New York: Guilford Press.

Burns, B. J., Schoenwald, S. K., Burchard, J. D., Faw, L., & Santos, A. B. (2000). Comprehensive community-based interventions for youth with severe emotional disorders: Multisystemic therapy and the wraparound process. *Journal of Child and Family Studies, 9,* 283–314.

Chamberlin, P., & Smith, D. K. (2003). Antisocial behavior in children and adolescents: The Oregon multidimensional treatment foster care model. In A. E. Kazdin & J. R. Weisz (Eds.), *Evidence-based psychotherapies for children and adolescents* (pp. 282–300). New York: Guilford Press.

Christophersen, E. R., & Mortweet, S. L. (2001). *Treatments that work with children: Empirically supported strategies for managing childhood problems.* Washington, DC: American Psychological Association.

Chorpita, B. F., Daleiden, E. L., & Weisz, J. R. (2005). Identifying and selecting the common elements of evidence-based interventions: A distillation and matching model. *Mental Health Services Research, 7,* 5–20.

Cicchetti, D., & Toth, S. L. (2003). Child maltreatment: Past, present, and future perspectives. In R. P. Weisberg, H. J. Walberg, M. U. O'Brien, & C. B. Custer (Eds.), *Long-term trends in the well-being of children and youth: Issues in children's and families' lives* (pp. 181–205). Washington, DC: CWLA Press.

Coppolillo, H. P. (1987). *Psychodynamic psychotherapy of children: An introduction to the art and the techniques.* Madison, CT: International Universities Press.

Edwards, D. J. A. (1996). Case study research: The cornerstone of theory and practice. In M. A. Reineke, F. M. Dattilio, & A. Freeman (Eds.), *Cognitive therapy with children and adolescents: A casebook for clinical practice* (pp. 10–17). New York: Guilford Press.

Eisenberg, L. (2001). The past 50 years of child and adolescent psychiatry: A personal memoir. *Journal of the American Academy of Child and Adolescent Psychiatry, 40,* 743–748.

Evans, D. L., Foa, E. B., Gur, R. E., Hendin, H., O'Brien, C. P., Seligman, M. E. P., & Walsh, T. (Eds.). (2005). *Treating and preventing adolescent mental health disorders: What we know and don't know.* Oxford, England: Oxford University Press.

Fonagy, P., Target, M., Cottrell, D., Phillips, J., & Kurtz, Z. (2002). *What works for whom? A critical review of treatments for children and adolescents.* New York: Guilford Press.

Frank, J. D., & Frank, J. B. (1991). *Persuasion and healing: A comparative study of psychotherapy* (3rd ed.). Baltimore: Johns Hopkins University Press.

Franklin, R. D., Allison, D. B., & Gorman, B. S. (Eds.). (1997). *Design and analysis of single-case research*. Mawah, NJ: Erlbaum.

Friedman, R. M. (2001). The practice of psychology with children, adolescents, and their families: A look into the future. In J. N. Hughes, A. M. La Greca, & J. C. Conoley (Eds.), *Handbook of psychological services for children and adolescents* (pp. 3–22). New York: Oxford University Press.

Haley, J. (1975). Why a mental health clinic should avoid family therapy. *Journal of Marriage and Family Counseling, 1*, 3–13.

Hansen, M. (2002). The need for competence in children's public mental health services. In D. T. Marsh & M. A. Fristad (Eds.), *Handbook of serious emotional disturbance in children and adolescence* (pp. 93–111). New York: Wiley.

Hibbs, E. D., & Jensen, P. S. (2005). *Psychosocial treatments for child and adolescent disorders: Empirically based strategies for clinical practice* (2nd ed.). Washington, DC: American Psychological Association.

Hoagwood, K. (2005). The research, policy, and practice context for delivery of evidence-based mental health treatments for adolescents: A systems perspective. In D. L. Evans, E. B. Foa, R. E. Gur, H. Hendin, C. P. O'Brien, M. Seligman, & T. Walsh (Eds.), *Treating and preventing adolescent mental health disorders: What we know and don't know* (pp. 545–560). Oxford, England: Oxford University Press.

Hoagwood, K., & Olin, S. S. (2002). The NIMH blueprint for change report: Research priorities in child and adolescent mental health. *Journal of the American Academy of Child and Adolescent Psychiatry, 41*, 760–767.

Hobbs, N. (1975). *The futures of children*. San Francisco: Jossey-Bass.

Hodges, K. (2004). Using assessment in everyday practice for the benefit of families and practitioners. *Professional Psychology: Research and Practice, 35*, 449–456.

Holden, E. W., & Brannan, A. M. (2002). Evaluating systems of care: The comprehensive community mental health services for children and their families program [Special issue]. *Children's Services: Social Policy, Research, and Practice, 5*(1).

Jacobs, L., & Wachs, C. (2002). *Parent therapy: A relational alternative to working with children*. Northvale, NJ: Jason Aronson.

Jellinek, M. S. (1999). Changes in the practice of child and adolescent psychiatry: Are our patients better served? *Journal of the American Academy of Child and Adolescent Psychiatry, 38*, 115–117.

Jensen, P. S., Weersing, R., Hoagwood, K. E., & Goldman, E. (2005). What is the evidence for evidence-based treatments? A hard look at our soft underbelly. *Mental Health Services Research, 7*, 53–74.

Kataoka, S. H., Zhang, L., & Wells, K. B. (2002). Unmet needs for mental health care among U.S. children: Variation by ethnicity and insurance status. *American Journal of Psychiatry, 159*, 1548–1555.

Kazdin, A. E. (1988). *Child psychotherapy: Developing and identifying effective treatments*. Elmsford, NY: Pergamon Press.

Kazdin, A. E. (2000). *Psychotherapy for children and adolescents: Directions for research and practice*. New York: Oxford University Press.

Kazdin, A. E. (2005). *Parent management training*. Oxford, England: Oxford University Press.

Kazdin, A. E., & Kendall, P. C. (1998). Current progress and future plans for developing effective treatments: Comments and perspectives. *Journal of Clinical Child Psychology, 27*, 217–226.

Kazdin, A. E., & Weisz, J. R. (2003). *Evidence-based psychotherapies for children and adolescents*. New York: Guilford Press.

Kolko, D., Brent, D., Baugher, M., Bridge, J., & Birmaher, B. (2000). Cognitive and family therapies for adolescent depression: Treatment specificity, mediation and moderation. *Journal of Consulting and Clinical Psychology, 68*, 603–614.

Lonigan, C. J., Elbert, J. C., & Johnson, S. B. (1998). Empirically supported psychosocial interventions for children: An overview. *Journal of Clinical Child Psychology, 27*, 138–145.

Lyons, J. S., Howard, K. I., O'Mahoney, M. T., & Lish, J. D. (1997). *The measurement and management of clinical outcomes in mental health*. New York: Wiley.

Marsh, D. T. (2004). Serious emotional disturbance in children and adolescents: Opportunities and challenges for psychologists. *Professional Psychology: Research and Practice, 35*, 443–448.

Mash, E. J., & Hunsley, J. (2005). Evidence-based assessment of child and adolescent disorders: Issues and challenges. *Journal of Clinical and Adolescent Psychology, 34*, 362–379.

Mufson, L., & Moreau, D. (1999). Interpersonal psychotherapy for depressed adolescents (ITP–A). In S. W. Russ & T. H. Ollendick (Eds.), *Handbook of psychotherapies for children and families* (pp. 239–253). New York: Kluwer Academic/Plenum Publishers.

Munson, C. E. (2002). *Handbook of clinical social work supervision*. New York: Haworth Press.

Norcross, J. C., Hedges, M., & Castle, P. H. (2002). Psychologists conducting psychotherapy in 2001: A study of the Division 29 membership. *Psychotherapy: Theory, Research, Practice, Training, 39*, 97–102.

Paul, G. L. (1967). Strategy of outcome research in psychotherapy. *Journal of Consulting and Clinical Psychology, 31*, 109–118.

Pelham, W. E., Wheeler, T., & Chronis, A. (1998). Empirically supported psychosocial treatments for attention deficit hyperactivity disorder. *Journal of Clinical Child Psychology, 27*, 190–205.

Peterson, C., & Seligman, M. E. P. (2004). *Character strengths and virtues: A handbook and classification*. New York: American Psychological Association and Oxford University Press.

Peterson, L., Homer, A., & Wonderlich, S. (1982). The integrity of independent variables in behavior analysis. *Journal of Applied Behavior Analysis, 15*, 477–492.

Phelps, L., Brown, R. T., & Power, T. J. (2002). *Pediatric psychopharmacology: Combining medical and psychosocial interventions*. Washington, DC: American Psychological Association.

Prilleltensky, I. (1994). *The morals and politics of psychology: Psychological discourse and the status quo.* Albany: State University of New York Press.

Reisman, J. M., & Ribordy, S. (1993). *Principles of psychotherapy with children* (2nd ed.). New York: Lexington Books.

Russ, S. W., & Ollendick, T. H. (Eds.). (1999). *Handbook of psychotherapies with children and families.* New York: Kluwer Academic/Plenum Publishers.

Safer, D. J., Zito, J. M., & dosReis, S. (2003). Concomitant psychotropic medication for youth. *American Journal of Psychiatry, 160,* 438–449.

Sameroff, A. J., McDonough, S. C., & Rosenblum, K. L. (2004). *Treating parent–infant relationship problems.* New York: Guilford Press.

Schroder, C. S., & Gordon, B. N. (2002). *Assessment and treatment of childhood problems: A clinician's guide* (2nd ed.). New York: Guilford Press.

Shirk, S. R., & Russell, R. L. (1996). *Change processes in child psychotherapy: Revitalizing treatment and research.* New York: Guilford Press.

Torralba-Romero, J. (1998). Recruitment, retention, training, and supervision of mental health staff. In M. Hernandez & M. R. Isaacs (Eds.), *Promoting cultural competence in mental health services* (pp. 81–93). Baltimore: Brookes Publishing.

Toth, S. L., & Cicchetti, D. (1999). Developmental psychopathology and child psychotherapy. In S. W. Russ & T. H. Ollendick (Eds.), *Handbook of psychotherapies with children and families* (pp. 15–44). New York: Kluwer Academic/Plenum Publishers.

Wampold, B. E. (2001). *The great psychotherapy debate: Models, methods, and findings.* Mawah, NJ: Erlbaum.

Weersing, V. R., & Weisz, J. R. (2002). Mechanisms of action in youth psychotherapy. *Journal of Child Psychology and Psychiatry, 42,* 3–29.

Weisz, J., Donenberg, G., Han, S., & Kauneckis, D. (1995). Child and adolescent psychotherapy outcomes in experiments versus clinics: Why the disparity? *Journal of Abnormal Child Psychology, 23,* 83–106.

Weisz, J. R., & Hawley, K. M. (1998). Finding, evaluating, refining, and applying empirically supported treatments for children and adolescents. *Journal of Clinical Child Psychology, 27,* 206–216.

Weisz, J. R., & Kazdin, A. E. (2003). Concluding thoughts: Present and future of evidence-based psychotherapies for children and adolescents. In A. E. Kazdin & J. R. Weisz (Eds.), *Evidence-based psychotherapies for children and adolescents* (pp. 439–451). New York: Guilford Press.

Woody, S. R., Detweiler-Bedell, J., Teachman, B. A., & O'Hearn, T. (2003). *Treatment planning in psychotherapy: Taking the guesswork out of clinical care.* New York: Guilford Press.

Zero to Three: National Center for Infants, Toddlers, and Families. (1994). *Diagnostic classification of mental health and developmental disorders of infancy and early childhood.* Washington, DC: Author.

3

ETHICS AND ACCOUNTABILITY IN SUPERVISION OF CHILD PSYCHOTHERAPY

JAMES J. CLARK AND ELIZABETH L. CRONEY

Doing ethics is fundamental to clinical practice. Because professionals pledge to fulfill socially necessary duties to their clients and colleagues and to society at large, they enjoy the privilege to practice (Koehn, 1994). New practitioners, overwhelmed by the technical and emotional demands of their work, can lose sight of this mandate. The desire to do good or to be a successful clinician sometimes outweighs the prudence necessary for ethical

The statements and opinions published in this chapter are the responsibility of the authors. Such opinions and statements do not represent official policies, standards, guidelines, or ethical mandates of the American Psychological Association (APA), APA's Ethics Committee or Office of Ethics, or any other APA governance group or staff. Statements made in this chapter neither add to nor reduce requirements of the APA "Ethical Principles of Psychologists and Code of Conduct" (2002), hereinafter referred to as the APA Ethics Code or the Ethics Code, nor can they be viewed as a definitive source of the meaning of the Ethics Code Standards or their application to particular situations. Each ethics committee or other relevant body must interpret and apply the Ethics Code as it believes proper, given all the circumstances. Any information in this chapter involving legal and ethical issues should not be used as a substitute for obtaining personal legal and/or ethical advice and consultation prior to making decisions regarding individual circumstances.

The authors dedicate this chapter to the late John Ballantine, MSW, supervisor and friend extraordinaire.

clinical work. For example, modern bioethics has demonstrated that "good intentions" are not sufficient to prevent violations of clients' basic rights (Rae, Brunnquell, & Sullivan, 2003). Paternalism (i.e., acting for the apparent good for others without respecting their own right to decide and act) is a special danger, and well-meaning clinicians are sometimes tempted to use aggressively helpful approaches that deprive clients of their freedom and autonomy (Kopelman, 1998).

Supervision is the place where ethical choices must be recognized, evaluated, and modeled.

> We acquire habits of conduct not by constructing a way of living upon rules or precepts learned by heart and subsequently practiced, but by living with people who habitually behave in a certain manner: We acquire habits of conduct in the same way as we acquire our native language. (Oakeshott, 1991, p. 468)

If this is true, no ethics code or course can replace the consistent presence and modeling of a supervisor who actively helps the supervisee to integrate the principles of ethical, clinical practice with the supervisee's pre-existing moral framework (Handelsman, Gottlieb, & Knapp, 2005).

PROFESSIONAL BOARD REGULATIONS

Much ethical instruction tends to be conducted by reviewing professional codes, board regulations, or, more starkly, examples of professionals' broad exposure to civil litigation (Besharov & Besharov, 1987). Indeed, research on medical malpractice litigation reveals those patients who perceive their health care providers as disrespectful and unresponsive are more likely to sue (Hickson et al., 2002). The public's growing awareness of medical errors, shrinking confidence in health care systems in part because of managed care, rising expectations of positive outcomes, and witnessing of zealous plaintiffs' attorneys are associated with the increase in malpractice claims (Studdert, Mello, & Brennan, 2004).

Although committees in professional associations define and monitor the ethical activities of their members, actual professional regulation rests with boards created by state legislatures. Those who mistake state boards as lenient guild organizations acting on the professional's behalf make a grave error. The state boards' mandate is *consumer* protection (Clark, 1999; Hedges & Thatcher, 2000). They issue, monitor, and revoke professional licenses—they literally begin and end careers. Supervisors must teach and apply regulations governing the jurisdictions where they practice.

Under U.S. case law, the supervisor is almost always vicariously responsible for their supervisees' misadventures. The principle of *respondeat superior* implies that "in supervision, responsibility is multiplied, it is never divided" (Saccuzzo, 2003b, p. 17). Attempts to sever supervisor from supervisee in the course of a lawsuit almost always prove to be fruitless (Perlin, 1994; Saccuzzo, 2003a, 2003b). Regulatory boards typically hold this perspective as they consider complaints filed by the public.

CHILD CLINICIANS, WELL INTENDED OR NOT, ARE SUBJECT TO ETHICAL LAPSES

Child mental health professionals sometimes fail to adequately meet ethical challenges. Melton, Ehrenreich, and Lyons (2001) argued that "many of the most egregious intrusions on the rights of children have been in the name of treatment" (p. 1089). They asserted that most ethical failures flow from clinicians who are uninformed or insensitive to their obligation to respect children's rights. What causes such problematic behavior? Decision research robustly shows that clinicians can overestimate their knowledge of ethical and legal standards, often substituting personal views in making ethical judgments (Grob, 1998). Turk and Salovey (1989) demonstrated that cognitive errors and biases were common in clinical work and were usually undetected by clinicians or supervisors. Pressures to appear all knowing can lead to mistakes born of self-deception (Crawshaw, 1987). Therapies that result in transference or strong emotional connections may distort clinical judgment and lead to unethical decisions (Clark, 1999). Workplace flaws also facilitate unethical behavior (Reid, 2004). Agency and managed care policies can pressure clinicians to limit the quantity and quality of care, avoid case coordination, skimp on assessments, or inflate diagnoses. Such pressures point to the need for organizations to make ethical behavior an important dimension of their mission (Cooper, 1994).

DOING ETHICS AND BEING ACCOUNTABLE IN THE SUPERVISORY RELATIONSHIP

Supervisors should be prepared to teach supervisees a pragmatic, defensible framework for ethical decision making—one that is useful across cases and crises. Rae and Fournier (1999) suggested ethical decision making involves four steps: (a) identify the ethical issues and dilemmas, (b) analyze the situation, (c) implement the decision, and (d) evaluate the decision. Clinicians should be insightful about values and biases animating their preferences, know the ethics codes germane to their practice, cultivate a network of colleagues to assist with complex decisions, and establish policies and procedures reflecting ethical standards of practice (pp. 79–81).

Gert (2004), a philosopher who specializes in professional codes of ethics, applied fundamental moral rules to ethical conflicts as they arose in practice situations. These rules can be helpful for supervisors who wish to teach pragmatic moral reasoning. Gert delineated the basic moral principles of respect for persons, autonomy, beneficence, veracity, confidentiality, fidelity, and justice. He has specified a basic set of moral rules: (a) do not kill, (b) do not cause suffering, (c) do not disable, (d) do not deprive of freedom, (e) do not deprive of pleasure, (f) do not deceive, and (g) do not cheat. Problematic cases usually involve conflict among these moral rules, which are so-called, ethical dilemmas. In such cases, it is crucial to examine the relevant moral principles, the desires and beliefs of the persons involved, and the potential harm and benefits attached to all possible decisions.

Ultimately, supervisors need to use their chosen, sanctioned ethical framework to assist supervisees as they think through their responses to problematic cases with children and families. The decision-making process will frequently involve a consideration of both ethical obligations and legal duties. It is clear that a person assuming a supervisory role should possess the intellectual rigor and the experience to apply and teach a viable framework for ethical decision making.

Supervisor Competence

There is significant variation in the knowledge and experiences of professionals who supervise work with children (Munson, 1993). The first duty for prospective supervisors is to ensure that they have attained the qualifications, experiences, and knowledge necessary to be effective. To do so, supervisors require a solid background in child mental health and experience in effective clinical work. They should understand and be able to apply ethics codes, board regulations, and laws concerning their practice. In addition, they should understand and respect the boundaries and roles that create effective and nonexploitative supervision relationships (Heru, Strong, Price, & Recupero, 2004). One might be a competent clinician, but, as Stoltenberg, McNeill, and Delworth (1998) noted, "Not all players make good coaches" (p. xi). In fact, research examining supervision relationships has shown that ineffective supervisors can harm their supervisees—this is the so-called *dark side* of supervision (Ladany, 2004). Ladany, Lehrman-Waterman, Molinaro, and Wolgast (1999) surveyed 151 therapists and found that 51% of the respondents reported at least one ethical violation by their supervisors; the most frequently cited violations were inadequate performance evaluations, confidentiality issues in supervision, and theoretical–clinical inflexibility. It is important to note that nonadherence to ethical guidelines appeared to be positively related to weak supervisory alliances and to overall low supervisee satisfaction. Clinicians planning to enter supervisory roles should seek supervision training to build the knowledge and skills necessary for developing and maintaining strong supervisory alliances; theoretical–clinical pluralism; and consistent, ethical supervision practices. Prospective supervisors must have their own houses in order—that is, they should have worked through personal and professional issues to the degree that allows for continuous self-analysis, careful use of self, proper management of supervisory countertransference, and sound capacity to repair ruptured supervisory alliances (Ladany, Constantine, Miller, Erickson, & Muse-Burke, 2000).

Assessing Supervisee Readiness to Act Ethically

At the outset, supervisors should emphasize to supervisees that ethical analysis is central to clinical practice. In initial meetings, supervisors have a duty to clarify the requirements of the profession, the employing organization, and the supervisor, while allowing the supervisee to join the discussion by identifying areas of strength and areas of weakness that need work in supervision (Bradley & Ladany, 2001). Supervisors cannot presume therapists have a working knowledge of ethics. Supervisees' credentials can range from paraprofessionals who have never read an ethics code to seasoned, doctoral practitioners, but even graduate-level practitioners may have scant memory or grasp of ethical principles. By discussing prospective supervisee's thoughts, emotions, and choices in previous ethical struggles, the supervisor can informally gauge the supervisee's ethical "intelligence." This inquiry includes two broad domains: (a) the knowledge of ethics codes and legal duties and (b) the capacity to act ethically, the distinction between knowing good and doing good. A supervisor interested in infusing ethical analysis into the supervisory relationship must understand their supervisee as a thinker, judger, and actor.

Supervisees' Reactions to Need for Ethical Analysis

In orientations to ethics and risk management, some supervisees readily discuss the importance of ethical issues. Others may not value ethical reflection apart from dangers looming in a particular case. The supervisor should offer examples of how ethical analysis protects the client, the organization, and the supervisee. If the supervisee resists such ideas or comments on their triviality, the supervisor should think carefully about accepting the supervisee and exposing him or her to clients.

Building an Ethical Base

The supervisor should have an effective blueprint to help the supervisee build his or her fund of ethical understanding and legal duties, as well as a plan for experiences to enhance the supervisee's capacities to act ethically (Besharov & Besharov, 1987; Handelsman et al., 2005). The stakes are high for the supervisor (i.e., the rule of *respondeat superior*), the supervisee, the organization, and the children and families they serve.

Examples of Specific Supervision Techniques

Formats for supervision have ethical and risk management implications. Ladany (2004) argued that the development of a strong supervisor–supervisee alliance is critical for the effective and ethical treatment of clients. From their important work toward a conceptual model of the supervision process, Ladany, Friedlander, and Nelson (2005) described *markers* that indicate a particular supervisory action or focus. For example, the authors' discussion of countertransference alerted supervisors to markers hinting at supervisee reactions that may complicate therapy or supervision or that may lie at the root of ethical errors—statements indicative of positive or negative bias, overlooking important issues, over activity, tardiness, or behaviors simply uncharacteristic of the trainee. It is hoped sensitive responses to such markers will result in resolutions that will enhance supervisees' self-awareness, knowledge, and skills, while enhancing the supervisory alliance. The ultimate goal is greater clinician self-efficacy and better services for clients. Ladany et al. identified six critical events that supervisors should be prepared to address: (a) remediating skill deficits, (b) heightening multi-cultural awareness, (c) negotiating role conflicts, (d) managing sexual attraction, (e) repairing gender-related misunderstandings, and (f) addressing problematic behaviors (pp. 18–19).

Consistent with this process model, Walker and Clark (1999) recommended a proactive supervision style that included sensitive assessment of personal and professional pressures facing supervisees, special attention to supervisees' narratives about their interactions with clients, and use of guided exploration as opposed to passive listening or intrusive cross-examination. They urged attention to emergent themes across cases, such as strong feelings about clients, business, or monetary transactions and client contacts that portend serious boundary violations. Consider the following case example.

> Phyllis, a talented, new therapist, began her supervision session by discussing Tony, a 16-year-old client diagnosed with depression and oppositional defiant disorder. Tony flattered Phyllis by asking for special sessions. She also gave Tony her home phone number. Through empathetic questioning, the supervisor explored Phyllis' clinical rationale for these actions, and Phyllis found that her decisions were based on her emotional responses to Tony, especially her unrecognized fears that she might not be helpful because of her inexperience. The supervisor also expressed concern that these favors were unusual, because they were

not granted to other clients and they might reflect Tony's skill at manipulating others by seeming needy. Resistant to supervisory direction at first, Phyllis subsequently began to connect Tony's behavior with his historical problems with authority and his previous therapists. Phyllis began to re-establish boundaries by restricting phone calls and tapering off special sessions. At the same time, she worked to help Tony see the destructive aspects of his manipulations with others and within the therapy relationship.

The supervisor continued to help Phyllis be more confident with such challenging strategies and be more tolerant of Tony's anger when he struggled in this new relationship that demanded more honesty and consideration. In a later supervision session, Phyllis remarked that she had begun to understand she could be more therapeutic by maintaining professional boundaries and agency guidelines. It is remarkable that she was able to discuss the parallel process experience of learning to follow the rules herself as a supervisee and employee, as she was counseling Tony to do in his life.

Complex, clinical interactions usually require the supervisor to use different sources of data to inform the supervision process. Saccuzzo (2003b) strongly recommended combining supervisee self-reports, reviewing supervisee records, using live observation, using videotapes and audiotapes, as well as doing therapy as a team. Supervisors should document their supervision sessions. We have found that regular chart audits and independent contacts with clients to ascertain their satisfaction with ongoing treatment are very helpful, especially for monitoring supervisees' work in homes, in schools, and in neighborhoods.

REPRESENTATIVE LEGAL AND ETHICAL PROBLEMS IN CHILD WORK

Legal and ethical problems in adult therapy usually arise in the clinician–patient relationship. But in the child's world, family members, teachers, ministers, coaches, physicians, attorneys, and mental health professionals, as well as schools, welfare agencies, hospitals, and courts may stake claims. Supervisors considering the contextual differences between work with children and with adults can profitably turn to the important works by Melton et al. (2001) and Schetky and Benedek (2002), which informed the following discussion.

For adults, case law generally guides supervisors when dealing with problems of informed consent, refusal of and right to treatment, and confidentiality. These problems are more complex for children because child cases are decided at the nexus of conflicting interests held by the child, their caregivers, and the state (Rae & Fournier, 1999). It bears repeating that statutes and case laws pertaining to these issues will vary among states.[1]

Obtaining Informed Consent and Protecting Confidentiality

Informed Consent

Typically, children are involuntary clients referred by their parents or by their state acting in its *parens patriae* capacity (e.g., a state foster care agency). Practitioners are advised to treat children only when they have obtained the informed consent of the children's legal custodians. In cases of separation, divorce, or referral by temporary caregivers, it is wise for practitioners to copy and file documentation of custody. Joint custody arrangements may award medical decision making to one or both parents, and this should be determined during the intake process. Though young children are unable to give legally informed consent, it is ethically preferable to clarify every child's understanding about therapy and to actively seek assent from the child when possible.

Rae and Fournier (1999) provided an excellent overview of the four elements of informed consent that can assist a clinical supervisor. They emphasized (a) developing information commensurate to children's stages of cognitive development, (b) structuring a noncoercive environment for children and adolescents, (c) ensuring complete and understandable information about assessment and treatment, and (d) using fact sheets and other standardized documentation to fully inform all parties. Clinicians should explain the services and their risks and benefits to the child and should address the expectations of the child. Supervisors might consider modeling such clinical interactions with adult and child clients, having new clinicians process what they observe, and then discussing what they have learned. Such sessions can be followed by joint supervisor–supervisee sessions and then by videotaped sessions where the clinician takes the lead with the supervisor providing feedback. Supervisors should also help clinicians document the informed consent process, which includes obtaining signatures that indicate consent from caregivers, from adolescents, and, if appropriate, from older children. Such respect for the children's participation can be an empowering and therapeutic experience for them. It is also important that clinicians disclose to clients that their work is being supervised by a specific person who is sanctioned by the agency and that the assessment and treatment process will be monitored by that professional. Optimally, clients

---

[1]The American Psychological Association publishes the series *Law and Mental Health Professionals*, which is edited by Bruce D. Sales and Michael O. Miller. Each volume contains the relevant mental health law for a particular state, and is an excellent resource for clinical supervisors.

should be informed that they have the right to contact the supervisor when necessary.

There are exceptions to the need for parental consent in many states, such as when services are delivered in emergencies or to emancipated minors or when they are provided under special consent statutes. Such statutes may stipulate that minors can independently consent to help for substance abuse, pregnancy, or sexually transmitted diseases. These statutes allow treatment for children at risk, who might avoid care if their parents discovered their situation. Supervisors in school-based and in community health clinics will routinely face such issues and must be aware of local exceptions that allow children to seek help without a caregiver's knowledge. Jurisdictions vary regarding a child's right to receive mental health treatment, to seek hospitalization without parental consent, or to demand a hearing and legal representation when adults seek a child's hospitalization. They also vary with regard to a child's right to refuse treatment. Supervisors should develop their knowledge base through consultations with attorneys, forensic mental health professionals, and relevant publications. See footnote 1.

Confidentiality of Client Records

The implementation of the Health Insurance Portability and Accountability Act (HIPAA) has prioritized the protection of patients' health information. In most jurisdictions, release of information to third parties (e.g., insurance companies) requires the written permission of the child's legal custodian, and parents have the right to review their child's mental health records. Some jurisdictions grant exceptions for adolescents, and federal law grants significant protection to teens seeking substance abuse treatment. Supervisors should advise trainees that HIPAA violations carry severe legal sanctions. Therefore, knowledge of these regulations and an agency's procedures to implement HIPAA is important.

Supervisors should warn therapists that records can often be read by parents, and by extension, children. What information might be problematic if the parent or child were to know? When is it responsible or irresponsible to put this information in the record? Although the law may stipulate access to the child's productions in treatment, practitioners can seek some autonomy, particularly for teens, by developing agreements as to what information will be shared that will suit caregivers and children (Behnke & Kinsherff, 2002a). Such arrangements enhance the child's freedom to disclose painful and private thoughts. Supervisors can help clinicians develop case-specific approaches to documentation, especially when child treatment is conducted as family treatment. In some cases, Behnke and Kinsherff used approaches where clinicians and adolescent clients worked together to document their sessions to enhance communication, cooperation, and trust.

Clinicians should assume that patient records ultimately will be disclosed. In child custody or child protection cases, records are available to many interested parties. Guidance in these areas can prepare supervisees for discussions with clients during the informed consent process. Supervisees should understand the legal processes required to disclose records (e.g., subpoenas, court orders, and confidentiality waivers). Observing a supervisor seek consultation about confidentiality problems can be especially instructive. A supervisee compelled to testify in court should be well prepared by the supervisor or a clinician with forensic experience.

Confidentiality During the Treatment Process

Rae and Fournier (1999) described difficulties therapists and supervisors may face in preserving confidentiality in child therapy. Some of these may be avoided by developing specific agreements, which stipulate what information will and will not be shared with caregivers, during the initial family session with children and adults (House, 2002). Supervisors can oversee the development of these agreements, share the ethical and clinical basis for key decisions, and monitor respect for these agreements during treatment.

Representative Situations With Special Risks

Suspicion of Child Abuse or Neglect and Domestic Violence

A central purpose of supervision is to protect patients from harm. This includes respecting the legal duty to report child neglect and abuse. Child mental health professionals must understand forms of child maltreatment and their clinical signs (Finlayson & Koocher, 1991). Practitioners need such assessment skills in any setting that serves children, such as churches, schools, and camps. There is so little discretion about reporting reasonable suspicion of abuse or neglect to child protection authorities that supervision is focused on *how* rather than *if* (Kalichman, 1999). The form and timing of reporting often requires supervisory oversight and sometimes involves consultation with child protection officials (Behnke & Kinscherff, 2002b). When domestic violence occurs between a child's caregivers, a supervisee may fear losing his child client if he reports it. Supervisors need to help supervisees sort through such emotional reactions; one approach is to assist the clinician to develop and present the data supporting a child's need for protection (Stern, 1997).

Suicidal Clients

Rising rates of child and adolescent suicide are especially troubling (U.S. Department of Health and Human Services, 1999). Shea (1999) recommended that supervisors help clinicians use advanced interviewing skills to enhance the validity of self-disclosures in suicidal youth. Such disclosures should be assessed for their likely enactment and for the need to consult with caretakers and to seek crisis stabilization or hospitalization. Supervisors should also ensure that at-risk youth see qualified therapists (see chap. 10, this volume). A prudent supervisor, especially of an inexperienced clinician, sometimes needs to directly observe or assess a suicidal youth. Litigation is a risk; although Baerger (2001) found that in cases where therapists were sued after a client fatality, fewer than 10% actually went to trial and almost 80% were won by the clinician (Gutheil, 1992; Litman, 1982). A commitment to follow reasonable standards of care and to document the clinical decision-making process greatly lowers risks in litigation.[2]

Other Threats to Self or Others

Sullivan, Ramirez, Rae, Razo, and George (2002) engaged the problem of maintaining the therapeutic alliance when adolescents trigger confidentiality dilemmas by disclosing high-risk behaviors. Supervisors must help clinicians identify, weigh, and confront the level of danger involved. Again, delineating contingencies to the client and the family during initial sessions facilitates clinical responses when crises arise in treatment. In most jurisdictions, when clients threaten to harm others, the clinician must assess the likelihood that such threats will be enacted and warn the intended target and pertinent law enforcement authorities if the threats seem plausible. Although some threats may spring from childish bravado, they should not be casually dismissed, as recent school shootings tragically demonstrate. Supervisors and clinicians should ascertain a child's access to weapons, explosives, knives, or baseball bats. Youth with mood disorders, comorbid substance abuse, and dangerous sexual activity can present vexing challenges in threat assessment, as exemplified in the following example.

> After many weeks of work, 13-year-old John has developed a positive alliance with his clinician. John struggled with symptoms of posttraumatic stress disorder (PTSD), the sequelae of many years of sexual abuse. John disclosed that he has been having compulsive sex and using nonprescribed benzodiazepines every day. Fearful of being kicked out of his foster home and new school, he begged the clinician not to tell anyone. This outcome, he warned, would make life not worth living. In supervision, the clinician appeared overwhelmed with the possible consequences of John's activities but also felt guilty about disclosing them to authorities and was fearful that disclosing them to the supervisor would be an admission of failure. After empathically exploring the

---

[2] The authors are indebted to Joe Hansel for the discussion of Baerger's treatment of risk in treating suicidal clients. This was originally developed for chapter 12, but steered to this chapter by the editor.

clinician's emotional responses and identifying the situation as a typical dilemma facing those who work with high-risk clients, the supervisor explored what clinical approaches had been taken. On determining that John has persisted in his behaviors despite standard interventions, the supervisor examined the possibility that John was so out of control that his disclosures were a way to signal his desperation and his terror that therapy was not working.

After the supervisor reframed the situation as a complex case requiring multiple treatment providers and possibly requiring hospitalization to protect John, the clinician became more comfortable with objectively reviewing evidence-based approaches to comorbid PTSD and addictive behaviors. He saw John for an emergency session, and with John present, he contacted the foster care worker and foster parents. A behavioral contract was established that would reward John by maintaining his current placement if he immediately participated in inpatient treatment. John completed his inpatient treatment and, after discharge, resumed outpatient work where he and the clinician were able to use the strengthened therapeutic alliance and behavioral contracting to maintain his treatment gains.

In this case, John's situation required immediate attention from a clinical supervisor. Various risks, such as arrest for drug possession, addictive disorder, transmission of HIV, suicide, and injury to others, must be weighed against possible disruption of the therapeutic alliance. Children and teens often bargain for secrecy when they are hoping for decisive help from the clinicians, the parents, or the community. Supervisors can support clinicians through the emotional turbulence of such cases, and then step back to consider best practices. In John's case, the supervisor helped negotiate with the foster care officials, foster parents, and school to develop a behavioral contract that could motivate John's recovery. This produced an optimal outcome, but sometimes systems of care are less responsive, and decisions are made that respect only the payment options or foster agency policies rather than the child's needs. In such cases, supervisors and clinicians must advocate for their clients, sometimes enlisting advocacy agencies to access necessary treatment.

Therapy Outside the Agency and Contacts With Clients in the Community

Wrap-around treatment approaches require that clinicians meet and work with children and teens in homes, parks, schools, and employment settings. Although best practices in this area of practice are nascent, it is clear that supervision needs to address the capacities of the supervisee to follow agency policies, ethics codes, and the law without benefit of daily contact with supervisors and colleagues in an agency building. This autonomy can create special supervisory challenges, as exemplified in the following example:

Candace, a compassionate clinician, moved from an outpatient agency to one providing community-based services. She began treating 5-year-old Hattie, who lives in a marginally neglectful home. Child protection workers determined that the family is poor, but not guilty of maltreatment. Candace managed her anger at Hattie's situation by loaning Hattie's single mother rent money and by taking Hattie to restaurants on unsanctioned outings. Because she learned from her supervisor in orientation that personal gifts to clients are against agency policy and create boundary problems, Candace hid these activities from her supervisors. The supervisor learned about them from another agency client.

In this case, Candace's supervisors put her on probation for violating policy and for deceiving the agency. Supervision became focused on helping Candace deal with the emotional toll of in-home work and with her boundary violations. Candace became aware of her inordinate need to rescue children from the kind of impoverished childhood she herself had experienced. Countertransference issues and deficits in the skills required for community-based treatment became the foci of supervision. After several weeks, Candace mustered the courage to enter personal therapy to work on the issues that compromised her professional competence, and she ultimately achieved considerable success.

Dual Relationships and Casual Contacts

Lazarus and Zur (2002) protested negative perspectives toward dual relationships, arguing that these relationships were unavoidable, especially in rural areas, and could often be helpful to clients. However, most experts counsel caution (Walker & Clark, 1999). Because of blurred or violated boundaries in their past, vulnerable and needy persons are often unable to negotiate complex relationships. They may personalize the professional roles clinicians play in their lives. Rural clinicians inevitably buy groceries or attend church with some clients; yet developing close relationships is usually contraindicated.

When encountering adolescents or families in the community, clinicians should take cues from the client before making contact. With young children, it is better to acknowledge them after eye contact. Not doing so may be viewed as rejection. Children might make unrealistic requests of the therapist, such as "Buy me some ice cream!" Therapists can usually deflect such demands by stating their current purpose, "Right now I am buying groceries, but I'll see you next week." It is good to discuss such encounters in supervision. For example, meeting a therapist and her children at a local event may be overwhelming for a child nurturing fantasies of being adopted by the therapist. Consider the following example:

Ron, a clinical social worker in a small community, worked with a family with three children. The treatment plan required that he spend hours in the family home. With Ron's guidance, Barbara, an attractive single mother, has made great progress in parenting her children. At a church picnic, she saw Ron and invited him to sit with her and her kids to enjoy pizza. The following week, Barbara saw an opening for a secretarial job at Ron's agency and asked him to recommend her. Simultaneously, the children were clamoring for a special outing to reward their improved behavior. They even offered to clean Ron's yard to earn money for the trip. Ron felt pressured to help this family, because they have worked so hard in treatment.

In this case, Ron reported these issues in supervision, where it was suggested that he find prudent approaches to reinforce the family's gains. He gave Barbara the number of a job coach to help her assemble a resume and job applications. Later, Ron and a colleague took the children for an authorized outing to affirm their progress. He was encouraged to be friendly to the family when he saw them in the community but to beware of developing multiple relationships.

Problems With Termination

Clinical relationships ideally end with children at a point of enduring, positive improvement. Many factors work against such optimal endings. Too often terminations are driven by organizational needs—loss of insurance payments or the need to use inpatient beds for other youth. "Many, perhaps most, decisions made in the discharge planning process are based on policy and precedent without the identification or deliberate examination of the ethical issues that the situation presents" (Cohen, 1995, p. 11). Supervisors, aware that administrative rationales for termination usually do not release the agency or clinician from the duty of care established at the beginning of therapy, must ensure transfer of the child to qualified providers, even if poverty is a barrier. To do otherwise is to abandon the client—an undeniably unethical and potentially actionable decision (Hoge, 1995).

Supervisors need to monitor transitions from care and to educate supervisees about transfers when a family moves, a clinician departs, or the school year ends. Developmentally appropriate preparation, termination rituals, and transfer procedures, such as personally introducing the child to his or her new clinician, lower the risk of retraumatizing a child who has experienced multiple losses or abandonment, as demonstrated in the following example.

Seven-year-old Susan, diagnosed with a bipolar disorder, had suffered physical abuse by her incarcerated father. She lived in a high-crime, urban neighborhood and was being treated by Ann, a female clinician from a community outreach program. During a recent home session, neighbors strolled in and out, interrupting the session. Also, Susan's stepfather made sexual advances toward Ann. Confused and afraid, Ann ran from the home, which frightened and confused Susan. The next day, Ann announced to her supervisor her decision to immediately terminate work with Susan and her family.

In this case, the supervisor helped the therapist with three critical issues. First, she offered support, helping Ann deal with her own anxiety and sense of disorganization. Second, the supervisor gently reminded Ann that she should have taken a colleague with her into that particular area, as stipulated by agency policy. Third, she worked with Ann to find a safe, productive setting for Susan's sessions and to develop approaches to managing the stepfather. Finally, the supervisor worked with agency officials to screen for homes that clinicians should not enter alone and to develop safety training to help clinicians manage such crises in the future. These supervisory initiatives served the ethical and clinical goals of persevering with treatment at a critical point for Susan and of helping all community-based clinicians in the agency who faced similar circumstances.

More problematic are cases where a family terminates in anger, arbitrarily changes providers, or pulls the plug on therapy that has become emotionally threatening to them. Supervisors have an obligation to assist clinicians in managing their negative reactions (e.g., anger or betrayal), so they can proactively address termination issues with caregivers. Sometimes this can keep the child in therapy. When efforts are unsuccessful, the supervisor and clinician should document the problems and seek permission to communicate with any new therapists.

A child who requests termination or refuses to participate in therapy may unsettle supervisees, who may take it as a personal statement that they are unlikable or incompetent. Supervisors need to help clinicians work through their feelings and to develop useful hypotheses about what is happening. Often such impasses are overcome. Maltreated children may behave this way to test a clinician's reliability and resilience and may tweak emotional vulnerabilities. If the child is distressed and unshakable in the desire to terminate, the supervisee needs guidance in approaching caregivers about a therapeutic exit. Intense clinician disappointment with such experiences merits ongoing supervisory attention, because it affects future work with children.

Therapists may need explicit instructions about contacting children who have terminated treatment. Although letters or brief calls might be indicated, recontact may inadvertently re-establish a duty of care and should be managed to meet the child's needs, not to meet the supervisee's. However, children who enter a potential round robin of state placements may need not only follow-up treatment but also ongoing advocacy (Knitzer, 1989). Supervisors should be on hand to assist clinicians in following and advocating for these youth.

Entangling Clinical and Forensic Roles

We have noted a recent and troubling phenomenon. Some clinicians are tempted to augment their incomes by engaging in forensic work, often without proper supervision or training. Forensic roles carry very different duties than treatment roles, and the ethics codes of the American Psychological Association and the American Psychiatric Association stipulate that a clinician shall not enter into dual roles of treatment provider and forensic expert for the same client (see Rae & Fournier, 1999; Strasburger, Gutheil, & Brodsky, 1997). At times, child therapists are drawn into litigation by virtue of their treatment relationships with the child and caregivers. In such cases, clinical supervisors should assist clinicians with understanding their roles as fact witnesses as opposed to experts, no matter what attorneys and caregivers might demand. A fact witness responds to questions regarding the assessment and treatment of the child and family but usually does not venture recommendations regarding custody or other legal outcomes under consideration, as do experts.

Evaluating Incompetent and Impaired Professionals

Supervisors have the responsibility of developing measures of accountability and performance for their supervisees that respect due process and serve as valid, reliable instruments for evaluation. Ladany et al. (2005) took up the difficult issue of sorting out supervisees who should be counseled out of the mental health professions. There is a vast difference between trainees who are unable to advance beyond very basic skill levels and are, therefore, not competent to assess and treat children and those who have become impaired because of emotional exhaustion or workplace circumstances. Supervisors should encourage those in the former group to find other professional fields or other practice settings. These issues present significant challenges to supervisors who, as clinicians themselves, may be reluctant to give up on any supervisee. However, supervisors owe clinicians and their clients a realistic appraisal and a decisive action in cases where progress is highly unlikely. Friendships with clinicians, fears of supervisory failure, or countertransference issues can present significant obstacles to enacting this important ethical obligation, so it is advisable for supervisors facing such situations to seek collegial support and consultation.

Clinicians in the second group should be assisted through enhanced supervision and linkages to appropriate help. Clients need to be protected from clinicians who refuse to or fail to benefit from such assistance. Compassion for supervisees is necessary and desirable, but proper care of children and families is the supervisors' primary ethical responsibility and legal duty.

Criminality and Exploitation

It is unfortunate that some individuals, consciously or not, enter the helping professions to psychologically and sexually exploit children. The consequences of such behaviors are catastrophic (Gonsiorek, 1995). All professional ethics codes forbid sexual relationships with clients, and demand that such behavior be reported to regulatory boards. Reports must also be made if a supervisor discovers a clinician's sexual involvement with a child's caregiver or other family member. Supervisors must never cover-up a situation, though there might be pressures to do so from the trainee, agency officials, or even the victim and the caregivers. The supervisor is also responsible for alerting agency superiors who would join him or her in forbidding further clinician contact with all clients while issues in the case are clarified, and, if warranted, in investigating the clinician's relationships with all previous clients.

It often falls to supervisors in the field to identify and remove pedophiles and other predators, who pass undetected through academic settings, from clinical practice. If a clinician sexually exploits a child, a serious felony has been committed, and the supervisor must ensure that law enforcement and child protection agencies are notified. Although the supervisor should be careful to make such reports after thoroughly reviewing and weighing the facts, it is usually not desirable for the agency to undertake an independent investigation, which might taint an official criminal or child protection investigation. The supervisor should immediately begin to collaborate with law enforcement professionals. When a supervisor faces such a disaster in his or her own practice, it can evoke intense emotional and moral reactivity. Consultation among the attorneys representing the agency and the supervisor should begin as early as possible to ensure that clear-headed, fair, legal, and ethical actions are taken and that due process is accorded to all persons involved. The supervisor may also need to seek collegial and therapeutic support.

INSTITUTIONAL AND SOCIAL ETHICS:
THE "BIG" PICTURE AND CLINICAL SUPERVISION

Are supervisors able and ready to address social justice issues and organizational corruption as part of their supervisory activities? If so, how might these issues be approached in contemporary practice? Following are a few situations in which clinicians might turn to supervisors:

- children abused, neglected, or exploited in systems of care that serve them;
- children victimized by vengeful, postdivorce, custody disputes;
- diagnoses inflated to ensure access to services or hospital payment;
- children poorly educated because of school failure or budget shortfalls;
- children denied access to basic health and behavioral health care; and
- adolescents faced with unwarranted "adult" punishments in the criminal justice system.

Children have almost no power in society, and advocacy is a natural corollary of working with them (chap. 1, this volume). "The healer . . . cannot evade the problem of assuring ethical vitality to all lives saved from undernourishment, morbidity, and early mortality. Man's technical ability and social resolve . . . makes every child conceived a subject of universal responsibility" (Erikson, 1964, p. 238). This responsibility extends beyond the "do no harm" mandate that undergirds tort law. It includes activities such as going to court on behalf of children in jeopardy and becoming politically involved when policies that impact children are at stake. "Admirable mentors" are critical to the development of such practitioners and "the moral milieu of graduate and professional school and of people's first jobs" is critical (Gardner, Csikszentmihalyi, & Damon, 2004, pp. 246–247). Although much of the prior discussion emphasized managing or avoiding risk, advocacy often involves embracing risks.

If professional life is animated by the pledge to serve the common good, clinical supervision must advance the common good for children, especially those who count few caring adults in their lives. Indeed, for those children, there is

> a redemptive side: eyes that can sustain a spell of moral vision, ears that can pick up the ethical heart of a given matter . . . indeed, we can . . . be both hopeful, because of the moral possibilities in this world, and full of sadness, because so often those possibilities are wasted, or more forcibly, crushed outright. (Coles, 1980, pp. 140–141)

All supervisors are challenged by such a moral and ethical call. Ultimately, the practice of ethics is not primarily concerned with avoiding trouble, but instead, as the Greeks argued long ago, it is primarily concerned with helping people pursue "flourishing" lives that provide the foundation for a healthy and good society (Nussbaum, 1994).

REFERENCES

American Psychological Association. (2002). Ethical principles of psychologists and code of conduct. *American Psychologist, 57,* 1060–1073.

Baerger, D. R. (2001). Risk management with the suicidal patient: Lessons from case law. *Professional Psychology Research and Practice, 32,* 359–366.

Behnke, S. H., & Kinscherff, R. (2002a). Confidentiality in the treatment of adolescents. *Monitor on Psychology, 33,* 44–45.

Behnke, S. H., & Kinscherff, R. (2002b). Must a psychologist report past child abuse? *Monitor on Psychology, 33,* 56–57.

Besharov, D. J., & Besharov, S. H. (1987). Teaching about liability. *Social Work, 32,* 517–522.

Bradley, L. J., & Ladany, N. (2001). *Counselor supervision: Principles, process, & practice.* Philadelphia: Brunner-Routledge.

Clark, J. (1999). Clinical risk & brief psychodynamic therapy: A forensic mental health perspective. *Journal of Psychoanalytic Social Work,* 6(3/4), 219–235.

Cohen, M. H. (1995). Ethical issues in discharge planning for vulnerable infants and children. *Ethics and Behavior, 5,* 1–13.

Coles, R. (1980, April). Children as moral observers. *The Tanner Lectures on Human Values.* Lecture presented at the University of Michigan, Ann Arbor. Retrieved December 14, 2005, from http://www.tannerlectures.utah.edu/lectures/coles81.pdf

Cooper, T. L. (1994). *Handbook of administrative ethics.* New York: M. Dekker, Inc.

Crawshaw, R. (1987). Lying. In R. J. Bulger (Ed.), *In search of the modern Hippocrates* (pp. 182–194). Iowa City: Iowa University Press.

Erikson, E. H. (1964). *Insight & responsibility.* New York: Norton.

Finlayson, L. M., & Koocher, G. P. (1991). Professional judgment and child abuse reporting in sexual abuse cases. *Professional psychology: Research and practice, 22,* 464–472.

Gardner, H., Csikszentmihalyi, M., & Damon, W. (2004). *Good work: Where excellence and ethics meet.* New York: Basic Books.

Gert, B. (2004). *Common morality: Deciding what to do.* New York: Oxford University Press.

Gonsiorek, J. C. (1995). *Breach of trust: sexual exploitation by health care professionals and clergy.* Thousand Oaks, CA: Sage.

Grob, H. N. (1998). *Studying the clinician: Judgment research and psychological assessment.* Washington, DC: American Psychological Association.

Gutheil, T. G. (1992). Suicide and suit: liability after self-destruction. In D. Jacobs (Ed.), *Suicide and clinical practice* (pp. 147–167). Baltimore: Williams & Wilkins.

Handelsman, M. M., Gottlieb, M. C., & Knapp, S. (2005). Training ethical psychologists: An acculturation model. *Professional psychology: Research and practice, 36,* 59–65.

Hedges, L. E., & Thatcher, P. (2000). *Facing the challenge of liability in psychotherapy practice*. New York: Jason Aronson.

Heru, A. M., Strong, D. R., Price, M., & Recupero, P. R. (2004). Boundaries in psychotherapy supervision. *American Journal of Psychotherapy, 58,* 76–89.

Hickson, G. B., Federspiel, C. F., Pickert, J. W., Miller, C. S., Gauld-Jaeger, J., & Bost, P. (2002, December 18). Patient complaints and malpractice risk. *Journal of the American Medical Association, 287,* 2951–2957.

Hoge, S. K. (1995, May). Your legal responsibilities in a managed care environment. *Journal of Practical Psychiatry and Behavioral Health,* 62–63.

House, A. E. (2002). *The first session with children and adolescents: Conducting a comprehensive mental health evaluation*. New York: Guilford Press.

Kalichman, S. C. (1999). *Mandated reporting of suspected child abuse: Ethics, law, and policy* (2nd ed.). Washington, DC: American Psychological Association.

Knitzer, J. (1989). Children's mental health: The advocacy challenge "and miles to go before we sleep." In R. M. Friedman, A. J. Duchnowski, & E. L. Henderson (Eds.), *Advocacy on behalf of children with serious emotional problems*. Springfield, IL: Charles C Thomas.

Koehn, D. (1994). *The ground of professional ethics*. London: Routledge.

Kopelman, L. M. (1998). Beyond autonomy: Health care decisions for cognitively impaired individuals. *Advances in Bioethics, 4,* 255–275.

Ladany, N. (2004). Psychotherapy supervision: What lies beneath. *Psychotherapy Research, 14,* 1–19.

Ladany, N., Constantine, M., Miller, K., Erickson, C., & Muse-Burke, J. L. (2000). Supervisor countertransference: A qualitative investigation into its identification and description. *Journal of Counseling Psychology, 47,* 102–115.

Ladany, N., Friedlander, M. L., & Nelson, M. L. (2005). *Critical events in psychotherapy supervision: An interpersonal approach*. Washington, DC: American Psychological Association.

Ladany, N., Lehrman-Waterman, D., Molinaro, M., & Wolgast, B. (1999). Psychotherapy supervisor ethical practices: Adherences to guidelines, the supervisory working alliance, and supervisee satisfaction. *Counseling Psychologist, 27,* 443–475.

Lazarus, A. A., & Zur, O. (Eds.). (2002). *Dual relationships in psychotherapy*. New York: Springer Publishing Company.

Litman, R. E. (1982). Hospital suicides: Lawsuits and standards. *Suicide and Life-Threatening Behavior, 12,* 212–220.

Melton, G. B., Ehrenreich, N. S., & Lyons, P. M. (2001). Ethical and legal issues in mental health services for children. In C. E. Walker & M. C. Roberts (Eds.), *Handbook of clinical child psychology* (pp. 1074–1093). New York: Plenum Press.

Munson, C. E. (1993). *Clinical social work supervision* (2nd ed.). Binghamton, NY: Haworth Press.

Nussbaum, M. C. (1994). *The therapy of desire: Theory and practice in Hellenistic ethics*. Princeton, NJ: Princeton University Press.

Oakeshott, M. (1991). *Rationalism in politics and other essays*. Indianapolis, IN: Liberty Fund.

Perlin, M. (1994). *Law & mental disability*. New York: Lexis.

Rae, W. A., Brunnquell, D., & Sullivan, J. R. (2003). Ethical and legal issues in pediatric psychology. In M. Roberts (Ed.), *Handbook of pediatric psychology* (3rd ed., pp. 32–49). New York: Guilford Press.

Rae, W. A., & Fournier, C. J. (1999). Ethical and legal issues in the treatment of children and families. In T. H. Ollendick & S. W. Russ (Eds.), *Handbook of psychotherapies with children and families* (pp. 67–83). Dordrecht, the Netherlands: Kluwer Academic Publishers.

Reid, W. H. (2004). Organizational liability: Beyond respondeat superior. *Journal of Psychiatric Practice, 10,* 258–262.

Saccuzzo, D. P. (2003a). Liability for failure to supervise adequately: Let the master beware (Part 1). *The Psychologist's Legal Update, 13,* 1–14.

Saccuzzo, D. P. (2003b). Liability for failure to supervise adequately: Let the master beware (Part 2). *The Psychologist's Legal Update, 13,* 15–22.

Shea, S. C. (1999). *Psychiatric interviewing*. Philadelphia: W.B. Saunders.

Schetky, D. H., & Benedek, E. P. (Eds.). (2002). *Principles and practice of child and adolescent forensic psychiatry*. Washington, DC: American Psychiatric Press.

Stern, P. (1997). *Preparing and presenting expert testimony in child abuse litigation: A guide for expert witnesses and attorneys*. Thousand Oaks, CA: Sage.

Stoltenberg, C. D., McNeill, B., & Delworth, U. (1998). *IDM supervision: An integrated developmental model of supervising counselors and therapists*. San Francisco: Jossey-Bass.

Strasburger, L. H., Gutheil, T. G., & Brodsky, A. (1997). On wearing two hats: Role conflict in serving as both psychotherapist and expert witness. *American Journal of Psychiatry, 154,* 448–456.

Studdert, D. M., Mello, M. M., & Brennan, T. A. (2004). Medical malpractice. *New England Journal of Medicine, 350,* 283–292.

Sullivan, J. R., Ramirez, E., Rae, W. A., Razo, N. R., & George, C. (2002). Factors contributing to breaking confidentiality with adolescent clients. *Professional Psychology: Research & Practice, 33,* 396–401.

Turk, D. C., & Salovey, P. (1989). *Reasoning, inference, and judgment in clinical psychology*. New York: Free Press.

U.S. Department of Health and Human Services. (1999). *Mental health: A report of the surgeon general—Executive summary*. Rockville, MD: Author.

Walker, R., & Clark, J. J. (1999). Heading off boundary problems: Clinical supervision as risk management. *Psychiatric Services, 50,* 1435–1439.

4

CROSS-CULTURAL ISSUES AFFECTING THE SUPERVISORY RELATIONSHIP IN COUNSELING CHILDREN AND FAMILIES

TAMARA L. BROWN, IGNACIO DAVID ACEVEDO-POLAKOVICH, AND ANDREA M. SMITH

Ethnic diversity among supervisees in the mental health disciplines is growing at a rate nearly five times faster than the rate of diversification among faculty trainers (American Psychological Association, 1997). This means that European Americans are increasingly supervising trainees whose cultural background differs from their own. In a similar way, cross-cultural supervisory relationships are virtually the rule for supervisors from ethnic minority groups, because European American supervisees continue to vastly outnumber ethnic minority supervisees. The scant research on cross-cultural supervision (e.g., Leong & Wagner, 1994; McNeill, Hom, & Perez, 1995) makes it clear that special challenges arise in these relationships. Challenges are only complicated when the culture of the client is also different (Brown & Landrum-Brown, 1995) and may be intensified in work with children because cultural perspectives on child rearing are so basic, personal, and deeply held. This chapter will detail specific strategies for avoiding difficulties in cross-cultural supervision using examples from child psychotherapy.

In this chapter, the term *cross-cultural supervision* will refer to relationships where the supervisor and supervisee come from different cultural backgrounds. Cultural themes may arise in supervision from many sources, among them are: a person's racial experience, ethnic socialization, social class, religious orientation, gender identity, and sexual orientation (Helms & Cook, 1991). A thorough discussion of how all, or even most, of these cultural factors may influence supervision, individually or in combination with one another, is beyond the scope of this chapter. We have chosen to focus on differences in ethnicity, culture, ethnic identity, and race to illustrate how these issues can arise in supervision, especially in work with children and families. We use the terms *culture* and *cultural background* broadly in this chapter. Our aim is to provide strategies for resolving differences between supervisors and supervisees when race and ethnicity impact the supervisory relationship. This chapter presumes at least a working understanding of the constructs of racial and ethnic identity. Readers who are unfamiliar with these constructs are referred to Helms and Cook (1991, especially chap. 14) who provide a thorough review of the research on how racial issues, including racial identity, affect supervision. The chapter concentrates on practical strategies rather than developing a model for cross-cultural supervision. Ancis and Ladany (2001) offered a solid discussion of two comprehensive models of multicultural supervision.

STRATEGIES FOR INCORPORATING CULTURAL ISSUES INTO SUPERVISION

Supervisors and supervisees bring their own values, world views, and experiences to supervision. These cultural perspectives shape the supervisory relationship, its structure, and its process (Duan & Roehlke, 2001).

Strategy 1: Supervisors Become Aware of Their Own Cultural Perspectives

In instances of cross-cultural supervision, the role of the supervisor is to help discover how the interplay of differing perspectives can promote, rather than impede, the growth of the trainee and the well-being of the client. This is of special concern because the majority of supervisors have never received formal training in cultural issues (Constantine, 1997), and many may lack the cultural competence to meet this challenge.

The academic attainment of cultural knowledge and counseling skills is necessary but is not sufficient for effective cross-cultural work (Sue & Sue, 1999). Effective cross-cultural supervision also requires knowledge of one's own racial or ethnic identity and one's own cultural biases (Richardson

& Molinaro, 1996). Supervisors who have not developed this self-knowledge often make crucial mistakes in cross-cultural supervision, including misjudging or dominating supervisees, fostering misunderstanding, failing to provide or elicit critical feedback, and giving or receiving unintended offense (Garrett et al., 2001). Consider the following vignette:

> A European American supervisor viewed the video of an African American therapist working with an African American adolescent. The therapist confronted the adolescent's flippancy by changing her tone, accent, and jargon to that of the street. The supervisor questioned the professionalism of the shift. The therapist responded angrily that she was challenging the youth's effort to dismiss her by implying she was too White.

A constructive outcome requires a supervisor with: more cultural sensitivity than suggested in the vignette, openness by both parties, and willingness to let the needs of the client take priority over the ego of either professional.

Several self-assessment instruments are available for supervisors who wish to examine their own cultural competence. A brief description of two scales may give the reader a sense of how such measures can be helpful. The Multicultural Supervision Inventory—Supervisors Version (Pope-Davis, Toporek, & Ortega, 1999; Pope-Davis, Toporek, & Ortega-Villalobos, 2003) is designed to help supervisors assess their own multicultural performance (e.g., "I helped my supervisee understand his or her ethnic identity and how that relates to counseling," and "My supervisee would feel comfortable telling me if we had misunderstandings because of our cultural differences"). The Multicultural Counseling Knowledge and Awareness Scale is a measure with two subscales: one assessing supervisors' awareness of their own cultural socialization and biases (e.g., "I believe all clients should maintain direct eye contact during counseling") and the other assessing supervisors' knowledge of basic, cross-cultural, counseling issues and familiarity with the work of leading scholars in multicultural counseling (e.g., "I am familiar with the research and the writings of Janet E. Helms, and I can spontaneously discuss her work at length"; Ponterotto, Gretchen, Utsey, Rieger, & Austin, 2002). Constantine and Ladany (2001) offered a more thorough review and evaluation of measures and of other approaches to assessing multicultural competence.

Supervisors do well to also assess the cultural context of the organization where they supervise. Organizations that fail to promote and to value cultural diversity may directly and indirectly impact the supervisory process (Peterson, 1991). Supervisees may question the sincerity of supervisors when the training institution itself appears insensitive to cultural issues. Minority supervisees report that the knowledge, the commitment, and the appreciation for diversity in their training institutions affect their supervision and training (Fukuyama, 1994; Tinsley-Jones, 2001). The Multicultural Environment Inventory—Revised (Pope-Davis, Liu, Nevitt, & Toporek, 2000) is an example of an instrument for evaluating training sites. It assesses multiculturalism in the coursework, in the supervision, and in the priorities of a training program from the trainee's perspective. Training programs would ideally use such an instrument to assess, enhance, and maintain their multicultural climate (Toporek, Liu, & Pope-Davis, 2003). This goes beyond training and attitude—fees, location, hours of operation, and décor may exclude important client groups.

Strategy 2: Supervisors Strive to Develop Their Cultural Awareness and Competence

At a child guidance clinic serving many Appalachian residents, a supervisor invited an anthropologist to discuss parenting in Appalachia with the clinic staff. This led to active discussions of the practice of cosleeping (i.e., parents and children sleeping together in the same bed) that persists until many children reach school age, or beyond for the youngest child, in Appalachia. Often, therapists consider cosleeping pathological, but it occurs in many cultures and can only be understood relative to a family's history (Abbot, 1992; Landrine & Klonoff, 1996). Supervisors must strive to understand various cultural practices to avoid misdiagnosis and pathologizing the culturally normative. Porter (1994) has outlined four stages through which supervisors progress to become culturally competent. The first stage involves increasing their awareness of cultural issues and of how their world views affect the way they perceive their own and others' experiences. Those who have not completed this stage assume that their world views have no bearing on the clinical or supervisory context and may even claim a scientific objectivity. Mastery of this stage leads to the recognition that one's views are influenced by one's culture and that individuals from other cultures have different, equally valid, ways of thinking and perceiving that demand respect.

At the second stage, supervisors explore how discrimination, oppression, power, and other sociocultural forces affect the mental health of minorities. Supervisors understand that some behaviors that appear pathological may be culturally embedded or may even be adaptive ways of coping with real sociocultural problems. Paranoia, for example, may be a reality-based adaptation to pervasive experiences of discrimination (Whaley, 2001; see also the discussion of treating children's reality-based anxieties in chap. 7, this volume)

Having recognized that culture influences world views and behaviors, supervisors at stage three are ready to explore their own biases, stereotypes, racism, and classism. Honest self-reflection is necessary to uncover one's hidden biases and stereotypes, but it is hard to imagine such reflection in the absence of a cross-cultural challenge. Supervisors need to identify how their own culture shapes their theoretical orientation, case conceptualization, and treatment planning. Pipher's (2002) delightful account of her work with international refugees described the regularity with which her social and clinical assumptions were upended. For example, in contrast to the conventional view that trauma must be discussed and that the client must be desensitized, she cited the Vietnamese proverb, "A wound will only heal if it is left alone" (p. 282). She described how many refugees resolved horrendous trauma in ways vastly different from the traditional approaches of European American mental health. When a therapist sees a traumatized child from another culture, the supervisor may encourage special attention to the family's expectations about both the outcome and the process of therapy.

In the fourth stage, supervisors, through advocacy and working to empower exploited groups, expand their interventions beyond individual clients to social action to address the social forces that stress their clients (see chaps. 1 and 3, this volume). If the problem for which ethnic minority children and families seek treatment originates in the external environment, moving beyond the individual level to intervene at the external-sources level of the problem is required. Advocacy implicitly recognizes that in certain cases individual-level interventions are inappropriate and may be victim blaming.

To provide adequate cross-cultural supervision, supervisors grow toward the fourth stage (Aponte & Johnson, 2000). Culturally-competent supervisors must also guide supervisees through these stages as part of their professional development and must also seek opportunities for increasing their own and their supervisees' multicultural awareness.

Strategy 3: Supervisors Teach Cultural Competence by Modeling Cultural Competence

Supervisees look to their supervisors as sources of knowledge, models for their professional identity, and examples of how to behave in difficult professional situations (Bradshaw, 1982). As a consequence, supervisors who openly discuss cultural issues with their supervisees both increase the effectiveness of communication in the supervisory relationship (Garrett et al., 2001) and normalize honest dialogue regarding cultural similarities and differences (Constantine, 2003). Situations where supervisor and therapist differ actually provide excellent opportunities to model how to discuss differences with clients. Supervisors who do not enter such dialogue may imply that discussions of culture are inappropriate and unsafe in supervision or in therapy, as exemplified in the following example.

An African American supervisor questioned why a European American therapist chose to see a 12-year-old Salvadoran girl in individual therapy.

The therapist said that she wanted to help the girl deal with her father's unreasonable rules that restricted the girl's normal friendships and noted that the girl spoke better English than her parents. The supervisor acknowledged that interpreters were not readily available but were often necessary. He acknowledged that he is not an expert on Salvadoran culture but asked how the therapist's strategy would permit either a necessary alliance with the parents or resolve the father–daughter conflict. The supervisor noted that such conflicts were common in first generation immigrant families. He suggested readings on acculturation for the therapist while he consulted with a colleague experienced with Central American families.

Supervisors whose cultural competence exceeds that of their supervisees are in the best position to guide them to higher levels of development. However, many training programs now incorporate multicultural preparation, and supervisees may now have a higher level of multicultural development than their supervisors. Unaddressed, such differences can lead to dissatisfaction (Ladany, Hill, Corbett, & Nutt, 1996) and to nondisclosure (Ladany, 2004). It is likely that the supervisee's candor will decrease when the supervisor is perceived as culturally insensitive. Supervisors with less cross-cultural development than their supervisees may feel threatened and may become overly controlling to assert their authority. Even if they do not feel threatened, negotiating the supervisory relationship can be difficult when the person in the position of power and authority has less expertise than the person being trained. Negative consequences can be avoided if supervisors directly and comprehensively address differences. Situations in which supervisees have competencies their supervisors lack are also discussed in chapter 1 of this volume.

Strategy 4: Supervisors Initiate the Discussion of Cultural Issues

Supervisors create a safe environment for cultural discussions by initiating them (Norton & Coleman, 2003). A safe atmosphere, depth of dialogue, and frequent opportunities to discuss cultural issues contribute to better alliances, increasing satisfaction, professional growth, validation, and trust (Gatmon et al., 2001), thereby allowing supervisor and supervisee to share their world views and assumptions and to examine their effect on both supervisory and client relationships. Such discussions are important for all supervisees; a supervisor from a cultural background similar to the supervisees' should not assume such discussions are unnecessary. Minority supervisees may even approach supervisors from the same minority with suspicion, viewing them as part of the "White establishment" (Boyd-Franklin, 1989). Alternatively, having received most of their instruction from European Americans, ethnic minority supervisees may doubt whether ethnic minorities are equipped to supervise (Priest, 1994). A supervisory dyad from a common minority background may experience conflict and express different biases, if they are at different stages in the development of their ethnic identity (Cook, 1994).

An ethnic minority supervisor may be the first non-European American instructor a supervisee encounters, and the supervisee may anticipate a negative supervision outcome (McRoy, Freeman, Logan, & Blackmon, 1986) or may doubt the supervisor's expertise (Priest, 1994). Hence, many ethnic minority supervisors continually feel compelled to prove themselves. Minority supervisors may also find themselves the target of a supervisee's racial misconceptions and antagonism and may expend considerable energy contending with the feelings aroused by such prejudice (Priest, 1994). In such cases, conversations about cultural issues may need to be ongoing and may require the supervisor to candidly address a supervisee's ethnic misconceptions (Priest, 1994).

Despite evidence of their importance for the supervisory alliance and supervisee satisfaction (e.g., Brown & Landrum-Brown, 1995; Morgan, 1984), cultural issues are discussed infrequently in supervision, and it is supervisees who typically initiate the discussion (Gatmon et al., 2001). When a supervisee is the first to raise cultural issues, the supervisor's response is crucial. A dismissive supervisor may slam the door on cultural dialogue. Supervisors who disclose their own vulnerabilities and struggles in cross-cultural work may keep it open. Consider the following vignette:

> In an initial meeting, a Korean American supervisor explained that she was adopted internationally and raised by an American family in New Mexico. As an adult, she sought information about her birth family but found little. She said she also pursued knowledge of Korean culture and has developed a hybrid approach to living, adopting what appeals to her from her Southwest United States upbringing and from her Korean explorations. She humorously warned her supervisee that she can become preoccupied with cultural issues and that they will need to work to strike a mutual balance in considering the clinical impact of culture.

Because of the power differential inherent in supervisory relationships, supervisors bear responsibility for cultural discussions even if supervisees first raise the issue (Hird, Cavalieri, Dulko, Felice, & Ho, 2001). When European Americans supervise ethnic minority trainees, the power differential is often exaggerated. According to Bernard (1994), "when an unaware White supervisor works with a culturally sensitive person of color, the situation is skewed toward a negative outcome" (p. 162). A supervisor with culturally ascribed privilege (McIntosh, 1988) can undermine the supervision process by ignoring alternative perspectives, unconditionally applying a Eurocentric approach, and pathologizing differences. The cost of such insensitivity is typically borne by those with the least power—supervisees and clients (Hird et al., 2001).

Some European American supervisors feel they act without discrimination and, therefore, culture is irrelevant. Such Eurocentrism has been called *hallucinatory whitening* (Jones, Lightfoot, Palmer, Wilkerson, & Williams, 1970) or *illusion of color blindness* (Proctor & Davis, 1989). Some supervisors avoid cultural discussions because they lack training or familiarity with the subject (Bradshaw, 1982). Some supervisors fear supervisees who appear more culturally competent than they are. Some supervisors emphasize assumed cultural differences, thereby reinforcing stereotypes (Arkin, 1999). A candid discussion of each person's history may avoid stereotyping while helping supervisors remain cognizant of the ways in which their actions and their supervisees' actions may be culturally motivated (Torres-Rivera, Phan, Maddux, Wilbur, & Garret, 2001).

Strategy 5: Use Open-Ended Questions to Facilitate Discussion

Constructive discussions about culture occur when the entire supervisory process is framed as a venture in collaborative learning (D'Andrea & Daniels, 1997; Daniels, D'Andrea, & Kyung Kim, 1999). Hird et al. (2001) compiled a number of suggestions offered by supervisees for facilitating cultural discussion:

> One way that a supervisor could introduce cultural issues into supervision is to acknowledge the demographic differences that exist between the supervisor and [the] supervisee. For example, a supervisor might say, "An important component of my supervision model includes developing a trusting relationship with my supervisee. As we sit here, I notice that there are a lot of differences that exist between the two of us, such as gender, race and ethnicity, and age. I'm wondering how that might affect our ability to develop a strong working relationship. Let me tell you some of my thoughts. I'd also be interested in hearing yours as well." As the supervision progresses, it would be important to keep revisiting in a more holistic manner how cultural differences affect the supervisory relationship. For example, a supervisor would want to spend some time sharing their [sic] respective worldviews [sic], their [sic] individual definitions of multicultural competence, and how cultural differences unfold in their therapeutic relationships. (p. 124)

The approach espoused by Hird et al. (2001) used open-ended questions (e.g., "How might our differences affect our ability to develop a strong working relationship?") that tend to generate greater disclosure and discussion. Closed-ended questions (e.g., "Do you think our differences will affect our ability to develop a working relationship?") tend to inhibit discussion. Consider the following vignette:

In supervision, a social worker reported seeing a Bosnian refugee family whose son was referred for academic problems. During intake, the son sat awkwardly on the edge of a plastic chair. When encouraged to sit back and make himself comfortable, he said his bottom was too sore. The father smiled and comfortably acknowledged spanking his son, indicating it was routine if the boy teased his sister. In the interview, the boy showed no fear and appeared to have a warm relationship with his father. The social worker made no mention of a referral to child protective services. The supervisor asked the social worker what he thought of spankings. He described growing up in a rural German American community where he and his friends were all spanked if they "crossed the line." He had a deep respect and affection for his father and said spankings never harmed him.

In this case, the supervisor's open-ended question set the table for the constructive discussion of cultural, personal, legal, ethical, and parenting issues that followed.

Strategy 6: Supervisors Adapt Their Communication to the Cultural Needs of Their Supervisees

Communication and communication styles are key factors in the supervisory relationship. Communication styles are influenced by race, ethnicity, culture, and gender (Sue & Sue, 1999). Cultural differences in communication styles involve a wide variety of behaviors—how close to each other people sit, use of hand gestures, volume of speech, and body language. For this reason, effective cross-cultural counseling and supervision depends heavily on the ability to accurately and appropriately send and receive verbal and nonverbal messages (Sue & Sue, 1999). Two aspects of communication that are particularly important in culturally appropriate supervision are context and complementarity.

Communication styles vary from high-context cultures to low-context cultures. Communication in high-context cultures is more relational, collectivist, and contemplative. In these cultures, communication is anchored in the environment and relies heavily on nonverbal signals and on group identification. Typically, communication is more formal, indirect, nonverbal, and person-centered, and language is more polite and deferential. Latin graciousness may be mistaken for commitment, and many Asian cultures so value the maintenance of social harmony that when expressing disagreement they may avoid direct use of the word *no*. As a consequence, understanding an Asian supervisee's sentiments may require extra attention to nonverbal cues such as tone of voice, facial expressions, gestures, and posture. In many high-context cultures, the development of trust is a critical first step in any interaction. Communication in low-context cultures, such as the United

States, tends to be informal and direct, and communicators are expected to be straightforward and concise. Miscommunication can easily occur between a supervisor who, accustomed to low-context communication, narrowly focuses on words and ignores the nonverbal cues provided by a supervisee from a high-context culture. Supervisees in this situation may feel they are communicating thoughts and feelings clearly but are being ignored.

Complementarity is based on the notion that communication occurs across three important levels: universal, group, and individual (Leong, 1996). The universal level incorporates similarities that cut across racial, ethnic, and cultural groups. The individual level incorporates the idiosyncratic features of a person's communication. The group level, which is often overlooked in cross-cultural communication, incorporates features associated with the groups to which an individual belongs (e.g., racial, ethnic, cultural, religious, etc.). Each instance of interpersonal interaction involves all three levels. Complementarity occurs when both supervisor and supervisee are operating on the same level of communication. As illustrated in the following example, complementarity is a constantly changing characteristic of communication.

> A European American supervisor and a Latino supervisee both began their initial sessions, regarding an African American teen with depression, at the universal level, and experienced complementarity. During the next two sessions, the supervisee discussed group-level issues that may play a role in the teen's depression (e.g., racism among school peers and in-group pressure against entering advanced classes) while the supervisor discussed biological hypotheses. At this point, the supervisee has begun communicating at the group level, and the supervisor has remained at the universal level. Unrecognized and unaddressed, such noncomplimentarity may lead to decreased rapport.

However, if the supervisor attends to the group-level issues raised, complimentarity can be restored, and the issues identified by the supervisee can be examined. Many factors can lead to shifts between levels. Effective supervisors will recognize that all three levels of communication exist in every supervisory situation, that both supervisor and supervisee may shift back and forth between these levels, and that communication problems result when there is noncomplimentarity in communication between the supervisor and supervisee (Leong, 1996).

In the supervisory relationship, mismatched communication can subtly undermine rapport and trust leading supervisees to suppress important information about themselves and their clients. In the clinical relationship, mismatches can leave the client feeling misunderstood and lead to premature termination (Sue & Sue, 1999). In both the clinical and supervisory relationships, it will be important for the supervisor to recognize mismatches, point them out, and process them with the supervisee. No one style of communication or counseling is appropriate for every cultural group and for every situation. Supervisors must adapt to meet the needs of different supervisees and must teach their supervisees to make similar adaptations in their counseling with children and families (Ivey, 1981, 1986).

Strategy 7: Supervisors Seek Out Opportunities for Cross-Cultural Activities

Developing a culturally sensitive approach to supervision is a lengthy and labor-intensive endeavor. Supervisors who aspire to cross-cultural competence will benefit from continued involvement in course work; readings; practical and personal experiences; and professional memberships, workshops, and conferences that foster cultural sensitivity (Hird et al., 2001). These experiences afford in vivo opportunities for them to observe and to become facile with cultural subtleties, and to practice verbal and nonverbal communication skills. Consultation with colleagues from culturally different groups who are willing to be open, honest, and vulnerable, and with whom they can discuss their reactions to these experiences, enrich their understanding and mastery of cultural content. Appendix 4.1 lists examples of resources for improving cross-cultural competence.

CONCLUSION

Cross-cultural supervision, increasingly common as the helping professions become more diverse, presents unique challenges for supervisors, many of whom are having to train themselves to be culturally competent. This chapter emphasizes that both supervisor and supervisee bring to supervision a rich blend of experiences, values, and world views that, left unexamined, can lead to problematic interactions, withholding of important clinical information, and perpetuation of stereotypes and misconceptions. Our hope is that the strategies presented in this chapter, although not exhaustive, will help supervisors address some of the challenges that arise in cross-cultural supervision.

APPENDIX 4.1:

RESOURCES FOR IMPROVING
CROSS-CULTURAL COMPETENCE

Many professional organizations promote cultural competence. Here are a few examples:

- Society for the Psychological Study of Ethnic Minority Issues (http://www.apa.org/divisions/div45/)
- Asian American Psychological Association (http://www.aapaonline.org/)
- Society of Indian Psychologists (http://www.okstate.edu/osu_orgs/sip/)
- Association of Black Psychologists (http://www.abpsi.org/)
- National Latina/o Psychological Association (http://www.nlpa.ws)
- Network for Multicultural Training in Psychology (http://www.nmtp.org/)
- Association of Multicultural Counseling and Development (http://www.amcd-aca.org/)
- Society for the Clinical Psychology (http://www.apa.org/divisions/div12/)
- National Association of Black Social Workers (http://www.nabsw.org/)
- Latino Social Work Organization (http://www.lswo.org/)

In addition, programs of minority studies at large universities can suggest reading lists to enhance one's cultural perspective. Among this chapter's references, Pipher's (2002) work on helping refugees is an easy starting point. Professional references include the following: *Promoting Cultural Competence in Children's Mental Health Services* (Hernandez & Issacs, 1998); *Handbook of Multicultural Competencies in Counseling and Psychology* (Pope-Davis, Toporek, & Ortega-Villalobos, 2003); *Counseling the Culturally Different* (Sue & Sue, 1999); *Counseling American Minorities* (6th ed.; Atkinson, 2004); and *Mental Health: Culture, Race, and Ethnicity* (http://www.mentalhealth.org/cre/default.asp).

As well, several professional journals feature material on culture and its relation to mental health, including the *Journal of Multicultural Counseling and Development, Cultural Diversity and Ethnic Minority Psychology*, the *Journal of Black Psychology*, the *Hispanic Journal of Behavioral Sciences*, and *Culture, Medicine, and Psychiatry*.

REFERENCES

Abbot, S. (1992). Holding on and pushing away: Comparative perspectives on an eastern Kentucky child-rearing practice. *Ethos, 20,* 33–65.

American Psychological Association, Commission on Ethnic Minority Recruitment, Retention, and Training in Psychology. (1997). *Diversity and accreditation.* Washington, DC: American Psychological Association.

Ancis, J. R., & Ladany, N. (2001). A multicultural framework for counselor supervision. In N. Ladany & L. J. Bradley (Eds.), *Counselor supervision: Principles, process, and practice* (3rd ed., pp. 63–90). New York: Brunner-Routledge.

Aponte, J. F., & Johnson, L. R. (2000). Ethnicity and supervision: Models, methods, processes, and issues. In J. F. Aponte & J. Wohl (Eds.), *Psychological intervention and cultural diversity* (pp. 268–285). Boston: Allyn & Bacon.

Arkin, N. (1999). Cultural sensitive student supervision: Difficulties and challenges. *The Clinical Supervisor, 18,* 1–16.

Atkinson, D. R. (2004). *Counseling American minorities* (6th ed.). Boston: McGraw-Hill.

Bernard, J. M. (1994). Multicultural supervision: A reaction to Leong and Wagner, Cook, Priest, and Fukuyama. *Counselor Education and Supervision, 34,* 159–171.

Boyd-Franklin, N. (1989). *Black families in therapy: A multisystems approach.* New York: Guilford Press.

Bradshaw, W. H., Jr. (1982). Supervision in Black and White: Race as a factor in supervision. In M. Blumenfield (Ed.), *Applied supervision in psychotherapy* (pp. 199–220). New York: Grune & Stratton.

Brown, M. T., & Landrum-Brown, J. (1995). Counselor supervision: Cross-cultural perspectives. In J. G. Ponterotto, J. M. Casas, L. Suzuki, & C. Alexander (Eds.), *Handbook of multicultural counseling* (pp. 263–286). Thousand Oaks, CA: Sage.

Constantine, M. G. (1997). Facilitating multicultural competency in counseling supervision: Operationalizing a practical framework. In D. B. Pope-Davis & H. L. K. Coleman (Eds.), *Multicultural counseling competencies: Assessment, education and training, and supervision* (pp. 290–309). Thousand Oaks, CA: Sage.

Constantine, M. G. (2003). Multicultural competence in supervision: Issues, processes, and outcomes. In D. B. Pope-Davis, H. L. K. Coleman, W. M. Liu, & R. L. Toporek (Eds.), *Handbook of multicultural competencies in counseling and psychology* (pp. 383–391). Thousand Oaks, CA: Sage.

Constantine, M. G., & Ladany, N. (2001). New visions for defining and assessing multicultural counseling competence. In J. G. Ponterotto, J. M. Casas, L. A. Suzuki, & C. M. Alexander (Eds.), *Handbook of multicultural counseling* (2nd ed., pp. 482–498). Thousand Oaks, CA: Sage.

Cook, D. A. (1994). Racial identity in supervision. *Counselor Education & Supervision, 34,* 132–141.

D'Andrea, M., & Daniels, J. (1997). Multicultural counseling supervision: Central issues, theoretical considerations, and practical strategies. In D. B. Pope-Davis & H. L. K. Coleman (Eds.), *Multicultural counseling competencies: Assessment, education and training, and supervision* (pp. 290–309). Thousand Oaks, CA: Sage.

Daniels, J., D'Andrea, M., & Kyung Kim, B. S. (1999). Assessing the barriers and changes of cross-cultural supervision: A case study. *Counselor Education and Supervision, 38,* 191–204.

Duan, C., & Roehlke, H. (2001). A descriptive "snapshot" of cross-racial supervision in university counseling center internships. *Journal of Multicultural Counseling and Development, 29,* 131–146.

Fukuyama, M. (1994). Critical incidents in multicultural counseling supervision: A phenomenological approach to supervision research. *Counselor Education and Supervision, 34,* 142–151.

Garrett, M. T., Borders, L. D., Crutchfield, L. B., Torres-Rivera, E., Brotherton, D., & Curtis, R. (2001). Multicultural supervision: A paradigm of cultural responsiveness for supervisors. *Journal of Multicultural Counseling and Development, 29,* 147–158.

Gatmon, D., Jackson, D., Koshkarian, L., Martos-Perry, N., Molina, A., Patel, N., & Rodolfa, E. (2001). Exploring ethnic, gender, and sexual orientation variables in supervision: Do they really matter? *Journal of Multicultural Counseling and Development, 29,* 102–113.

Helms, J. E., & Cook, D. A. (1991). *Using race and culture in counseling and psychotherapy: Theory and process.* Boston: Allyn & Bacon.

Hernandez, M., & Isaacs, M. R. (1998). *Promoting cultural competence in children's mental health services.* Baltimore: Brookes Publishing.

Hird, J. S., Cavalieri, C. E., Dulko, J. P., Felice, A. A. D., & Ho, T. A. (2001). Visions and realities: Supervisee perspectives on multicultural supervision. *Journal of Multicultural Counseling and Development, 29,* 114–130.

Ivey, A. E. (1981). Counseling and psychotherapy: Toward a new perspective. In A. J. Marsella & P. B. Pedersen (Eds.), *Cross-cultural counseling and psychotherapy.* New York: Pergamon Press.

Ivey, A. E. (1986). *Developmental therapy.* San Francisco: Jossey-Bass.

Jones, B. E., Lightfoot, O. B., Palmer, D., Wilkerson, R. G., & Williams, D. H. (1970). Problems of Black residents in White training institutes. *American Journal of Psychiatry, 127,* 798–803.

Ladany, N. (2004). Psychotherapy supervision: What lies beneath. *Psychotherapy Research, 14,* 1–19.

Ladany, N., Hill, C. E., Corbett, M. M., & Nutt, E. A. (1996). The nature, extent, and importance of what psychotherapy supervisees do not disclose to their supervisors. *Journal of Counseling Psychology, 43,* 10–24.

Landrine, H., & Klonoff, E. A. (1996). Traditional African American family practices: Prevalence and correlates. *Western Journal of Black Studies, 20,* 59–62.

Leong, F. T. L. (1996). Toward an integrative model for cross-cultural counseling and psychotherapy. *Applied and Preventive Psychology, 5,* 189–209.

Leong, F. T. L., & Wagner, N. S. (1994). Cross-cultural counseling supervision: What do you know? What do we need to know? *Counselor Education & Supervision, 34,* 117–131.

McIntosh, P. (1988). *White privilege and male privilege: A personal account of coming to see correspondences through work in women's studies.* Wellesley, MA: Wellesley College, Center for Research on Women.

McNeil, B. W., Hom, K. L., & Perez, J. A. (1995). The training and supervisory needs of racial and ethnic minority students. *Journal of Multicultural Counseling and Development, 23,* 246–259.

McRoy, R. G., Freeman, E. G., Logan, S. L., & Blackmon, B. (1986). Cross-cultural field supervision: Implications for social work education. *Journal of Social Work Education, 22,* 50–56.

Morgan, D. W. (1984). Cross-cultural factors in the supervision of psychotherapy. *The Psychiatric Forum, 12,* 61–64.

Norton, R. A., & Coleman, H. L. K. (2003). Multicultural supervision: The influence of race-related issues in supervision process and outcome. In D. B. Pope-Davis, H. L. K. Coleman, W. M. Liu, & R. L. Toporek (Eds.), *Handbook of multicultural competencies in counseling and psychology* (pp. 114–134). Thousand Oaks, CA: Sage.

Peterson, F. K. (1991). Issues of race and ethnicity in supervision: Emphasizing who you are, not what you know. *The Clinical Supervisor, 7,* 27–40.

Pipher, M. (2002). *The middle of everywhere: The world's refugees come to our town.* New York: Harcourt.

Ponterotto, J. G., Gretchen, D., Utsey, S. O., Rieger, B. P., & Austin, R. (2002). A revision of the Multicultural Counseling Awareness Scale (MCAS). *Journal of Multicultural Counseling and Development, 30,* 153–180.

Pope-Davis, D. B., Liu, W. M., Nevitt, J., & Toporek, R. L. (2000). The development and initial validation of the Multicultural Environmental Inventory. *Cultural Diversity and Ethnic Minority Psychology, 6,* 57–64.

Pope-Davis, D. B., Toporek, R. L., & Ortega, L. (1999). *The Multicultural Supervision Scale.* College Park, MD: Authors.

Pope-Davis, D. B., Toporek, R. L., & Ortega-Villalobos, L. (2003). Assessing supervisors' and supervisees' perceptions of multicultural competence in supervision using the multicultural supervision inventory. In D. B. Pope-Davis, H. L. K. Coleman, W. M. Liu, & R. L. Toporek (Eds.), *Handbook of multicultural competencies in counseling and psychology* (pp. 211–224). Thousand Oaks, CA: Sage.

Porter, N. (1994). Empowering supervisees to empower others: A culturally responsive supervision model. *Hispanic Journal of Behavioral Sciences, 16,* 43–56.

Priest, R. (1994). Minority supervisor and majority supervisee: Another perspective of clinical reality. *Counselor Education & Supervision, 34,* 152–158.

Proctor, E. K., & Davis, L. E. (1989). *Race, gender, and class: Guidelines for practice with individuals, families, and groups*. Englewood Cliffs, NJ: Prentice Hall.

Richardson, T. O., & Molinaro, K. I. (1996). White counselor self-awareness: A prerequisite for multicultural competence. *Journal of Counseling and Development, 74,* 238–242.

Sue, D. W., & Sue, D. (1999). *Counseling the culturally different: Theory and practice* (3rd ed.). New York: Wiley.

Tinsley-Jones, H. A. (2001). Racism in our midst: Listening to psychologists of Color. *American Psychologist, 32,* 573–580.

Toporek, R. L., Liu, W. M., & Pope-Davis, D. B. (2003). Assessing multicultural competence of the training environment: Further validation for the psychometric properties of the Multicultural Environment Inventory—Revised. In D. B. Pope-Davis, H. L. K. Coleman, W. M. Liu, & R. L. Toporek (Eds.), *Handbook of multicultural competencies in counseling and psychology* (pp. 183–190). Thousand Oaks, CA: Sage.

Torres-Rivera, E., Phan, L. T., Maddux, D., Wilbur, M. P., & Garret, M. T. (2001). Process versus content: Integrating personal awareness and counseling skills to meet the multicultural challenge of the 21st century. *Counselor Education & Supervision, 41,* 28–40.

Whaley, A., (2001). Cultural mistrust: An important psychological construct for diagnosis and treatment of African Americans. *American Psychologist, 32,* 555–562.

5

SUPERVISION IN PLAY AND FILIAL THERAPY

DEE C. RAY

Play is a powerful force in the life of children. Unlike the stereotype of play as simple entertainment, play is necessary for the exploration and mastery of a child's world. Bruner (1976) described the developmental role of play as critical in humans. It is the workshop for adult mental development. In play, children tenaciously vary and try new skills without the frustrations inherent in real-life performance; in play, possibilities are conceived, explored, and practiced; the seeds of creativity are sown (Singer, 2002). Play can be symbolic and can constitute or augment the language of the child. Interactive play with adults can enable children to tolerate novel situations or risk new activities. Behaviors modeled by adults are enacted or reworked in play, helping children acquire social conventions or aberrations. Play can reflect a child's own experiences and perceptions of himself, of his relationships, and of the world in general.

Play therapy enlists this powerful medium to understand and help children. In most play therapies, the child is allowed a freedom inconsistent with his or her usual experience with adults. The child is encouraged to express feelings, thoughts, and behaviors, and it is assumed that the child's preoccupations will come to the fore. In play therapy, a child might express himself in complex metaphors, become aggressive toward the therapist or the toys, repeat certain themes, or refuse to play or speak. It is the symbolic function of play that is significant. Toys are viewed as the child's words, and play is the child's language (Landreth, 2002a). Children more comfortably, safely, and meaningfully express their inner world through concrete, symbolic representation in play. Through toys or role-playing, children have the opportunity to develop a sense of control over their world as they reenact their experiences in the safety of the playroom. In play therapy, regardless of the reason for referral, the therapist has the opportunity to enter and experience the child's world and to actively deal with issues that brought the child to therapy.

A therapist who would engage children in play must be grounded in child development, attentive to the child's unique perceptions and experiences, and ready to function nonverbally or verbally in the experiential and symbolic world of childhood. Play therapists acquire the elements of their profession through classwork, discussions, reading, workshops, role-playing, and observing experienced play therapists. However, it is in supervision that knowledge of development, theories of change, self-awareness, and continuous assessment become integrated into clinical practice (Guerney, 1983; Landreth, 2002a).

SUPERVISION AND MODELS OF PLAY THERAPY

Play therapy is not so unique as to escape the theoretical camps that define much of psychotherapy, and supervision is shaped by the supervisor's orientation. Like many therapies, play therapy has roots in the psychoanalytic model. Anna Freud (1965) and Melanie Klein (1932) offered nondirective methods for working with children by providing toys and interpreting play to children. Anna Freud used play as a way to build the relationship with the child. Once the relationship was established, she could move to the verbal modalities of free association and dream analysis. Klein recognized play as a substitute for verbal expression in children and interpreted directly from the child's play. Supervisors of a Freudian or Kleinian orientation emphasize interpretation and insight as mechanisms of change in children. In contrast, Jungian play therapists believe the child's psyche is capable of healing itself when engaged in symbolic play in a free, protected environment while in a transference relationship with a supportive therapist (De Domenico, 1994).

Kottman (2003) applied Adlerian concepts to play therapy by incorporating the importance of social embeddedness, thereby encouraging the play therapist to work more directly with all systemic variables in the child's life. In addition, Adlerian play therapists address the cognitive world of the child through investigating lifestyle and private logic. Brody (1997) introduced developmental play therapy, heavily influenced by attachment theory. Brody emphasized the reparative relationship between the child and the therapist. Developmental play therapy encourages physical and structured activities between therapist and child to improve the child's ability to build positive relationships.

Cognitive–behavioral and ecosystemic play therapies are newer approaches in the field. Cognitive–behavioral play therapy presents play therapy as an opportunity for the therapist to model cognitive change strategies to children to improve coping capacity (Knell, 1999). Ecosystemic play therapy focuses on the balance between the child, biological forces, development, cognitive processes, systemic influences, therapeutic relationship, pathology, and play (O'Connor, 2000).

Because of the prevalence of the child-centered philosophy in the application of play therapy, this chapter will focus on the supervision of the child-centered play therapy (CCPT) approach to supervising therapists in play therapy. CCPT is based on the person-centered principles of Carl Rogers (1951) and is reviewed in more detail later in this chapter. In a survey of members of the Association of Play Therapy, most play therapists identified themselves as being trained in CCPT (Ryan, Gomory, & Lacasse, 2002). In an earlier survey, Phillips and Landreth (1995) found that play therapists identified CCPT and eclectic models as the most used forms of play therapy. The heavy representation of child-centered play therapists can probably be attributed to the formalization of this approach in the classic writings of Virginia Axline (1947, 1964), to its elaboration in the work of Guerney (1983) and Landreth (1991, 2002a), and to the training available in this approach. The child-centered model offers a solid base for understanding children and for learning how to work therapeutically with them. Most theories incorporate the basics of the child-centered approach in teaching initial play therapy skills. Filial therapy offers a person centered approach to parent education. This chapter will focus on the supervision of CCPT and its important affiliate, filial therapy.

CHILD-CENTERED PLAY THERAPY

Building on her developmental understanding of children and her child-centered philosophy, Axline (1947) identified eight basic principles that guide the play therapist. These principles include (a) developing a warm, friendly relationship with the child; (b) accepting the child unconditionally without wishing the child were different in some way; (c) establishing an atmosphere of permissiveness so the child feels free to express himself or herself; (d) recognizing and reflecting the feelings of the child to convey understanding; (e) respecting the child's innate ability to solve his or her own problems and offering the child opportunities to assume responsibility; (f) allowing the child to lead the way and avoiding attempts to direct the child's actions or conversation; (g) recognizing the gradual nature of the child's process and not rushing the therapy; and (h) establishing only those limitations that are necessary to anchor the child's therapy to the world of reality.

SUPERVISION OF BASIC PLAY THERAPY

The supervisor should be trained in play therapy and should limit supervision to the theoretical models of play therapy in which he or she is trained. The following descriptions assume that supervision is occurring in the context of a formal training program. However, it is common for therapists without child clinical training to begin seeing children and then to seek supervision. Ethically, this is problematic—children are a population for which therapists should receive special training. In such cases, the supervisor must decide what is appropriate. If they accept supervision in such a situation, then they become instructor and trainer, teaching basic skills to the novice therapist. The supervisor must be ready to devote extra time to orientating and monitoring the supervisee through readings, additional supervision, and limiting the number and kinds of cases that the therapist accepts. Supervisors bear a strong responsibility to ensure that the child's caretakers are aware of the training status of the therapist and that they are able to contact the supervisor.

Kranz and Lund (1994) emphasized the supervisor as a role model demonstrating acceptance and genuineness and reflecting the feelings of students. Because play therapy is solidly aligned with a belief in the importance of the therapist–child relationship, play therapy supervision also follows a similar belief. The supervisory relationship typically follows a developmental trajectory moving from a highly structured teaching relationship to an increasing independence of the supervisee, where the supervisor adopts the role of consultant (Whiting, Bradley, & Planny, 2001). Supervisees are initially very concrete and dependent, in need of specific skills and feedback. As the supervisory relationship grows, the supervisee feels confident enough to move into the role of peer, seeking mutual consultation and discussion. Guerney (1978) discussed the importance of beginning by teaching skills, followed by regular live supervision of the play therapist. Once the basic skills are mastered, supervisors can then concentrate on theoretical integration into the play therapy process.

STRUCTURING PLAY THERAPY SUPERVISION

The Center for Play Therapy at the University of North Texas structures supervision and training of play therapists around direct or video
observation of sessions using the Play Therapy Skills Checklist (PTSC; see
Appendix 5.1 at the end of this chapter). On the basis of Landreth's (1991)
original text on the application of CCPT, the PTSC evolved over the last
20 years as an instrument that is used to provide feedback to new and
experienced play therapists to increase their skill levels. It is not used for
collecting data, so it has not been formally reviewed for reliability or validity.
The PTSC reflects contributions from many play therapy faculty, students,
and supervisees over decades of play therapy supervision and practice. The
PTSC reviews skills essential to developing effective therapeutic relationships, including nonverbal communication and therapist response skills.
Supervisors rate whether each skill is demonstrated too much, too little,
not at all, or appropriately. The supervisor records examples of the therapist's
actual responses in each category and suggests responses that might have been
more effective. The category *other possible responses* is crucial for beginning
therapists, guiding them in choosing better responses.

A second section of the PTSC addresses limit setting, connectedness,
and identified themes. This section offers the supervisor more room to
provide subjective comments. These four areas often require more explanation, from reviewing the details of limit setting to suggesting more effective
interventions. A final section allows the supervisor to evaluate the therapist's
strengths and areas for growth. When completed, the checklist allows the
supervisor to provide an overall impression of the session and the therapist's
skills. The rationale and descriptions of basic and advanced skills that are
evaluated using the PTSC are given in the following section.

Application of the Play Therapy Skills Checklist

Following a developmental model of supervision, the PTSC can be
tailored to meet the supervisee's professional needs. In the initial training,
the supervisor completes the PTSC and discusses it with the supervisee. In
the middle stages of supervision, both the supervisor and the supervisee fill
out separate forms and compare them in supervision. In latter stages, when
the supervisor has moved into more of a consultant role, the supervisee
completes the PTSC to review sessions of concern and to share this concern
with the supervisor.

The use of the PTSC is based on visual observation of play therapy
sessions through live supervision or through video recording of sessions.
The PTSC can be used on a limited basis through audio recording, but
audio recording reduces the PTSC's effectiveness, especially feedback on

nonverbal communication. In supervising experienced play therapists, a supervisor might use supervisees' self-reports on the PTSC to encourage self-review and continued growth. This use of the instrument would not necessitate video recording of sessions.

BASIC SKILLS

Certain skills are basic to the play therapy process (Axline, 1947; Guerney, 1983; Kottman, 2003; Landreth, 2002a; Moustakas, 1997; O'Connor, 2000). Basic nonverbal skills include leaning forward, appearing interested, seeming comfortable, applying a tone congruent with the child's affect, and applying a tone congruent with the therapist's response. Among basic verbal skills are tracking behavior, reflecting content, reflecting feeling, facilitating decision making, facilitating creativity, esteem building, and facilitating the therapeutic relationship. These specific skills are likely to be demonstrated in most play therapy sessions. The extent to which they are used depends on the needs of the child and, possibly, the theoretical orientation of the therapist. In play therapy supervision, it helps to provide new therapists with the skills to structure their work. Even experienced play therapists can profit from reviewing the basics when they are feeling unfocused or confused about a case.

Nonverbal Skills

Focus on Child

Play therapy relies heavily on nonverbal skills. The play therapist leans forward, moving as the child moves so that he or she is always squarely facing the child. Arms and legs are positioned to convey a sense of openness to the child. The therapist appears interested, focusing on the child throughout the session and guarding against becoming preoccupied with other thoughts. The therapist communicates comfort and acceptance of the child and the situation, though such reassurance may be difficult during the expression of emotionally laden or traumatic material.

Congruence

The play therapist's actions are congruent with the child's. The therapist matches the tone and level of affect of the child. Often, new therapists are overly animated, the way many adults relate to children. Newer therapists may feel their role is to make the child happy, and they use their tone to this end. Such incongruent affect is no more appropriate with children than with adults. Therapists should convey a sense of genuineness. Matching the emotional tone of one's verbal response with the child's verbal or nonverbal response is symptomatic of the therapist's investment in the child. A therapist would not flatly mumble, "You're excited by how you made the bubbles," but would comment in a way that reflects the child's excitement. Some therapists who are still tentative in their skills may end definitive responses in a higher tone, suggesting a question. This is confusing and leaves the child to figure out how to respond.

Verbal Skills

Tracking Behavior

In tracking behaviors, the play therapist simply states what she observes, allowing the child to know that she is interested and engaged. Tracking helps the therapist immerse herself in the child's world—as the child runs in a circle, she says, "You're running around and around."

Reflecting Content

Reflecting content in play therapy is identical to reflecting content in adult talk therapy. The therapist paraphrases the account of the child. Reflecting content validates the children's perceptions of their experience and helps them clarify their understanding of themselves (Landreth, 2002a). If a child enacts a dollhouse scene and verbalizes the content of the scene, the therapist might respond, "The sister got to go away with the dad, but the brother had to stay home."

Tracking behavior and reflecting content are the most basic verbal skills in play therapy. They help to build a relationship so the child can benefit from other therapeutic responses.

Succinctness

Play therapy recognizes children's limited language ability, so therapeutic responses are short. Supervisors help therapists to communicate in as few words as possible. A maximum of ten words is a good guideline. Lengthy or abstract responses quickly lose the child's interest, may confuse the child, and often convey a therapist's lack of understanding.

Rate of Response

The therapist's communication style should match the child's. If the child is quiet and reserved, then the play therapist will slow his responses. If the child is interactive and talkative, the therapist will match this energy with increased responses. Initially, therapists may speak more, because silence can be uncomfortable for the child in a new situation. In subsequent sessions, the therapist will assume a pace that matches the child's. Both length of responses and rate of responses can be problematic for beginning therapists, but these skills are quickly acquired and usually are not an issue with experienced play therapists.

The following verbal skills are slightly more advanced than the basic verbal skills: reflecting feeling, facilitating decision making and returning responsibility, facilitating creativity and spontaneity, esteem building and encouraging, and facilitating relationship. They aim to build self-concept, develop self-responsibility, create awareness, and fortify the therapeutic relationship.

Reflecting Feeling

Responding to emotions expressed by children in play requires attuned awareness and sensitivity by the therapist. Children are quite emotive, yet they rarely describe their feelings explicitly. Reflecting their feelings can be threatening to some children and should be done carefully. Reflecting feelings can help a child become aware of emotions and can lead to appropriate acceptance and expression of feelings. A child unsuccessfully tries several times to take the top off a marker and then throws the marker on the floor. Avoiding adult words such as *frustrated*, the therapist responds, "You're really *mad* with that marker."

Facilitating Decision Making and Returning Responsibility

One of the play therapist's goals is to help the child experience his or her own capacity and take ownership of his or her abilities. The therapist does not do for a child what a child can do for him- or herself (Landreth, 2002a). Responses that facilitate decision making or return responsibility empower a child. A child wants to draw a picture and asks, "What color should the car be?" The therapist affirms, "In here, you decide what color you want it to be." Without making an attempt, a child asks, "Can you get the ball from behind the shelf for me?" The therapist suggests, "That looks like something you can do."

Facilitating Creativity and Spontaneity

Freeing a child to experience his or her own creativity is another goal of play therapy. Acceptance and encouragement of experimentation and creativity affirms the child as special in his or her own way. Children in therapy are often trapped in rigid ways of acting and thinking. Experiencing freedom of expression allows them to become more flexible in thought and action. A child who moves from one project to another can be affirmed, "You changed to do just what you want."

Esteem Building and Encouraging

Encouraging a child to feel better about him- or herself is a constant objective in play therapy. Esteem-building statements acknowledge children as capable. If a child tries a few ways to reach the top shelf, the therapist can admire the effort, "You're not giving up; you just keep trying."

Supervisors help therapists recognize how esteem-building responses are more effective than simple praise. Simple praise, such as, "That's a pretty picture" or "I like the way you did that" encourages the child to perform for the therapist and to continue seeking external reinforcement, thereby eroding a sense of self. Esteem-building responses, such as, "You're really proud of your picture," or "You made that just the way you wanted," encourage a child to trust his or her own capacity for self-evaluation.

Facilitating Relationship

Responses focused on the relationship between the play therapist and child help the child experience a safe, positive relationship. Because the therapy relationship models participation in intimate relationships, the therapist should respond to any attempt by the child to address the relationship. Relational responses help the child both learn effective communication and express the therapist's care for the child. For example, a child building in sand stops to look at the therapist but says nothing. The therapist comments, "You're wondering what I think about that." The therapist sneezes, and the child gives him or her a bowl saying, "Eat the soup, you'll feel better." The therapist responds, "You really want to take care of me." In response to a limit set by the therapist, the child screams, "I hate you. I hate you." The therapist acknowledges, "You're really angry with me for this." Relationship responses should always include a reference to the child and to the therapist.

SUPERVISION OF ADVANCED SKILLS IN PLAY THERAPY

Basic skills are integrated early in the development of play therapists. A supervisor might revisit these skills but can usually progress to advanced skills that remain foci for supervision and consultation throughout a therapist's career. This section addresses four such skills: (a) enlarging the meaning, (b) identifying play themes, (c) connecting with children, and (d) limit setting.

Enlarging the Meaning and Facilitating Understanding

Enlarging the meaning is the most advanced of the play therapy skills but has the least explanation in play therapy instruction or literature. In the absence of literature on enlarging the meaning, this section is based primarily on years of play therapy experience. According to his or her theoretical orientation, a therapist might enlarge the meaning by commenting on patterns in the child's play (e.g., "You always make sure to play with the Mommy doll") or by interpreting (e.g., "You seem to want to make things better with your Mommy"). Enlarging the meaning provides the child with awareness of the significance of his or her play and allows the child to feel the therapist's broader empathy and understanding for his or her intentions and motivations.

Jungian, Gestalt, Psychoanalytic, and Adlerian play therapies all support some level of interpretation in the play therapy process. Child-centered, play therapists are hesitant to offer interpretation but enlarge the meaning by bringing observed and felt experiences to the child's awareness—"Sometimes, when you come into the playroom, you really want to be the one in charge." From any theoretical perspective, enlarging the meaning is difficult, and timing is critical. Supervisors often discourage new therapists from enlarging the meaning, because it can be damaging if used without skill. Children may experience enlarging the meaning as evaluative and invasive and may become less engaged. It is recommended that supervisors get to know a supervisee's case well before introducing the technique of enlarging the meaning. The supervisor might want to role-play this skill prior to the therapist's using it with the child.

Identifying Play Themes

As patterns begin to emerge, play therapists attempt to identify play themes. A play theme is a coherent metaphor through which the child communicates the meaning he or she has attributed to his or her experience. Play themes allow clinicians to intuit and conceptualize the subjective experience of the child. Identification of play themes offers the therapist responses for enlarging the meaning, ways to converse about the child, and frameworks for communicating issues and progress to parents. Common play themes include power–control, dependency, revenge, safety–security, mastery, nurturing (i.e., self or others), grief and loss, abandonment, fear–protection, separation, perfectionism, hopelessness, and anxiety.

Many supervision sessions will center on the attempt to understand a child's play. The supervisor should look to multiple threads of convergent evidence in identifying play themes. Play themes are not fixed. In one session, a theme may seem perfectly clear, but play therapists need to be open to rethinking that theme in subsequent sessions. As a child is a dynamic changing being, so is his or her play. Experience suggests that play themes should always be conceptualized outside of the playroom. When therapists attempt to analyze play themes during therapy, they lose sight of connecting with the children in the moment. Because play themes derive from the subjective understanding of the therapist, their interpretation is limited by the therapist's own experiences and by assumptions outside of the therapist's awareness. Play therapists, operating from their own childhood experiences, may burden children with misperceptions. Supervisors must be aware of the personal histories of supervisees and their resultant professional limitations and must be aware of how these histories might affect the children with whom they work.

Connecting With Children

Although it seems basic that play therapists would be able to connect with children, this is often a concern in supervision. Because the children play therapists frequently work with have experienced damaged relationships, their ability to damage the play therapy relationship can be high. Some children are skilled in rejectful, hurtful, and vengeful behavior. Even the most experienced play therapist can be challenged in connecting with a child. In supervision, it helps to process the supervisee's anger, frustration, hurt, or even vengeance. The supervisor can generally help the therapist come to a constructive understanding of his or her feelings. The way the therapist feels often reflects feelings the child has experienced from someone in his or her life. This awareness can lead to increased empathy for the child.

Therapists who choose play therapy may expect to experience a fun, working environment where they receive emotional affirmation regarding their skills, caring, and personality from the children. With such expectancies, therapists can become sorely disillusioned with play therapy and with their child clients. Supervisors must help such supervisees assess their career path and evaluate the therapists' ability to change or choose another career.

Limit Setting

What limits to set, how to set them, and what to do when limits are violated are generally top concerns of play therapists (Kranz & Lund, 1993; Landreth, 2002b). The supervisor's and the therapist's theoretical orientations and personal preferences will impact decisions about limit setting. In an attempt to provide an environment that allows a child's self-direction and self-responsibility, minimal limits are encouraged in play therapy. The goal is to help the child move toward self-control. This permissive philosophy may be antithetical to the beliefs of many adults. Hence, play therapists struggle with their own belief system regarding limit setting.

Typically, limits are set when a child attempts to injure him- or herself or another person or to damage expensive or irreplaceable toys or furnishings or when a child's behavior impedes therapist acceptance. The guidelines limiting damaging behavior seem clear. However, setting limits to promote therapist acceptance is often controversial and subject to individual preferences. The purpose of therapist acceptance is to send the message that the therapist maintains a constant regard and respect for the child regardless of behavior, thereby allowing the child to feel that the person of the child is more important than the behavior of the child (Landreth, 2002b). One play therapist might be accepting when a child paints his or her face; another play therapist might find this interferes with his or her ability to accept the child fully, becoming annoyed or angry with the child. One play therapist might feel positive about a child making a huge mess in the playroom; another play therapist might have a second client directly following this client and cannot clean up the room in the time allotted. Limit setting is more complicated when the therapist does not have access to a dedicated playroom but must use an area of his or her office. It is helpful to address decisions about limits in supervision, helping the therapist clarify his or her own concerns regarding working with children. In discussing limits, the supervisor will want to assess the impact of a specific limit on the therapeutic work of a child.

Landreth (2002a) proposed a widely adopted approach to setting a limit in the playroom. The A-C-T model of limit setting involves (a) *acknowledging* the feeling, (b) *communicating* the limit, and (c) *targeting* an alternative. The play therapist addresses the child's feelings in the moment; sets a short, concrete limit; and provides an alternative to the action, "You're really angry with me, but I'm not for hitting. You can hit the Bop bag." When children have intense, directed energy, it is important to provide them with an alternative for that energy, so they do not act on destructive impulses. Although there are other methods for setting limits, the A-C-T model is short, direct, and effective.

Limit violations can be immediate and unexpected, so play therapists need to be prepared. Occasionally, children are so seriously out of control as to require physical limits. Access to help, safety issues, and guidelines regarding such situations need to be clarified before therapy begins.

When delivered in a firm, matter-of-fact way, the A-C-T model works with most children. However, play therapists will deal with many cases where children do not respond to limits. The therapist and supervisor should generate a list of ideas to help this particular child choose a course of action with likelihood of success that is within the competence and comfort level of the therapist, and practice limit setting in supervision. If success does not occur, careful reassessment is required. Experience in play therapy teaches that the majority of significant, limit-setting problems are preventable (Landreth, 2002b). When the supervisor and supervisee can identify the context and intent of the child's response, a solution to the problem is more likely. The following are case examples of preventable limit setting.

A 5-year-old girl with strong needs for attention was excited about coming to play therapy. The therapist arranged to consult with the parent during the first 15 minutes of the session. While they were in consultation, the child ran around the clinic screaming for her mother and ignoring limits set by the child-care worker. When the therapist and mother returned, the child refused to enter the play therapy session.

After this case was staffed, it was decided that the therapist would move parent consultations to the last 15 minutes of the session or to a time when the child did not accompany the parent.

> A 7-year-old boy, identified as needing power and control, was consistently aggressive toward the therapist. In therapy, the child moved from throwing play materials around the room to throwing them close to the therapist to throwing them directly at the therapist. The therapist began to dread preparing for sessions. After a few weeks of tense response to the aggressive play, the therapist began a session by saying; "You cannot throw things at me anymore." The child threw materials directly at the therapist while laughing.

In supervision, the therapist discussed feelings of rejection and discomfort with the child's aggression and reviewed use of the A-C-T model of limit setting. Saying, "I'm not for hitting," rather than, "You cannot . . . ," is less likely to challenge the child to demonstrate aggressive power.

> An 8-year-old boy referred for impulsive, aggressive behavior had an extremely conflicted relationship with his mother and had just learned that his emotionally distant father had cancer. The therapist had difficulty keeping the boy in the playroom. When he ran out of and around the clinic, he passed his mother, usually hitting or kicking her.

In staffing, it was decided to offer filial therapy for the mother to learn to set limits and to build a more positive relationship with her son; the father refused to participate.

In all these cases, the child's limit breaking was an attempt to meet a need, and the solutions were successful for that child. If the supervisor and play therapist can identify a child's specific need, they are more likely to target successful alternatives to limit setting (Landreth, 2002b).

FILIAL THERAPY

Filial therapy is the parent education component of CCPT and offers the therapist a model to work with parents based on child-centered principles. Because filial therapy integrates basic play therapy skills, advanced play therapy skills, group dynamics, parent education, and parent consultation, the therapist should be well trained and supervised in all of these arenas. The filial therapist has also become a supervisor of the parent's efforts. Filial therapy requires that therapists remain philosophically consistent with child-centered theory while facilitating a therapeutic parenting role. Supervision of filial therapy requires that the supervisor be experienced in facilitating filial groups and be able to offer the supervisee practical knowledge regarding expectations and methods.

Recognizing the power of child-centered play, Bernard and Louise Guerney developed filial therapy in the early 1960s. Their model was designed to enhance the relationship between a parent and child by facilitating empathy, genuineness, and acceptance on the part of the parent. The Guerneys offered training to parents in groups, over 12 to 18 months, and required weekly play sessions between parent and child (B. Guerney & Stover, 1971). VanFleet's (1994) version of their model narrowed training to 3 or 4 months and introduced the model of working with individual families in addition to working with parent groups. Landreth (2002a) designed a filial therapy, training model in a 10-week psychoeducational and support format. Therapists instructed parents in a group setting on principles of CCPT, then parents conducted 30-minute play sessions with their children on a weekly basis. Landreth and Bratton (2006) offered detailed outlines for each week's instruction and guidelines for facilitating play sessions. In filial therapy, the therapist supervises parents in developing their relationship skills with their children, often while the therapist is being supervised.

Although Guerney, VanFleet, and Landreth offered alternate time or group–individual formats for filial therapy delivery, the principles of intervention are common among all three approaches. These mutual assumptions include (a) focus on the relationship between parent and child instead of on the individual parent or child, (b) belief that parents are partners in the process, (c) belief that parents are capable of learning new skills, and (d) reverence for the importance of the parent's role in the child's life (VanFleet, Ryan, & Smith, 2005).

In the psychoeducational phase of filial therapy, the therapist teaches parents the basic child-centered skills outlined earlier. Filial therapy also addresses limit setting, which may be more complicated for parents because of the quantity and intensity of limits needed in a home. Following the education phase, the parents begin videotaped sessions with their children. If a parent does not have access to video equipment or to play materials, a filial therapist might allow the parent to use his playroom. Each week, a parent will present a play session to be reviewed by the parent group and the therapist. Unlike clinical supervision, filial therapists are trained to look for and to build on anything positive in the play sessions (VanFleet et al., 2005). If a parent responds negatively through most of the session but makes two or three effective filial responses, the therapist will focus on the parent's positive responses and the child's responses. A filial therapist supervising parent tapes concentrates on how the parent is feeling, how the child is feeling, which responses the parent is particularly proud of, how the child responds to the parents, and what the parent would like to change about the session. In filial therapy, techniques of enlarging the meaning and identifying themes are not used. Although these skills help to understand the child, they tend to distract parents from their goal of developing a nurturing, positive relationship. Relational skills are the focus in supervising filial sessions.

Filial therapy is the intervention of choice when dealing with strained parent–child relationships. Filial therapy helps parents to strengthen their relationships with all their children, to create understanding and acceptance for their children, to develop warm memories, and to rediscover the joy of parenting (Guerney & Stover, 1971; Landreth, 2002a; VanFleet, 1994). In addition, strong outcome research supports the efficacy of the filial model (Ray et al., 2001). VanFleet (1994) warned of inappropriate uses of filial training with parents who are incapable of comprehending the principles, who are so overwhelmed by their own needs they cannot focus on their children's needs, or who are abusive. In such situations, individual counseling for the parent and separate play therapy for the child are recommended. If parents can make necessary changes, then it might be appropriate to enter relational counseling with the child. In these cases, play sessions between parent and child are closely supervised, usually under controlled clinical conditions.

In deciding between the use of play and filial therapy, a supervisor might help the supervisee consider the following issues. Parents are probably the most effective agents of therapeutic change for very young children. For young children who have not experienced serious trauma, filial training seems to be appropriate and effective. When parents refer a child to therapy for relational problems (e.g., does not obey, is sullen or aggressive with family members, is unresponsive to parent, etc.) that do not permeate other settings, such as school, filial therapy might be the best choice (see chap. 2, this volume). Filial training can also provide a solid transition when a play therapist is ready to terminate play therapy with a child. Filial training allows (a) the child and the parents to experience less anxiety about termination, (b) the parents to gain skills to help their child, and (c) the child to have a continuing outlet for self-expression.

CONCLUSION

Play therapy is a unique, therapeutic modality in which the mental health professional is trained in the developmental knowledge of children, in the application of skills with children, in working with materials in a nonverbal setting, and in building therapeutic relationships. Supervision of play therapy requires extensive experience in these areas as well as expertise in clinical supervision. Effective supervision in play therapy involves the teaching and exploration of basic skills in working with children in a nonverbal modality. Therapists need assistance and encouragement in developing skills to both verbally and nonverbally communicate with children. This may be facilitated through the use of a well-designed checklist. Appendix 5.1 presents the Play Therapy Skills Checklist that can be used or modified to help play therapy supervisors give concrete and helpful feedback to supervisees.

Advanced skills in play therapy involve discovering and identifying the meaning of play, relating meaning to the child, and dealing with problems evolving in the play therapy relationship. In the supervision of advanced skills, the supervisor's role is to provide encouragement and knowledge of the play therapist's theoretical orientation and conceptual framework. From this framework, the play therapist will grow in his or her ability to understand, relate, and, ultimately, facilitate progress for a child. Through the supervision relationship, the play therapist will learn effective skills and use of self to support growth for the child. This chapter reviews areas that are difficult for new and experienced play therapists, including challenges to the therapist's ability to fully connect and accept the child as a person.

Filial therapy is a variation on play therapy in which the therapist teaches and supervises parents in the provision of therapeutic play with their children. Directed at strengthening the parent–child bond and at enhancing the skills of parents, filial therapy is a therapy of choice in selected family situations. Filial therapy requires that the filial therapist's supervisor ensure proper training of filial therapists, leading new therapists through the knowledge and skills of parent–child relationship dynamics, group process, play therapy, and teaching methods.

The unique circumstances of play therapy supervision necessitate advanced training of play therapy supervisors. As discussed, play and filial therapy supervision, at the very least, command working knowledge of the basics of counseling and therapy, a counseling supervision model, play therapy, child development, play behavior, parent education and consultation, and group dynamics. Such a broad and varied preparation appears to derive from a greater level of instruction and experience. This chapter offers a few guidelines to help play therapy supervisors build such experience and add to their toolbox of supervisory skills.

APPENDIX 5.1:

PLAY THERAPY SKILLS CHECKLIST
CENTER FOR PLAY THERAPY, UNIVERSITY OF NORTH TEXAS

Therapist: _____ Child/Age: _____ Date: _____

Observer: _____

Therapist's Nonverbal Communication

	Too Much	Appro-priate	Need More	None	Therapist Responses Examples	Other Possible Responses
Lean Forward/ Open						
Appeared Interested						
Relaxed Comfortable						
Tone/Expression Congruent With Child's Affect						
Tone/Expression Congruent With Therapist's Responses						

Therapist's Verbal Responses

	Too Much	Appro-priate	Need More	None	Therapist Responses Examples	Other Possible Responses
Tracking Behavior						
Reflecting Content						
Reflecting Feelings						
Facilitating Decisions Responsibility						
Facilitating Creativity Spontaneity						
Esteem Building Encouraging						
Facilitating Relationship						
Enlarging the Meaning/ Facilitating Understanding						
Succinct/ Interactive						
Rate of Responses						

Limit Setting:

Child Made Contacts/Connectedness:

Identified Themes:

Therapist's Strengths: Areas for Growth:

Note. From "Supervision of Basic and Advanced Skills in Play Therapy," by D. Ray, 2004, *Journal of Professional Counseling: Practice, Theory, and Research, 32,* p. 41. Copyright 2004 by the Texas Counseling Association. Reprinted with permission.

REFERENCES

Axline, V. (1947). *Play therapy*. New York: Ballantine Books.

Axline, V. (1964). *Dibs: In search of self*. Boston: Houghton Mifflin.

Brody, V. (1997). Developmental play therapy. In K. O'Connor & L. Braverman (Eds.), *Play therapy theory and practice: A comparative presentation* (pp. 160–183). New York: Wiley.

Bruner, J. S. (1976). Nature and uses of immaturity. In J. S. Bruner, A. Jolly, & K. Sylva (Eds.), *Play: Its role in development and evolution* (pp. 28–64). New York: Basic Books.

De Domenico, G. (1994). Jungian play therapy techniques. In K. O'Connor & C. Schaefer (Eds.), *Handbook of play therapy: Volume 2. Advances and innovations* (pp. 253–282). New York: Wiley.

Freud, A. (1965). *Normality and pathology in childhood*. New York: International Universities Press.

Guerney, B. G., Jr., & Stover, L. (1971). *Filial therapy* (Final report on MH 18254-01). Unpublished manuscript, Pennsylvania State University, University Park.

Guerney, L. (1978). Training and evaluation of students as consultants in an adult–child relationship enhancement program. *Professional Psychology, 9*, 193–198.

Guerney, L. (1983). Child-centered (non-directive) play therapy. In C. E. Schaefer & K. J. O'Connor (Eds.), *Handbook of play therapy* (pp. 21–64). New York: Wiley.

Klein, M. (1932). *The psychoanalysis of children*. London: Hogarth Press.

Knell, S. (1999). Cognitive–behavioral play therapy. In S. Russ & T. Ollendick (Eds.), *Handbook of psychotherapies with children and families* (pp. 385–404). New York: Kluwer Academic/Plenum Publishers.

Kottman, T. (2003). *Partners in play: An Adlerian approach to play therapy* (2nd ed.). Alexandria, VA: American Counseling Association.

Kranz, P., & Lund, N. (1993). Axline's eight principles of play therapy revisited. *International Journal of Play Therapy, 2*, 53–60.

Kranz, P., & Lund, N. (1994). Recommendations for supervising play therapists. *International Journal of Play Therapy, 3*, 45–52.

Landreth, G. (1991). *Play therapy: The art of the relationship*. New York: Brunner-Routledge.

Landreth, G. (2002a). *Play therapy: The art of the relationship* (2nd ed.). New York: Brunner-Routledge.

Landreth, G. (2002b). Therapeutic limit setting in the play therapy relationship. *Professional Psychology: Research and Practice, 33*, 529–535.

Landreth, G., & Bratton, S. (2006). *Child–parent relationship therapy: A 10-session filial therapy model*. New York: Routledge.

Moustakas, C. E. (1997). *Relationship play therapy*. Northvale, NJ: Jason Aronson.

O'Connor, K. (2000). *The play therapy primer* (2nd ed.). New York: Wiley.

Phillips, R., & Landreth, G. (1995). Play therapists on play therapy: I. A report of methods, demographics, and professional practices. *International Journal of Play Therapy, 4,* 1–26.

Ray, D. (2004). Supervision of basic and advanced skills in play therapy. *Journal of Professional Counseling: Practice, Theory, and Research, 32,* 28–41.

Ray, D., Bratton, S., Rhine, T., & Jones, L. (2001). The effectiveness of play therapy: Responding to the critics. *International Journal of Play Therapy, 10,* 85–108.

Rogers, C. (1951). *Client-centered therapy.* Boston: Houghton Mifflin.

Ryan, S., Gomory, T., & Lacasse, J. (2002). Who are we? Examining the results of the Association for Play Therapy membership survey. *International Journal of Play Therapy, 11,* 11–41.

Singer, J. L. (2002). Cognitive and affective implications of imaginative play in childhood. In M. Lewis (Ed.), *Child and adolescent psychiatry: A comprehensive textbook* (3rd ed., pp. 252–263). Philadelphia: Lippincott Williams & Wilkins.

VanFleet, R. (1994). *Filial therapy: Strengthening parent–child relationships through play.* Sarasota, FL: Professional Resource Press.

VanFleet, R., Ryan, S., & Smith, S. (2005). Filial therapy: A critical review. In L. Reddy, T. Files-Hall, & C. Schaefer (Eds.), *Empirically based play interventions for children* (pp. 241–264). Washington, DC: American Psychological Association.

Whiting, P., Bradley, L., & Planny, K. (2001). Supervision-based developmental models of counselor supervision. In L. Bradley & N. Ladany (Eds.), *Counselor supervision: Principles, process, and practice* (3rd ed., pp. 125–146). Philadelphia: Brunner-Routledge.

6

SUPERVISION OF COGNITIVE THERAPY WITH YOUTH

ROBERT D. FRIEDBERG AND CHRISTINA C. CLARK

Cognitive therapy with children offers several compelling advantages to supervisors and supervisees. The outcome literature indicates that cognitive therapy is a promising intervention for a myriad of conditions (Kaslow & Thompson, 1998; Kazdin & Weisz, 2003; Ollendick & King, 1998). Further, cognitive therapy owns a robust and a flexible conceptual framework that can be adapted for individual, family, and group modalities (Friedberg & McClure, 2002). Collaborative empiricism and guided discovery (J. S. Beck, 1995), the prototypical therapeutic stance variables, make cognitive therapy transparent to children and to their parents, include youth as partners in the change process, and honor children's phenomenological and subjective experiences. Moreover, these processes render therapy observable and measurable. Cognitive therapy's trademark session structure gives direction and momentum to clinical sessions. Homework makes cognitive therapy portable, so gain can generalize beyond clinicians' offices. Eliciting feedback empowers youth and makes perceptions of the treatment and of the therapist explicit. Finally, many intervention strategies founded on either a manually based (see chap. 7, this volume) or a modular approach to cognitive therapy contribute to numerous treatment options.

SUPERVISING THE BASICS

We recommend that supervisors and supervisees develop a supervision plan replete with operationalized goals and with associated learning processes. This game plan is akin to treatment plans completed with youth. Earlier chapters (1, 3, and 4) in this volume suggest other critical issues for the supervision contract. Training in case conceptualization lays the foundation for cognitive therapy supervision. We eschew bombarding supervisees with techniques until they have a basic understanding of case formulation. Case conceptualization provides supervisees with a clinical framework (J. S. Beck, 1995; Persons, 1989) that allows them to apply traditional cognitive techniques and to design innovative procedures to change thought, feeling, and behavior patterns.

Learning the cognitive model of psychopathology and personality is the first step in case conceptualization. In our work, we teach the hierarchical structural organizational model (A. T. Beck & Clark, 1988) that posits the roles of schemata, assumptions, and automatic thoughts in determining behavior. Trainees also learn the content-specificity hypothesis (A. T. Beck, 1976), which proposes that different cognitive content characterizes different emotional states.

Collaborative empiricism creates a milieu promoting a mutual search for possibilities. Children and therapists act like a team of detectives sifting through clues to assess the accuracy and the functional value of the child's beliefs (Kendall et al., 1992). Guided discovery is the process by which these possibilities are uncovered. Trainees are encouraged to adopt a curious stance (Padesky & Greenberger, 1995). Teaching supervisees to use Socratic questioning, homework, and behavioral experiments is a key supervisory task. A stance reflecting collaborative empiricism and guided discovery is invitational rather than confrontational. Supervisees learn to coach youth to evaluate their problematic thoughts rather than dogmatically refute irrational cognitions. I (Friedberg) fondly recall my supervisory experience with Christine A. Padesky who encouraged my own guided discovery. She taught that feelings of being stuck in therapy are just cues to ask more questions.

Training in cognitive therapy's prototypical session structure is another core element in supervision. The six components of session structure include (a) mood check-in, (b) homework review, (c) agenda setting, (d) processing session content, (e) homework assignment, and (f) eliciting feedback and summaries (J. S. Beck, 1995). The mood check-in provides a baseline and can be accomplished informally (e.g., How are you feeling? How did the last week go for you?) or can be accomplished formally with self-report inventories, such as the Children's Depression Inventory (Kovacs, 1992). Homework review involves processing the assignment designed in the previous session. Noncompliance with homework should always be addressed.

Data obtained from the mood check-in and homework review may be placed on the agenda. Agenda setting is the "table setter" for the session and helps both youths and their therapists allocate time for each issue. Setting an agenda is a collaborative endeavor with each therapeutic partner contributing to the menu. Friedberg and McClure (2002) suggested asking the patient, "What is it you absolutely, positively want to make sure we cover today?" to ensure all agenda items were placed on the table. Session content is derived from the agenda and is processed using guided discovery, empathy, behavioral techniques, and cognitive interventions. On the basis of the session content, homework assignments are collaboratively constructed. Homework assignments are best begun in session. Eliciting feedback gives the child opportunities to express satisfactions and dissatisfactions to the therapist. Obtaining treatment summaries from youth help to place a punctuation mark on the session. The patient has a chance to actively integrate session content, cull pivotal aspects, and construct a summary.

Managing the six components of session structure is a challenge for novice therapists. Friedberg and McClure (2002) drew an analogy between balancing session structure and juggling. They wrote, "like the balls jugglers toss and catch in their amazing balancing display[,] these clinical components must be kept in motion during therapy. Each separate component must be mindfully considered so that therapeutic momentum is maintained" (p. 45). Supervisors need to devote considerable effort to teaching trainees that these components are fluid and are not rigid, mechanical ways to manage sessions.

The opportunity to acquire tools for helping children attracts many supervisees to cognitive therapy. But they must learn the rudiments of theory and case conceptualization, before they focus their radars on technical targets. Practices, such as self-monitoring, behavioral activation (e.g., scheduling pleasant activities), relaxation procedures, systematic desensitization, exposure and performance attainment tasks, self-instruction, and rational analysis, are among the guts of technical training. Socratic dialogue may be one of the most difficult skills for trainees to develop. Although there are many types of Socratic dialogue, five classes of questions are commonly addressed to children's assumptions about their problems in cognitive therapy, including (a) What's the evidence? (b) What's an alternative explanation? (c) What are the advantages and the disadvantages? (d) How can I solve the problem? and (e) What's the worst that could happen? (i.e., decatastrophizing; Beal, Kopec, & DiGiuseppe, 1996; J. S. Beck, 1995). To facilitate Socratic questioning, we frequently recommend supervisees review articles by Overholser (1993a, 1993b, 1994), role-play the process, and watch videotape sessions of experienced cognitive therapists.

Experiential learning exercises can promote learning Socratic style. For instance, supervisees can gain practice building a Socratic dialogue around a common phrase such as, "If I step on a crack, I will break my mother's back" (Rutter & Friedberg, 1999). This phrase reflects an illusory correlation common to many inaccurate judgments made by young clients (e.g., "If I comply with my parents' commands, I will surrender total control"; "If I don't control other people, something bad will happen"). The supervisee is then asked to construct a line of questioning to test the thought (e.g., "Has your mother's back hurt when you have not stepped on a crack? Have you stepped on a crack, and your mother has been fine?") and then role play with the supervisor. Supervisors may frequently break role and give feedback during the dialogue process. Once the supervisee successfully completes this phase of practice, the supervisor proceeds to a clinical example (e.g., "If I stop worrying, disaster will follow"). The supervisee learns that a similar line of questioning will be effective in testing such beliefs. Supervisors may encourage the supervisee to keep a written log of effective questions.

SUPERVISORY STYLE

A supervisor's style parallels a cognitive therapist's clinical stance. A cognitive therapy supervisor is a coach who collaboratively shepherds trainees through the learning process via guided discovery. Collaborative empiricism also characterizes the partnership between supervisor and supervisee, as they mutually analyze the data. Data sources in supervision include verbal report, audiotape, videotape, objective testing results, patient satisfaction ratings, and competency-based rating scales (Liese & Beck, 1997). Hypotheses about clinical work are crafted and tested throughout the process. Learning occurs through the guided discovery process that makes use of empathy, Socratic questioning, behavioral experimentation, and homework to evaluate the supervisee's assumptions about a particular case, to broaden his or her knowledge and conceptual base, to increase his or her technical proficiency, and to foster professional development.

Teaching trainees and ensuring young clients receive proper treatment are two main supervisory responsibilities (Newman, 1998). To acquire the core competencies of cognitive therapy, therapists must first understand the theory. Then they can begin building skills to apply theory in a systematic and a structured way, to learn to develop a case conceptualization, to practice empirically based procedures in a creative way that appreciates clients' diverse contexts, and to become increasingly aware of interpersonal processes (Padesky, 1996). Teaching can use a range of methods, including didactic instruction, audiotape and videotape review, supervisor cotherapy, peer cotherapy, role-playing, Socratic dialogues, oral and written exams, reading assignments, and workshop attendance (Beal & DiGiuseppe, 1998; Newman, 1998; Padesky, 1993, 1996). Goals for each supervisee are individualized and are based on his or her developmental level. As supervisees progress, more emphasis is placed on complex skills, such as case formulation and attention to interpersonal processes, than on basic techniques. Several pivotal resources we encourage supervisees to review include work by A. T. Beck, Rush, Shaw, and Emery (1979); J. S. Beck (1995); Friedberg and McClure (2002); Kazdin and Weisz (2003); Kendall (1990, 2000); Kendall et al. (1992); Knell (1993); and Reinecke, Datillio, and Freeman (2003).

BASIC STRUCTURE OF THE SUPERVISION SESSION

Liese and Beck (1997) cogently outlined the basic structure of a cognitive therapy supervision session. It is not surprising that it approximated the structure of cognitive therapy and included check-in, agenda setting, bridge from previous sessions, follow-up from previous supervised cases, review of any homework, working of agenda items, homework assignment, and feedback. The check-in period allows for friendly chitchat with the supervisee. Agenda setting sets the stage for the supervision session and allows both parties to allocate time to relevant issues. Bridging from the previous session is a pivotal way to promote continuity and momentum in supervision. Liese and Beck offered useful questions, such as "What did you learn last time?" and "What did we discuss that was most important to you?" (p. 121) as ways to bridge between sessions. Follow-up on previous cases and reviewing any assignments are important ways that supervisors can monitor progress. Such follow-up shows supervisees that supervisors are committed to them. The focus of the individual session will vary depending on the agenda and may range from reviewing the supervisee's homework to reviewing the videotaped therapy sessions. Supervisors and supervisees may engage in didactic training, and assignments may be developed between sessions.

SUPERVISEE FEEDBACK

Feedback to the supervisee needs to be concrete, specific, constructive, and frequent (Beal & DiGiuseppe, 1998; Newman, 1998; Padesky, 1993, 1996). Beal and DiGiuseppe (1998, p. 130) outlined the following six pivotal lessons for supervisors to communicate to their supervisees: (a) errors are expected; (b) errors are understandable; (c) it is not horrible when one makes a mistake, it is only unfortunate; (d) a therapist is not a failure for making errors; he or she is only a fallible human being who lacks critical information or skills; (e) the supervisor can tolerate supervisee mistakes; and (f) people learn from mistakes. Supervisors are advised to build on a supervisee's strengths (Beal & DiGiuseppe, 1998; Padesky, 1996). Training plans should be graduated to match the supervisees' competence and training level (Padesky, 1996). For instance, processing interpersonal issues with a trainee who is still struggling with theory is counterproductive. Padesky recommends fostering strong case conceptualization skills and suggests paying attention to what the trainee does not talk about in supervision. Beal and DiGiuseppe designed a best-tape and worst-tape assignment to facilitate supervisee's presentation of hidden material.

TRAINING IN CASE CONCEPTUALIZATION

Case conceptualization is a dynamic process that starts at initial contact and continues through the course of treatment (J. S. Beck, 1995; Padesky, 1996). Supervisees are taught to craft a careful psychological picture, using cognitive behavioral constructs that enable comprehensive treatment planning and focused intervention. In teaching case conceptualization, supervisors (a) define case conceptualization and provide a rationale for formulating a case; (b) explicitly define the data necessary to complete a case conceptualization; (c) teach methods for gathering, organizing, and synthesizing information; and (d) model how hypotheses based on case conceptualization are tested and how interventions are developed.

Supervisees often need a template to integrate complex patient data. Excellent paradigms by Persons (1989), J. S. Beck (1995), and Padesky (1996) are available. We recommend a template developed by Friedberg and McClure (2002), which is based on these previous models and is specifically designed for children and adolescents. They propose a conceptual scheme that integrates cultural context, developmental history, cognitive structures, behavioral antecedents and consequences, physiological symptoms, moods, behavior, cognitions, and interpersonal processes. Templates or diagrams can also illustrate the dynamic interplay between variables. They can be condensed into one- or two-page summary sheets. Case summary forms facilitate the supervisory process (J. S. Beck, 1995; Padesky, 1996). As supervisors and their supervisees discuss each patient, the case formulation sheets are modified and amended. Written summaries can highlight what information has not been collected or has not been considered by the supervisees.

We find beginning supervisees feel pressure to get it right when conceptualizing cases. A pivotal task for supervisors is encouraging a curious, scientific attitude—one that promotes hypothesis testing. Assuring diffident supervisees of the value of revising case conceptualizations keeps them alert and learning. Flexibility is a skill that serves cognitive therapists well. Like Persons (1995), we urge supervisees to create simple conceptualizations rather than to paralyze themselves with complexity. Remembering the law of parsimony is a good strategy.

TRAINING IN TECHNIQUE

Applying basic cognitive and behavioral techniques with children requires sensitivity to developmental and cultural issues. Moreover, trainees need to be concrete, simple, engaging, and creative in their interventions. We provide a general menu of interventions to trainees including, but not limited to, self-monitoring, systematic desensitization, relaxation, contingency management, exposure, self-instruction, and rational analysis. We believe that the best learning occurs by doing.

We recommend trainees complete thought diaries when they feel strong emotions during supervision. If questionable automatic thoughts are identified, trainees can try self-instructional or rational analysis procedures. For instance, a psychiatric resident was reluctant to amplify a patient's anger and anxiety. The following thought record was identified in session.

Situation: Child becomes angry in session.
Feeling: Anxious.
Thought: I won't know what to do.

The thought record helped this astute resident locate the nature of his anxiety. He believed increased emotion in the child would leave him feeling incompetent and helpless. The supervisor and the resident then processed this belief through both testing evidence (e.g., "What is the evidence you will lose control? What is the evidence you will not lose control?") and decatastrophizing (e.g., "What's the worst thing that could happen? What is the best thing that could happen? What is the most likely thing to happen? How can you problem-solve if the worst thing happens? If you have a problem-solving strategy, how catastrophic can the worst thing be?"). In addition, this thought record led to a productive discussion of how the resident was colluding with the youth's own catastrophic predictions about emotional expression (e.g., "Expressing feelings means I will lose control").

Techniques are also learned during role-playing with the supervisee. For example, a panic induction by breathing through a straw might be practiced in session. Exposure trials are commonly role-played in session with supervisees. For instance, stepping supervisees through the sequential stages of graduated exposure is a good idea. It builds self-efficacy in the supervisee and helps him or her anticipate obstacles. When working with a supervisee who was treating an anxious child, I (Friedberg) role-played an exposure trial where balloons were burst randomly to create the dreaded startle response. Through role-playing, the supervisee learns how to Socratically process the child's discomfort while managing his or her own performance anxiety.

Supervisees also learn through homework assignments. A homework assignment might be to watch a favorite television show, to identify a character who seems plagued by inaccurate thinking, to make a daily thought record, and to design a self-instructional intervention. Finally, supervisees may observe supervisors applying these techniques in their clinical work by doing cotherapy, by watching through a one-way mirror, or by viewing videotapes. A caution here is that the supervisee needs to identify the pivotal aspects of the session and to identify with the supervisor. Therefore, we recommend that prior to any observation, the supervisee should be briefed on what to observe. Further, the supervisee should be debriefed to ensure that the observations were understood. Supervisees may also believe that they cannot do what the supervisor demonstrates because of lack of competence. If the supervisees see the gap between them and the supervisors as being too great, they will not identify with the supervisors and will fail to imitate the behavior.

WORKING WITH INTERPERSONAL PROCESSES

Cognitive–behavioral procedures all take place in a relationship. Thus, supervisors need to train supervisees to deal with the interpersonal processes in cognitive therapy with youth (Liese & Beck, 1997; Padesky, 1996). Interpersonal processes between supervisees and supervisors need similar attention. Adopting a collaborative approach, using guided discovery, and adhering to traditional session structure facilitate processing interpersonal issues in supervision (Padesky, 1996).

In general, supervisees who are competitive and resentful toward authority are less likely to profit from supervision than those who are not competitive and not resentful toward authority (Berger & Buchholz, 1993). Padesky (1996) suggested that "therapists who are not willing to participate in highly interactive therapy relationships are poor candidates for cognitive therapy training" (p. 270). These supervisees challenge the most experienced supervisors. For supervisees who are resentful and competitive, the supervisor is well advised to make this a focal point of supervision. Beliefs, expectations, and possibly self-schemata may need to be identified. For example, after completing 3 weeks of a 12-week rotation, a predoctoral psychology intern who resented learning cognitive therapy proclaimed, "I've learned everything I can from you." The supervisee was then asked, "What is it like training with someone you believe you cannot learn from?" The supervisee admitted it could be frustrating. After some additional Socratic dialogue, the supervisee remarked, "It is really frustrating having to learn something new after all of these years of training in a different model." This belief then became a new starting point for the supervision and the supervisory relationship. The key was to maintain a curious stance and to stay faithful to the notion of guided discovery.

Resentment toward supervision may also be associated with the supervisee's sense of status. One supervisee exclaimed, "I have to be the one who knows best. I shouldn't need anyone's suggestions. If I take someone else's recommendations, I am inferior to them." Socratic questioning focuses on the advantages and disadvantages of these beliefs and assumptions. After the supervisee listed "being isolated and alone in clinical work" as a disadvantage to this set of beliefs, the supervisor asked, "That's a lot of pressure to put on yourself at this point in your career. How helpful would it be to you if we worked together to relieve this excessive pressure and to help you get more support?" Once the supervisee began collaborating, rather than competing, the dialogue progressed to the expectations about taking feedback (e.g., "Do you have to take every recommendation? What is your role in evaluating supervisory feedback?"). Such interventions can increase competitive and resentful supervisees' collaboration in their own professional development. Adhering to guided discovery and collaborative empiricism not only facilitates testing supervisees' beliefs that buttress competition but also models the therapeutic position supervisors encourage supervisees to adopt.

Kaslow and Deering (1993) saw supervisory relationships as similar to parenting. In accordance with this, independence and dependence issues may erupt in supervision. Supervisees may overly rely on the supervisor, thereby undermining their own perceived competence. In these instances, supervisors should encourage experimentation with independence. The supervisor might have the supervisee log his or her own successes with youth and frequently refer to him or her to reinforce *felt* competence. Other supervisees may tug at the leash and may battle supervisors for control. They may fear supervisors are trying to dominate them or to convert them into clinical clones (Friedberg & Taylor, 1994). In these circumstances, the trainee might be invited to evaluate his or her all or none thinking about control and independence (e.g., "Is feedback always a form of control? What is the difference between learning or trying a new skill and being converted?").

Supervisees who worry excessively about their competence may fear negative evaluation and may present things that are only going well. A graduated approach to exposing their weaknesses or difficulties is a good strategy. Processing initial small disclosures about aspects of the therapy that did not go well is often productive (e.g., "What was it like for you to tell me your patient was dissatisfied with you? What went through your mind? How did you imagine I would react?"). In this way, supervisees face their catastrophic beliefs and learn that supervision is a place where trainees learn from mistakes.

The supervisee is only one side of the equation. Supervisors may be too nice, too controlling, or too focused on the feelings of the supervisee (Liese & Beck, 1997). The noncritical supervisor might believe constructive feedback will injure or wound a supervisee and might opt to provide only reassurance (Liese & Beck, 1997). For us, this is a unidimensional view of support. Rather than avoiding feedback in this instance, the supervisor should bring these thoughts and feelings into the supervisory relationship and process the negative feedback with the supervisee (e.g., "What goes through your mind when I give you criticism? What does it mean about you? What do you predict might happen to our relationship if I gave you more negative feedback?"). For some supervisees, criticism propels fears of poor evaluation or disapproval. For others, they fear that receipt of negative feedback reveals their incompetence. Supervisors also may worry that the supervisory relationship will be damaged if they offer negative feedback.

Alert supervisors will use guided discovery and behavioral experimentation to test their beliefs. After negative feedback is given, it should be Socratically processed, so inaccurate beliefs can be tested and problem-solving strategies can be created. Encouraging supervisees to present only the difficult cases where they have questions, self-doubts, and obstacles to therapeutic progress allows them to experiment with revealing weaknesses and deficiencies. Once a supervisee gains confidence that disclosing personal weaknesses is productive, he or she is on the road to genuine self-efficacy.

WORKING WITH ATTITUDINAL VARIABLES

Supervisees bring technical skills, interpersonal qualities, and attitudes to the supervisory process. Supervisors must work with what the supervisees bring to the table. Reflecting on her own growth as a cognitive therapist, Paolo (1998) remarked, "receiving supervision has required patience, persistence, and passion to learn" (p. 160). There are several attitudinal variables that novice cognitive therapy supervisees may hold that can interfere with their training.

The Therapeutic Relationship Is Unimportant in Cognitive Therapy

Cognitive therapy has long emphasized the necessity of building productive relationships with youth (A. T. Beck et al., 1979). Because of the central processes of guided discovery and of collaborative empiricism, much of the early work in therapy is focused on enlisting a child's collaboration.

The practice of eliciting feedback promotes the therapeutic relationship while it evokes implicit assumptions and beliefs that may facilitate or impede the therapy. Children's thoughts and feelings about themselves, their problems, their peers, their siblings, their parents, and their therapists are revealed only within a positive therapeutic relationship. When a child who fears negative evaluation forgets his or her homework, the time is ripe for identifying his or her predictions about what the therapist will think. After these beliefs are culled, the child can be prompted to test them.

Cognitive Therapy With Youth Is an Emotionless, Mechanical Endeavor

Many supervisees enter cognitive therapy training with the idea that cognitive therapy is a technical, sterile process where emotion is neglected. However, emotional arousal is the key cue for asking the seminal cognitive therapy question (e.g., "What's going through your mind right now?"). It also helps to increase supervisees awareness of the content–specificity hypothesis and the thought–feeling connection. Supervisees are often surprised to discover cognitive therapy sessions are punctuated by vivid here and now experiences (Knell, 1993). The child's immediate thoughts and feelings provide rich material. When a child loses at a game, it provides an in vivo opportunity to capture and to test dysfunctional thoughts, as well as to subsequently modify distressing feelings.

Trainees may initially be reluctant to experiment with agenda setting (Temple & Bowers, 1998). They may see agenda setting as imposing too much structure on the session and as limiting a child's spontaneity. It is important for supervisors to teach agenda setting as a rich and a fluid process. How a child responds to agenda setting is clinically significant. Trainees need to learn to work with children who have difficulty setting an agenda (e.g., "I don't know what to talk about. You decide."), who put too much on the agenda, who have difficulty sticking to the agenda, or who openly avoid agenda setting (e.g., "This sucks!").

Play Therapy and Cognitive Therapy Are Incompatible

Supervisees may think that sand play, dollhouses, checkers, and crayons have no place in cognitive therapy. Cognitive therapy readily uses play to facilitate therapeutic processes with children (Friedberg & McClure, 2002; Knell, 1993). Supervisees are taught that "play is the medium by which inaccurate internal dialogues are elicited and more adaptive coping methods are taught" (Friedberg & McClure, 2002, pp. 150–151). Automatic thoughts, such as "I must always get what I want," can be identified and evaluated in doll play or in games.

Cognitive Therapy Is All About Refutation and Disputation

Many trainees approach cognitive therapy believing they are to interrogate their young patients until they discover the truth. They are ready to dispute and to refute each negative thought until the child submits. The goal of cognitive therapy is not to argue but is to create doubt where error reigned with certainty (Padesky, 1988). Trainees who learn this simple but powerful axiom feel less pressure to change children's thinking than those who do not learn it. Trainees may begin to appreciate that cognitive therapy empowers children, changing how they process information as well as how they process their thought content.

In my (Friedberg) own training, I recall Christine Padesky teaching, "When the thought is accurate, we'll problem solve. When the thought is inaccurate, we'll teach you questions to make better sense of the situation." New cognitive therapists need to discern when a child's thought is inaccurate and when it represents a sad reality. A child's belief that his or her parents are critical and demanding may accurately reflect a distressing situation. However, the thought, "I am an awful son [or daughter] for disappointing my parents," is a destructive interpretation. Skillful use of collaborative empiricism and of guided discovery help supervisees discern these clinical subtleties.

CONCLUSION

Teaching new skills is a task of both practicing and supervising cognitive therapy with child therapists. A graduated approach that promotes acquisition of basic theory of cognitive therapy and child development, of case conceptualization, of session structure, of core techniques, and of sensitivity to interpersonal–attitudinal processes is recommended. With the increasing emphasis on evidence-supported treatments and the concomitant popularity of cognitive–behavioral approaches, cognitive therapy supervisors need to make sure supervisees gain a full appreciation of this evolving paradigm. In this way, a new generation of cognitive therapists can faithfully offer traditional and innovative intervention to young people.

REFERENCES

Beal, D., & DiGiuseppe, R. A. (1998). Training supervisors in rational emotive behavior therapy. *Journal of Cognitive Psychotherapy, 12,* 127–137.

Beal, D., Kopec, A. M., & DiGiuseppe, R. A. (1996). Disputing patient's irrational beliefs. *Journal of Rational–Emotive and Cognitive–Behavioral Therapy, 14,* 215–229.

Beck, A. T. (1976). *Cognitive therapy and the emotional disorders*. New York: International Universities Press.

Beck, A. T., & Clark, D. A. (1988). Anxiety and depression: An information processing approach. *Anxiety Research, 1,* 23–36.

Beck, A. T., Rush, A. J., Shaw, B. F., & Emery, G. (1979). *Cognitive therapy of depression: A treatment manual.* New York: Guilford Press.

Beck, J. S. (1995). *Cognitive therapy: Basics and beyond.* New York: Guilford Press.

Berger, S. S., & Buchholz, E. S. (1993). On becoming a supervisee: Preparation for learning in a supervisory relationship. *Psychotherapy, 30,* 86–92.

Friedberg, R. D., & McClure, J. M. (2002). *Clinical practice of cognitive therapy with children and adolescents: The nuts and bolts.* New York: Guilford Press.

Friedberg, R. D., & Taylor, L. A. (1994). Perspectives on supervision in cognitive therapy. *Journal of Rational–Emotive and Cognitive–Behavior Therapy, 12,* 147–151.

Kaslow, N. J., & Deering, C. G. (1993). A developmental approach to psychotherapy supervision of interns and postdoctoral fellows. *The Psychotherapy Bulletin, 28,* 20–23.

Kaslow, N. J., & Thompson, M. P. (1998). Applying the criteria for empirically supported treatments to studies of psychosocial interventions for child and adolescent depression. *Journal of Clinical Child Psychology, 27,* 146–155.

Kazdin, A. E., & Weisz, J. R. (2003). *Evidence-based psychotherapies for children and adolescents.* New York: Guilford Press.

Kendall, P. C. (1990). *Coping cat workbook.* Ardmore, PA: Workbook Publishing.

Kendall, P. C. (Ed.). (2000). *Child and adolescent therapy: Cognitive and behavioral procedures.* New York: Guilford Press.

Kendall, P. C., Chansky, T. E., Kane, M. T., Kortlander, E., Ronan, K. R., Sessa, F. M., & Siqueland, L. (1992). *Anxiety disorders in youth: Cognitive–behavioral interventions.* Boston: Allyn & Bacon.

Kovacs, M. (1992). *Children's Depression Inventory.* North Tonawanda, NY: Multi-Health Systems.

Knell, S. M. (1993). *Cognitive–behavior play therapy.* Northvale, NJ: Jason Aronson.

Liese, B. S., & Beck, J. S. (1997). Cognitive therapy supervision. In E. Watkins (Ed.), *Handbook of psychotherapy supervision* (pp. 114–133). New York: Wiley.

Newman, C. F. (1998). Therapeutic and supervisory relationships in cognitive–behavioral therapies: Similarities and differences. *Journal of Cognitive Psychotherapy, 12,* 95–108.

Ollendick, T. H., & King, N. J. (1998). Empirically supported treatments for children with phobic and anxiety disorders: Current status. *Journal of Clinical Child Psychology, 27,* 156–167.

Overholser, J. C. (1993a). Elements of the Socratic method, Part 1: Systematic questioning. *Psychotherapy, 30,* 67–74.

Overholser, J. C. (1993b). Elements of the Socratic method, Part 2: Inductive reasoning. *Psychotherapy, 30,* 75–85.

Overholser, J. C. (1994). Elements of the Socratic method, Part 3: Universal definitions. *Psychotherapy, 31,* 286–293.

Padesky, C. A. (1988, October). *Intensive training series in cognitive therapy.* Workshop series presented at Newport Beach, CA.

Padesky, C. A. (1993). Staff and patient education. In J. H. Wright, M. E. Thase, A. T. Beck, & J. W. Ludgate (Eds.), *Cognitive therapy with inpatients: Developing a cognitive milieu* (pp. 393–413). New York: Guilford Press.

Padesky, C. A. (1996). Developing cognitive therapist competency: Teaching and supervision models. In P. M. Salkovskis (Ed.), *Frontiers of cognitive therapy* (pp. 266–292). New York: Guilford Press.

Padesky, C. A., & Greenberger, D. P. (1995). *A clinician's guide to mind over mood.* New York: Guilford Press.

Paolo, S. B. (1998). Receiving supervision in cognitive therapy: A personal account. *Journal of Cognitive Psychotherapy, 12,* 153–162.

Persons, J. B. (1989). *Cognitive therapy in practice: A case formulation approach.* New York: Norton.

Persons, J. B. (1995, November). *Cognitive–behavioral case formulation.* Workshop presented at the annual meeting of the Association for the Advancement of Behavior Therapy, Washington, DC.

Reinecke, M. A., Dattilio, F. M., & Freeman, A. (Eds.). (2003). *Cognitive therapy with children and adolescents* (2nd ed.). New York: Guilford Press.

Rutter, J. G., & Friedberg, R. D. (1999). Guidelines for the effective use of Socratic dialogue in cognitive therapy. In L. Vandecreek, S. Knapp, & T. L. Jackson (Eds.), *Innovations in clinical practice: A sourcebook* (Vol. 17, pp. 481–490). Sarasota, FL: Professional Resource Press.

Temple, S., & Bowers, W. A. (1998). Supervising cognitive therapists from diverse fields. *Journal of Cognitive Psychotherapy, 12,* 139–152.

7

SUPERVISING A MANUAL-BASED TREATMENT PROGRAM IN THE UNIVERSITY AND THE COMMUNITY: A TALE OF TWO CITIES

MICHAEL A. SOUTHAM-GEROW AND PHILIP C. KENDALL

The growing evidence supporting child mental health treatments (Compton, Burns, Egger, & Robertson, 2002; Farmer, Compton, Burns, & Robertson, 2002) is creating optimism for empirically based practice in community settings (Chambless et al., 1996). Therapies with empirical support are typically manualized, making them well suited for dissemination as best practices. However, the adoption of evidence-based treatments in community settings has been slower than hoped (Norquist, Lebowitz, & Hyman, 1999; Schoenwald & Hoagwood, 2001). Scientists have long lamented the gap between science and practice. Research that closes this gap

Preparation of this article was supported in part by NIH Grants R01-MH59087 and U01-MH63747 to Philip C. Kendall.

Special thanks to John R. Weisz, Principal Investigator of the Youth Anxiety and Depression Study. We are grateful to our colleagues at the Child and Adolescent Anxiety and Disorders Clinic and Youth Anxiety and Depression Study and are grateful to Katherine Andrews for editorial assistance.

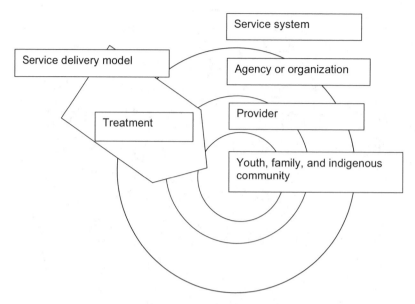

Figure 7.1. Dimensions relevant to treatment development, adaptation, and adoption. From "Effectiveness and Dissemination Research: Their Mutual Roles in Improving Mental Health Services for Children and Adolescents," by S. K. Schoenwald and K. Hoagwood, 2001, *Emotional & Behavioral Disorders in Youth, 2,* p. 4. Copyright 2001 by the Civic Research Institute. Adapted with permission.

is a major priority for the National Institutes of Health (Hoagwood & Olin, 2002).

Recent studies highlight differences between university-based, research clinics—where empirically supported treatments (ESTs) are often tested—and community-based clinics—where many children and families seek mental health services (e.g., Southam-Gerow, Weisz, & Kendall, 2003). As pictured in Figure 7.1, these contexts may differ by (a) client–family, (b) provider, (c) agency, and (d) service system (Southam-Gerow, Ringeisen, & Sherrill, in press). Of these, the provider (i.e., the therapist) has received little attention in the literature (e.g., Fehrenbach & Coffman, 2001; Martell & Hollon, 2001). The failure to fit newly developed treatments to providers may contribute to their slow deployment (Schoenwald & Hoagwood, 2001).

Surveys of providers regarding treatment adoption capture their concerns about the applicability of ESTs and their neglect of the research literature (e.g., Addis & Krasnow, 2000; Kazdin, Siegel, & Bass, 1990). When a treatment is evaluated in research, procedures are described in detail, usually in a manual. Manuals should facilitate dissemination (Kendall, 1998), yet they often create controversy. In a large survey, Addis and Krasnow (2000) revealed that one fifth of respondents had never considered use of treatment manuals. Manuals were viewed as both having a negative, dehumanizing effect on the process of psychotherapy and helpful in guiding empirically supported interventions to achieve positive outcomes. To state this ambivalence concisely, therapists believe manuals may improve outcomes but may worsen process. There is evidence for and against both of these ideas (e.g., Henry, Butler, Strupp, Schacht, & Binder, 1993; Huey, Henggeler, Brondino, & Pickrel, 2000; Kendall et al., 1997).

Besides attitudinal barriers toward manuals, there are differences between research–clinic and service–clinic therapists. Research–clinic therapists are often advanced graduate students in doctoral programs with small caseloads, who receive training and supervision from treatment experts or from treatment developers. Community–clinic therapists are usually licensed practitioners with large caseloads, many with master's of social work degrees. Such differences shape how therapists are trained and supervised. In our view, features of supervision are critical in the transportability and the adoptability of new treatments (Kendall & Southam-Gerow, 1995).

This chapter details our experiences with training and supervising clinicians in the use of a manualized, cognitive–behavioral therapy (i.e., the Coping Cat program; Kendall, 2002) for 7- to 13-year-old children and adolescents with anxiety disorders. We will discuss the similarities and the differences in two contexts—the Child and Adolescent Anxiety Disorders Clinic (CAADC) at Temple University in Philadelphia and the community clinics in the Youth Anxiety and Depression Study (YADS; Principal Investigator: John R. Weisz, MH-57347) in Los Angeles County.

THE COPING CAT TREATMENT MANUAL

Developed by Kendall and his colleagues at the CAADC, the Coping Cat program for childhood anxiety disorders has been evaluated in multiple settings and in individual, family, and group formats. Numerous studies support the program's efficacy, including those conducted by the developers and by independent investigators (see Chorpita & Southam-Gerow, 2006, for review). This chapter will focus on our work supervising the individual program.

The individual Coping Cat program is a manual-based, 16- to 20-session treatment that includes a skills training component and an exposure component (Kendall, 2002). After establishing rapport, youth are taught a four-step, coping plan called the FEAR steps. FEAR is an acronym for: *feeling* frightened, *expecting* bad things to happen, *actions* and attitudes to take, and *results* and rewards. The FEAR steps, taught over a series of sessions, include (a) the recognition of anxious feelings and somatic reactions, (b) the role of cognition and self-talk in exacerbating anxious situations, (c) the use of problem-solving skills and coping skills to manage anxiety, and (d) the use of self-evaluation and self-reinforcement strategies to facilitate and to maintain coping. After learning the FEAR steps, the remaining 8 to 12 sessions are dedicated to gradual exposure tasks. These tasks are viewed as critical to successful treatment and involve challenges for the therapist and the child because the therapist must arrange opportunities for the child to experience anxious distress in real situations (Kendall et al., 2005). Implementation of the coping plan is encouraged during individually tailored exposure tasks. Throughout treatment, behavioral strategies, such as *coping modeling*, in vivo exposure, role playing, relaxation training, and contingent reinforcement are used.

OVERVIEW OF COGNITIVE–BEHAVIOR THERAPY SUPERVISION MODEL

Essential to effective cognitive–behavior therapy (CBT) supervision is the supervisee's understanding of the underlying model (see chap. 6, this volume; Rosenbaum & Ronen, 1998). The CBT model views psychological problems as related to prior learning, which shape a child's attributions, expectations, misperceptions, and attentional biases. CBT emphasizes learning new skills to overcome problem behaviors. The CBT model is an integrative and interactive model, open to reformulation in accord with empirical evidence. For example, recent evidence on emotion processes led to an increased integration of emotion into the theory (Southam-Gerow & Kendall, 2002). Combining cognitive and behavioral intervention strategies into an expanding hybrid, the CBT model, which is data driven and hypothesis-testing in nature, is designed to respond actively and effectively to the heterogeneous problems that youth and their families face.

Rosenbaum and Ronen (1998) describe five key characteristics of supervision in CBT, they are (a) emphasis on the therapist being systematic and goal orientated, (b) emphasis on therapist practice or therapist rehearsal, (c) emphasis on the therapist–supervisor collaboration, (d) emphasis on the therapist as a change agent, and (e) emphasis aimed toward increasing therapist resourcefulness. We would add a sixth element, typical of our approach with Coping Cat—emphasis on focusing on the present. We briefly discuss the six key elements:

1. Manualized treatments systematize the flow of therapy in and across sessions. Sessions are organized in advance around specific skills, and supervision is concerned with fitting the session content to the specific child. Therapist and supervisor actively consider the myriad ways a skill can be taught and consider what should be emphasized. Optimally, the manual provides

a framework, but the details are determined by the individual child, the therapist, and the supervisor.

2. Supervision often includes practicing the strategies to be used in the sessions. Role-playing the teaching of problem-solving skills allows the therapist to gain confidence in applying the skills and permits the supervisor to observe in vivo and to detect possible misunderstandings or to suggest alternative presentations.

3. There is a high level of collaboration between supervisor and supervisee, paralleling the collaborative empiricism that typifies the therapy relationship in CBT.

4. The CBT therapist is an active change agent, facilitating the choice of goals and outcome measures and developing a flexible, working case conceptualization (Southam-Gerow & Kendall, 2000). Supervisors are similarly active in the development of the therapist.

5. A CBT supervisor works to facilitate therapists' sense of efficacy and resourcefulness in the clinical setting just as a CBT therapist seeks to maximize the client's strengths.

6. Finally, supervision of CBT is present-focused. Although client history is an integral part of the CBT conceptualization (Freeman & Miller, 2002), the CBT supervisor keeps the supervision meeting focused on creating change in a client's current life. The current events and the client's perceptions of those events take center stage. The CBT supervisor emphasizes formulations that are testable, so that data from the client and data from forthcoming sessions can be used to evaluate the case formulation.

SUPERVISION OF COPING CAT IN MULTIPLE SETTINGS

We believe that our experiences of supervising Coping Cat in sharply contrasting settings can contribute substantially to understanding the supervisory challenges that accompany the development and the dissemination of an innovative treatment. Our contrast is between the Temple University CAADC and YADS where we supervised therapists with scores of cases in six community mental health agencies in Los Angeles County.

Supervision in a Specialty Clinic Setting

Many features of the CAADC made it an easy place to supervise. Supervisees were select, highly motivated doctoral students in Temple

University's clinical psychology program. They chose Temple to work in the CAADC. Enrolled in a program with a strong cognitive–behavioral emphasis, therapists achieved great familiarity with CBT. Their caseloads ranged from three to eight cases at a time. This allowed ample time to learn Coping Cat.

Training Model at the CAADC

Potential CAADC therapists all work in the clinic for one to two semesters in their first year of study. They devote at least one year to do intakes and to follow up on assessment interviews before becoming therapy supervisees. During their assessment work, they become familiar with anxiety disorders in children and become comfortable with interacting with families about clinical issues. They also attend weekly group supervision meetings to learn from the work of senior therapists in the CAADC.

Formal therapy training begins with a session-by-session review of the Coping Cat manual. Over several meetings with a senior therapist, the supervisee learns the basic skills, practices them with the supervisor, and observes how the supervisor adapts sessions to particular children. Adaptation is crucial, because treatment manuals, though designed to be used with fidelity, are also meant to be applied flexibly (see Kendall, Chu, Gifford, Hayes, & Nauta, 1998). "Flexibility within fidelity" (Kendall, 1993) is an important description of the CBT approach.

Supervision Model at the CAADC

Supervision at the CAADC is typically conducted in a 2-hour, group meeting. There are currently three meetings at different times during the week with a nearly ideal ratio of 4:1 (supervisees:supervisor). All cases are reviewed weekly with peer and supervisor input. Therapists are encouraged to bring both problematic and positive issues to supervision. Because there is input from all members, group cohesion is high. The therapist can also receive individual supervision as needed. At almost any time of day, a senior clinician (including the second author of this chapter) is available for urgent consultation.

Supervision in Community Mental Health Program Settings

The YADS involved supervising dozens of therapists across six agencies. Supervisees differed considerably in training, from social work to psychology (i.e., master's or doctorate) to marriage and family counseling, and they also differed in experience, from having a first-time, 9-month internship to having 35 years of practice. Their familiarity with CBT and their motivation to learn Coping Cat varied greatly. The YADS therapists typically had over 20 clients a week and had quotas for billable hours. Because we, supervisors, worked at multiple clinics, we were not just down the hall from the supervisees.

Training Model in YADS

Because YADS is one of the first studies in training and supervising community-agency therapists in a research-based, manualized treatment, we initially sought to parallel the CAADC training and supervision. Therapists in the first year of the study attended a day-long training by the treatment developer (Kendall) similar to a 1-day workshop on Coping Cat. Training focused on (a) a normative and developmental perspective on childhood anxiety, (b) the role of children's cognitive processing in psychopathology and psychotherapy, and (c) the empirical support for the CBT approach. Participants explored avoidance learning, merits of exposure tasks, and parenting styles that maintain anxious avoidance in children. Each session included videotapes of selected sessions, including real cases. Although this training provided an overview and probably reduced some misperceptions (e.g., manuals cannot adapt to client needs), it was not considered sufficient. Following the one-day training, therapists engaged in weekly supervision meetings focused on mastering the treatment components session by session. Role-playing was used liberally and was often videotaped for review. Similar to the CAADC, training took additional weeks, or months, to increase therapists' familiarity with and comfort with Coping Cat. After this long training, therapists were assigned a study case and supervision proceeded.

As we, the YADS team, moved past the first year of the study, several limitations to this training were identified. First, therapist's attrition in the community agencies was higher than we expected. Many therapists were promoted or found new jobs within a year. Second, it was difficult to identify appropriate cases in the agencies. As a result, a number of trained therapists left before seeing a single case. Third, it became evident in supervision that our training skimped on the theory underlying Coping Cat. Working with therapists in an unfamiliar theoretical model posed many challenges (Kendall & Southam-Gerow, 1995).

The training process was shortened. The 1-day training emphasized basic cognitive–behavioral principles. The training also involved several basic CBT strategies that were not specific to Coping Cat, such as coping modeling, role playing, and therapist self-disclosure (Southam-Gerow & Kendall, 2000). Therapists were encouraged to discuss their reservations and comfort with CBT premises. Cases were assigned as soon after the training as possible.

Supervision Model in YADS

Early in supervision, the focus of supervision was on how to apply a CBT model to therapist cases. Furthermore, because some YADS therapists were licensed and more experienced than YADS supervisors, direct focus on this disparity was made a topic of conversation. The collaborative nature of CBT supervision helped greatly in this regard. Treating their experience as an asset, YADS supervisees were encouraged to share their personal approaches to each case, even if they were different from their perception of Coping Cat. YADS supervisors reassured therapists that the goal was not to change the way they did therapy for all of their cases. Furthermore, an emphasis was placed on therapists as partners in the research (Southam-Gerow, 2005), with supervision conceptualized as a way to help them implement CBT for the study cases. In this manner, these supervisory dialogues were a beginning to the bridge of the science–practice gap.

Almost none of the therapists had a cognitive–behavioral orientation. Many identified themselves as *eclectic*, and most were trained in psychodynamic or family systems approaches. The philosophical underpinnings of CBT, though not incompatible, are quite different from psychodynamic and family systems approaches (Kendall & Southam-Gerow, 1995; Overton, 1994). As therapists shared their misgivings or even challenged the techniques of the treatment program, they often targeted the perceived and real differences in YADS versus CAADC cases. Because therapist views about CBT were sometimes based on an incomplete understanding, the supervisory conversations were used as an opportunity to continue the training process by clarifying what the CBT is and is not. Some challenges—CBT was too "mechanistic" or manuals restricted therapist freedom and stifled creativity—were rare at CAADC, but they arose regularly at YADS.

Such challenges were addressed by making CBT theory a topic of discussion (Kendall, 2000; Southam-Gerow & Kendall, 2002) in supervision. Negative sentiments about CBT or therapy manuals were permitted, if not, encouraged. To address stereotypes of CBT as being overly structured and rigid and helpful for only simple problems, YADS supervisors used case examples to demonstrate how CBT actually requires therapist creativity and how it can adapt to complex, comorbid cases. In addition, in a crucial action, YADS supervisors asked therapists to conduct experiments to see if CBT techniques could help in both their study case(s) and with everyday problems experienced by members of the supervision group. YADS supervisors would choose a problem and apply a variety of CBT techniques to it. Further, homework was assigned to group participants to test if the strategy helped. Although Los Angeles residents are rarely thankful for their notorious traffic, YADS supervisors learned to make fruitful use of this aggravation. One therapist's reservations greatly decreased when he found cognitive strategies helped him feel less angry on his long commutes. Indeed, several of the most ambivalent therapists in YADS reported that seeing CBT work in their own lives led them to seeing its value for their clients.

Persuading YADS therapists to implement the exposure tasks within Coping Cat was one of our biggest supervisory challenges. Having someone confront his or her fears can test the mettle of the most experienced therapist (Becker, Zayfert, & Anderson, 2004). Students at CAADC were thoroughly familiar with CBT. A list of exposure tasks used in the past with anxious children in the clinic (Kendal et al., 2005) was provided. Because YADS supervisors anticipated cold feet on the part of some therapists, the supervisors recounted successes of other supervisees in helping children face and cope with their own fears. They reported gains children made after exposures as an additional training strategy.

At YADS, there were several barriers to implementing exposure tasks. Often, there were negative beliefs about the theory and the benefits of exposure (cf. Becker et al., 2004). Because YADS therapists rarely carried more than one Coping Cat case and because supervision groups were small, the pool of cases that could be shared was sharply reduced. In the absence of collective group experience, supervisors recounted exposure experiences with cases at other sites and suggested ways to surmount client and therapist anxiety. This was of limited help. The YADS therapists felt CAADC cases sounded less complex than theirs. Differences between lab and clinic samples figure heavily in the EST debate (Hammen, Rudolph, Weisz, Rao, & Burge, 1999; Weisz, 2000). In fact, there were differences between CAADC and YADS cases. Although both were selected for principal anxiety disorder diagnoses, and the severity of their anxiety was comparable, children from clinics participating in YADS had more externalizing behavior symptoms and greater sociodemographic disadvantages than children in the CAADC (Southam-Gerow et al., 2003). It also appeared that the foci for exposure tasks in YADS might need to be different. The following example demonstrates these differences and how they were addressed.

In YADS, one of us (Southam-Gerow) supervised the treatment of Rhonda, an 11-year-old Caucasian girl whose primary diagnoses included separation anxiety disorder and generalized anxiety disorder, as well as symptoms of major depressive disorder and oppositional defiant disorder. Her main fears concerned her mother's health and the possibility of returning home to find her mother gone. Rhonda called home from school several times a week. If her mother did not answer, she called many more times that day. She spent more time at home with her mother than typical preteens, eschewing peer activities. Typical exposure tasks would focus on increasing Rhonda's independence, working with her and her mother to reassure her about her mother's health, and helping both her and her mother adjust to her new autonomy. However, Rhonda's situation required another approach. Her mother had chronic, physical problems and was diagnosed with bipolar disorder I.

She was often in such pain or so depressed that rising from bed to answer the phone was more than she could muster. Past mood episodes had resulted in several hospitalizations. Rhonda's worries about her mother were not exaggerations. The likelihood of another separation from her mother was quite high. In collaboration with the therapist, exposure tasks were planned that included conversations between Rhonda and her mother about Rhonda's fears. The therapist worked with the mother to prepare her for these conversations and to promote their problem solving to reduce Rhonda's worries. In addition, the maternal grandmother, who often provided child care, was involved in some exposure tasks so that Rhonda could share her worries with her other caretaker.

Therapist-perceived differences between YADS and CAADC cases were partially inaccurate and accurate. Although a typical exposure engages the child in behaviors that he or she avoids but that are not likely to cause harm, such as riding elevators, making speeches, and meeting new kids in school, the worries of some YADS children were real—that is, separation from a parent for medical or legal reasons, peer victimization, or neighborhood dangers that limited the child's outside play. Although less common, CAADC therapists are also challenged by distressed, anxious youth who face real threats. Despite the perceived differences, applying the Coping Cat program in collaboration with the therapist generated exposure tasks to address reality-based worries in Los Angeles. Such adaptations are promising signs for applying the model across settings and confirming the importance of flexibility in treatment during the dissemination process (Kendall et al., 1998; Weisz, Southam-Gerow, Gordis, & Connor-Smith, 2003). As they experienced working with more cases like Rhonda's, cases similar to those they knew, YADS therapists gained comfort with exposure interventions. Exposure for therapists worked, too.

CONCLUSIONS AND FUTURE DIRECTIONS

Our experiences at the CAADC and YADS illustrate the centrality of clinical supervision in applying manualized treatments in multiple settings. We are confident that continued collaboration between research clinicians and practice therapists will improve mental health services for children and families (Martell & Hollon, 2001), yet we know challenges remain in moving evidence-based therapies to practice settings. Differences between cases seen in research settings and in practice settings are relevant, but therapist differences also loom large and warrant research. Our experience suggests therapist's reservations can be redressed with collaborative training and supervision. The collaboration we envision implies bidirectional, peer consultation rather than a mentor–mentee model (cf. Martell & Hollon, 2001). Such approaches fit the treatment to the setting and nurture the relationships necessary to enhance future success in the deployment and sustainability of ESTs (Weisz, 2000). The key role of supervision in bridging the gap between science and practice is as much one of collaboration and relationship building as it is one of program dissemination (Borkovec, Echemendia, Ragusea, & Ruiz, 2001; Chorpita et al., 2002; Fehrenbach & Coffman, 2001; Henggeler, Schoenwald, Liao, Letourneau, & Edwards, 2002).

Two issues to consider as these partnerships form are (a) the assessment of treatment fidelity and (b) the identification of the active treatment components. Although manuals need to be applied flexibly (Kendall et al., 1998), this must be balanced against evidence that therapist and supervisor fidelity to a treatment model determines treatment outcome (Henggeler et al., 2002; Huey et al., 2000). Research needs to identify where flexibility ends and where poor fidelity begins. While lab-based research continues, the literature remains largely silent on the issue of the mechanisms and the mediators of our treatments (see chap. 2, this volume). Some suggest identifying and disseminating empirically supported procedures and techniques rather than identifying and disseminating entire manuals to facilitate evidence based practice (Kazdin & Nock, 2003). Such research can and should occur in both our clinical labs and our practice contexts (Weisz, 2000).

As child and adolescent mental health researchers, we remain committed to identifying the optimal treatments for the variety of mental health problems facing youth and families. Our experience in YADS bolstered our impression that this mission is shared by those in the practice community.

REFERENCES

Addis, M. E., & Krasnow, A. D. (2000). A national survey of practicing psychologists' attitudes toward psychotherapy treatment manuals. *Journal of Consulting and Clinical Psychology, 68,* 331–339.

Becker, C. B., Zayfert, C., & Anderson, E. (2004). A survey of psychologists' attitudes towards and utilization of exposure therapy for PTSD. *Behaviour Research and Therapy, 42,* 277–292.

Borkovec, T. D., Echemendia, R. J., Ragusea, S. A., & Ruiz, M. (2001). The Pennsylvania Practice Research Network and future possibilities for clinically meaningful and scientifically rigorous psychotherapy effectiveness research. *Clinical Psychology: Science and Practice, 8,* 155–167.

Chambless, D. L., Sanderson, W. C., Shoham, V., Johnson, S. B., Pope, K. S., Crits-Christoph, P., et al. (1996). An update on empirically validated therapies. *The Clinical Psychologist, 49,* 5–18.

Chorpita, B. F., & Southam-Gerow, M. A. (2006). Treatment of anxiety disorders in youth. In E. J. Mash & R. A. Barkley (Eds.), *Treatment of childhood disorders* (3rd ed.). New York: Guilford Press.

Chorpita, B. F., Yim, L. M., Donkervoet, J. C., Arensdorf, A., Amundsen, M. J., McGee, C., et al. (2002). Toward large-scale implementation of empirically supported treatments for children: A review and observations by the Hawaii Empirical Basis to Services Task Force. *Clinical Psychology: Science and Practice, 9,* 165–190.

Compton, S. N., Burns, B. J., Egger, H. L., & Robertson, E. (2002). Review of the evidence base for treatment of childhood psychopathology: Internalizing disorders. *Journal of Consulting and Clinical Psychology, 70,* 1240–1266.

Farmer, E., Compton, S. N., Burns, J. B., & Robertson, E. (2002). Review of the evidence base for treatment of childhood psychopathology: Externalizing disorders. *Journal of Consulting and Clinical Psychology, 70,* 1267–1302.

Fehrenbach, P., & Coffman, S. (2001). Private practitioners in clinical trials: Supervision issues. *Behavior Therapist, 24,* 147–148.

Freeman, K. A., & Miller, C. A. (2002). Behavioral case conceptualization for children and adolescents. In M. Hersen (Ed.), *Clinical behavior therapy: Adults and children* (pp. 239–255). New York: Wiley.

Hammen, C., Rudolph, K., Weisz, J., Rao, U., & Burge, D. (1999). The context of depression in clinic-referred youth: Neglected areas in treatment. *Journal of the American Academy of Child and Adolescent Psychiatry, 38,* 64–71.

Henggeler, S. W., Schoenwald, S. K., Liao, J. G., Letourneau, E. J., & Edwards, D. L. (2002). Transporting efficacious treatments to field settings: The link between supervisory practices and therapist fidelity in MST programs. *Journal of Clinical Child and Adolescent Psychology, 31,* 155–167.

Henry, W. P., Butler, S. F., Strupp, H. H., Schacht, T. E., & Binder, J. L. (1993). Effects of training in time-limited dynamic psychotherapy: Changes in therapist behavior. *Journal of Consulting and Clinical Psychology, 61,* 434–440.

Hoagwood, K., & Olin, S. S. (2002). The NIMH blueprint for change report: Research priorities in child and adolescent mental health. *Journal of the American Academy of Child and Adolescent Psychiatry, 41,* 760–767.

Huey, S. J., Henggeler, S. W., Brondino, M. J., & Pickrel, S. G. (2000). Mechanisms of change in multisystemic therapy: Reducing delinquent behavior through therapist adherence and improved family and peer functioning. *Journal of Consulting and Clinical Psychology, 68,* 451–467.

Kazdin, A. E., & Nock, M. K. (2003). Delineating mechanisms of change in child and adolescent therapy: Methodological issues and research recommendations. *Journal of Child Psychology and Psychiatry and Allied Disciplines, 44,* 1116–1129.

Kazdin, A. E., Siegel, T. C., & Bass, D. (1990). Drawing on clinical practice to inform research on child and adolescent psychotherapy: Survey of practitioners. *Professional Psychology: Research and Practice, 21,* 189–198.

Kendall, P. C. (1993). Cognitive–behavioral therapies with youth: Guiding theory, current status, and emerging developments. *Journal of Consulting and Clinical Psychology, 61, 235–247.*

Kendall, P. C. (1998). Directing misperceptions: Researching the issues facing manual-based treatments. *Clinical Psychology: Science and Practice, 5, 396–400.*

Kendall, P. C. (2000). Guiding theory for therapy with children and adolescents. In P. C. Kendall (Ed.), *Child and adolescent therapy: Cognitive–behavioral procedures* (2nd ed., pp. 3–27). New York: Guilford Press.

Kendall, P. C. (2002). *Coping Cat therapist manual.* Ardmore, PA: Workbook Publishing.

Kendall, P. C., Chu, B., Gifford, A., Hayes, C., & Nauta, M. (1998). Breathing life into a manual. *Cognitive and Behavioral Practice, 5, 177–198.*

Kendall, P. C., Flannery-Schroeder, E., Panichelli-Mindel, S., Southam-Gerow, M., Henin, A., & Warman, M. (1997). Therapy for youths with anxiety disorders: A second randomized trial. *Journal of Consulting and Clinical Psychology, 65, 366–380.*

Kendall, P. C., Robin, J., Hedtke, K., Suveg, C., Flannery-Schroeder, E., & Gosch, E. (2005). Considering CBT with anxious youth? Think exposures. *Cognitive and Behavioral Practice, 12, 136–150.*

Kendall, P. C., & Southam-Gerow, M. A. (1995). Issues in the transportability of treatment: The case of anxiety disorders in youth. *Journal of Consulting and Clinical Psychology, 63, 702–708.*

Martell, C. R., & Hollon, S. D. (2001). Working together on shifting ground: Researcher and clinician collaboration in clinical trials. *Behavior Therapist, 24, 144–146.*

Norquist, G., Lebowitz, B., & Hyman, S. (1999). Expanding the frontier of treatment research. *Prevention and Treatment, 2,* np.

Overton, W. F. (1994). The arrow of time and the cycle of time: Concepts of change, cognition, and embodiment. *Psychological Inquiry, 5, 215–237.*

Rosenbaum, M., & Ronen, T. (1998). Clinical supervision from the standpoint of cognitive–behavior therapy. *Psychotherapy: Theory, Research, Practice, and Training, 35, 220–230.*

Schoenwald, S. K., & Hoagwood, K. (2001). Effectiveness, transportability, and dissemination of interventions: What matters when? *Psychiatric Services, 52, 1190–1197.*

Southam-Gerow, M. A. (2005, Summer). Using partnerships to adapt evidence-based mental health treatments for use outside labs. *Report on Emotional and Behavioral Disorders in Youth, 5, 58–60, 77–79.*

Southam-Gerow, M. A., & Kendall, P. C. (2000). Cognitive–behavior therapy with youth: Advances, challenges, and future directions. *Clinical Psychology and Psychotherapy, 7, 343–366.*

Southam-Gerow, M. A., & Kendall, P. C. (2002). Emotion regulation and understanding: Implications for child psychopathology and therapy. *Clinical Psychology Review, 22,* 189–222.

Southam-Gerow, M. A., Ringeisen, H. L., & Sherrill, J. T. (in press). Introduction to special issue: Integrating interventions and services research: Progress and prospects. *Clinical Psychology: Science and Practice, 13.*

Southam-Gerow, M. A., Weisz, J. R., & Kendall, P. C. (2003). Youth with anxiety disorders in research and service clinics: Examining client differences and similarities. *Journal of Clinical Child and Adolescent Psychology, 32,* 375–385.

Weisz, J. R. (2000, Spring). Lab–clinic differences and what we can do about them: I. The clinic-based treatment development model. *Clinical Child Psychology Newsletter, 15,* 1–3, 10.

Weisz, J. R., Southam-Gerow, M. A., Gordis, E. B., & Connor-Smith, J. K. (2003). Primary and secondary control enhancement training for youth depression: Applying the deployment-focused model of treatment development and testing. In A. E. Kazdin & J. R. Weisz (Eds.), *Evidence-based treatments for children and adolescents* (pp. 165–183). New York: Guilford Press.

8

MULTISYSTEMIC THERAPY SUPERVISION: A KEY COMPONENT OF QUALITY ASSURANCE

PHILLIPPE B. CUNNINGHAM, JEFF RANDALL, SCOTT W. HENGGELER, AND SONJA K. SCHOENWALD

Therapists are currently challenged to provide meaningful change for difficult youth in community settings. The discouraging outcomes in research on community-based treatment highlight the scope of this challenge. Multisystemic therapy (MST) is a comprehensive response to that challenge (Henggeler & Borduin, 1990; Henggeler, Schoenwald, Borduin, Rowland, & Cunningham, 1998; Henggeler, Schoenwald, Rowland, & Cunningham,

Preparation of this manuscript was supported by Grants MH59138, MH066905, and MH67361 from the National Institute of Mental Health; Grants DA17487, DA015844, and DA10079 from the National Institute on Drug Abuse; Grant AA122202 from the National Institute on Alcoholism and Alcohol Abuse; Grant H79TI14150 from the Center for Substance Abuse Treatment; and Grant 5 P01 HS10871 from the Agency for Healthcare Research and Quality; and the Annie E. Casey Foundation, and the John D. and Catherine T. MacArthur Foundation. The information represented in this chapter are those of the authors alone and do not necessarily reflect the opinions of the Annie E. Casey or the John D. and Catherine T. MacArthur Foundation.

The third and fourth authors are board members and stockholders of MST Services, LLC, the university-licensed organization that provides training in multisystemic therapy.

2002). Not only is MST a community-based treatment, but it is also a treatment that addresses adolescents presenting serious clinical problems (e.g., violence and drug abuse) and their families. However, MST is far from business as usual in community-based clinics, it is a highly structured approach to creative and flexible interventions. Supported by 10 published randomized clinical trials, MST has been identified by federal agencies (e.g., the National Institute on Drug Abuse, 1999, and the U.S. Public Health Service, 2001), leading reviewers (e.g., Weisz, 2004), consumer groups (e.g., the National Alliance for the Mentally Ill, 2003), and policy groups (e.g., the Annie E. Casey Foundation, the GAINS Center, and the Points of Light Foundation) as an effective treatment. Such recognition has contributed to the adoption of MST in practice settings in more than 30 states and 9 nations, annually treating approximately 12,000 serious, juvenile offenders.

Although several features of MST (e.g., addressing known risk factors, providing services in natural settings, integrating evidence-based therapies, and recognizing the key role of caregivers in long-term outcomes) are critical to its success, one of the most important features is the use of a multifaceted quality assurance and improvement protocol to support treatment fidelity. In light of the well-established association between therapist adherence to MST protocols and youth outcomes (Henggeler, Melton, Brondino, Scherer, & Hanley, 1997; Schoenwald, Henggeler, Brondino, & Rowland, 2000), the MST quality-assurance system is an integral part of every licensed MST program. A detailed supervisory process (Henggeler & Schoenwald, 1998) is central to this quality-assurance system, and evidence supports the linkage between that process and therapist adherence (Henggeler, Schoenwald, Liao, Letourneau, & Edwards, 2002).

This chapter focuses on MST clinical supervision and on its functions within the broader, quality-assurance system, especially supervisor training and consultation, measurement of supervisor performance, common problems encountered by MST supervisors, and strategies for managing these problems, such as therapist drift and frustration.

AN OVERVIEW OF MULTISYSTEMIC THERAPY TREATMENT

A comprehensive description of the MST treatment model for adolescent antisocial behavior can be found elsewhere (Henggeler et al., 1998). Suffice it to say that MST is an intensive and pragmatic family-based treatment that targets those factors in each youth's social ecology that contribute to his or her antisocial behavior.

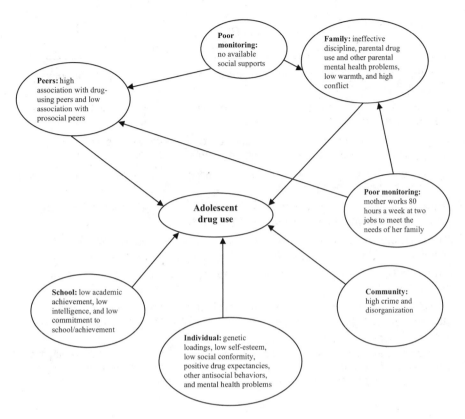

Figure 8.1. Example of a fit assessment for adolescent substance abuse.

Conceptual Basis of Multisystemic Therapy Treatment

MST is grounded in a theory of social ecology (Bronfenbrenner, 1979) that views human development as a product of reciprocal interactions between the individual and the multiple systems in which the individual is embedded. The term *fit* is MST shorthand for the process of viewing any behavior (i.e., clinical or supervisory) in terms of the environmental factors that promote it. MST analyses produce fit assessments and intervention strategies that are always hypotheses and are subject to continuous testing and revision. Using substance abuse as an example, research has shown that adolescent drug use is associated with (a) individual (e.g., genetic disposition and positive expectancies for drug effects); (b) family (e.g., ineffective monitoring and discipline and parental drug use); (c) peer (e.g., association with drug-using peers); (d) school (e.g., low academic achievement or low commitment); and (e) community (e.g., criminal and drug subculture) factors. These relationships can be depicted graphically using, in the vernacular of MST, a *fit circle* (see Figure 8.1). Interactions within and among these

EXHIBIT 8.1
Multisystemic Therapy Treatment Principles

Principle 1: The primary purpose of assessment is to understand the fit between the identified problems and their broader systemic context.

Principle 2: Therapeutic contacts should emphasize the positive and should use systemic strengths as levers for change.

Principle 3: Interventions should be designed to promote responsible behavior and decrease irresponsible behavior among family members.

Principle 4: Interventions should be present-focused and action-oriented, targeting specific and well-defined problems.

Principle 5: Interventions should target sequences of behavior within and between multiple systems that maintain identified problems.

Principle 6: Interventions should be developmentally appropriate and fit the developmental needs of the youth.

Principle 7: Interventions should be designed to require daily or weekly effort by family members.

Principle 8: Intervention effectiveness is evaluated continuously from multiple perspectives, with providers assuming accountability for overcoming barriers to successful outcomes.

Principle 9: Interventions should be designed to promote treatment generalization and long-term maintenance of therapeutic change by empowering caregivers to address family members' needs across multiple systemic contexts.

---

systems directly or indirectly influence adolescent substance use. For example, inadequate financial and social support might result in low parental monitoring, which can contribute to a teen's association with drug-using peers and to subsequent drug use.

Nine Treatment Principles and the Multisystemic Therapy Analytic Process

MST is specified by nine treatment principles (see Exhibit 8.1) that define the parameters for design and implementation of interventions. Interventions are monitored using researched instruments, quality assurance protocols, and specifically designed supervisory practices.

Multisystemic Therapy Analytic Process

The MST process begins with a carefully reasoned analysis of social networks and their influence on an adolescent's behavior. From the moment of referral to the end of treatment, MST supervisors and clinicians gather data from multiple sources regarding the most salient drivers (i.e., fit factors) of the problem behaviors. Hypotheses regarding these drivers are developed

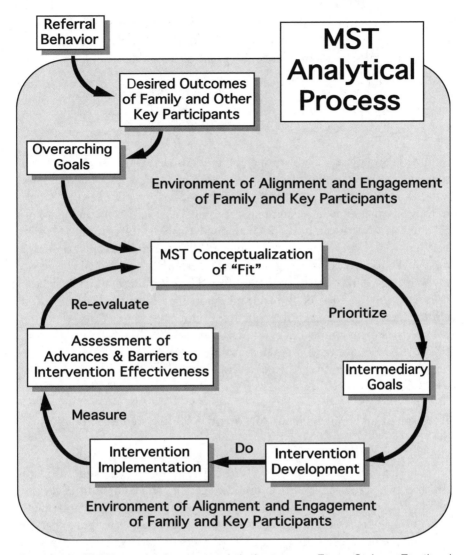

Figure 8.2. Multisystemic therapy analytical process. From *Serious Emotional Disturbance in Children and Adolescents: Multisystemic Therapy* (p. 18), by S. W. Henggeler, S. K. Schoenwald, M. Rowland, and P. B. Cunningham, 1998, New York: Guilford Press. Copyright 1998 by Guildford Press. Reprinted with permission.

and tested throughout MST interventions. This deductive and repetitive approach is encompassed within the *MST Analytical Process* (also known as the *MST Do-Loop*; Henggeler & Schoenwald, 1998; Henggeler et al., 1998) depicted in Figure 8.2. The MST Analytical Process is used continuously by supervisors and clinicians to develop, prioritize, implement, measure, and evaluate interventions. The MST principles and the MST Analytic

Process provide the pragmatic underpinnings of MST supervision; the only other caveat in selecting interventions is that supervisors and clinicians have empirical support in addressing a particular problem.

OVERVIEW OF MULTISYSTEMIC THERAPY QUALITY-ASSURANCE SYSTEM

MST supervision is a part of a comprehensive quality-assurance system to achieve favorable, short- and long-term, clinical outcomes for youth and families. Early experience with transporting MST to practice settings taught us that systematic quality-assurance was essential to achieving the outcomes obtained in MST research studies. Launched in 1996, Multisystemic Therapy Services, LLC (MSTS), strives to transport MST faithfully to new communities. MSTS has an exclusive licensing agreement with the Medical University of South Carolina for the transfer of MST technology and intellectual property. On the basis of the training and supervision used in the initial clinical trials, MSTS forged a quality-assurance system of six elements: (a) site assessment conducted by an MSTS employee, (b) a 5-day orientation, (c) on-site supervision, (d) weekly consultation with an MST expert, (e) quarterly booster training, and (f) feedback on therapist and supervisor adherence to MST protocols.

Assessment and Development of Potential Multisystemic Therapy Service Sites

A site assessment lasts 6 to 12 months and evaluates and cultivates the fit between the MST services and the agencies and communities seeking to establish an MST program. Philosophical, political, economic, and practical contingencies that can impact success are addressed, as are the organization and the culture of the host agencies. Program characteristics compatible with MST include (a) supportive agency–personnel policies, (b) a full-time commitment from MST therapists, and (c) a requirement that supervisors serve as both clinical and administrative supervisors for MST therapists. A comprehensive description of what is necessary for MST program design is found on the Web at http://www.mstservices.com.

Initial 5-Day Orientation for Multisystemic Therapy Therapists and Supervisors

Prior to orientation, each participant receives a copy of the MST treatment manual (Henggeler et al., 1998), and each supervisor receives a supervisory manual (Henggeler & Schoenwald, 1998). A 5-day orientation, provided by MSTS to all staff with clinical or supervisory responsibility for MST, offers an overview with five objectives: (a) familiarize participants with the causes and the correlates of serious problems addressed with MST; (b) explain the theoretical and the empirical underpinnings of MST; (c) describe family, peer, school, community, and individual intervention strategies used by MST; (d) train participants to conceptualize cases and interventions in terms consistent with MST principles; and (e) provide participants with opportunities to practice designing MST interventions.

On-Site Supervision of Multisystemic Therapy

On-site MST supervision is provided by clinicians with advanced training using the MST supervisory manual (Henggeler & Schoenwald, 1998). Teams of three or four MST clinicians have supervisors who devote at least half their time to the MST program. A major objective of MST supervision is to help clinicians develop the behavioral and the conceptual competencies required to adhere to MST principles (see Exhibit 8.1). Supervision of MST is a systematic and a pragmatic process for attaining treatment goals and targets all barriers to treatment success.

Weekly Consultation With an Off-Site Multisystemic Therapy Expert

To promote MST fidelity, a consultant offers weekly phone consultation and reviews the progress of each youth served by the local team. MST consultation is typically provided by doctorate-level practitioners (i.e., psychology, social work, or related field) with clinical competence in family therapy, behavior therapy, and child development. MST consultants have expertise in MST itself and in teaching clinicians to think and to act in accord with MST treatment principles (Schoenwald, 1998). The consultant ensures that assessment and intervention strategies developed during supervision are consistent with MST principles. Consultation also helps teams develop solutions to difficult clinical problems and to forge strategies to address barriers to program success (e.g., a local judge who favors incarceration of youth for minor infractions).

Quarterly Booster Training for Multisystemic Therapy Providers

Spanning 1.5 days, quarterly booster trainings focus on concerns identified locally. Consultants join staff in troubleshooting difficult cases encountered during the quarter. Booster trainings include didactic instructions, role-playing, modeling, and in vivo guidance. Home visits are often made during booster trainings to gauge the therapist's skill and adherence to the model. The MST consultant may also meet with managers and clinical leaders to address issues that might impact the sustainability of a quality MST program.

Feedback on Clinician and Supervisor Adherence

Therapist adherence to MST is tracked using the 26-item Therapist Adherence Measure (TAM) developed for MST clinical trials (Henggeler & Borduin, 1992). The TAM is completed monthly by caregivers via the Internet (http://www.mstinstitute.org; see Henggeler et al., 2002). In addition to the TAM, consultants instruct supervisors on use of audio recordings of family sessions to monitor and facilitate therapist adherence to MST principles. Supervisor adherence to MST is monitored using the Supervisor Adherence Measure (SAM; Schoenwald, Henggeler, & Edwards, 1998) completed on the Internet every 2 months by therapists.

MULTISYSTEMIC THERAPY SUPERVISION

Efficacy studies in child and adolescent psychotherapy demonstrate the importance of training and monitoring of clinician behavior to achieve adherence to empirically supported treatments (Weisz, Donenberg, Weiss, & Han, 1995; Weisz, Weiss, & Donenberg, 1992). The MST model of supervision evolved from the efficacy research in MST clinical trials. Using the MST Analytic Process as a guide, supervisors help clinicians identify and select specific interventions to attain desired outcomes with their families.

The goal of MST supervision is to help each MST clinician learn to effectively change the social ecology of youths and families in ways that lead to sustainable positive outcomes (Henggeler et al., 1998). To achieve this goal, supervision must be responsive to both the clinician's needs and strengths and the family's clinical needs and strengths.

Basic Assumptions of Multisystemic Therapy Supervision

The basic assumptions of MST Supervision and their corollaries, adapted from Henggeler and Schoenwald (1998), include the following:

1. "The purpose of MST supervision is to help clinicians adhere to the nine treatment principles of MST in all aspects of treatment—engagement of families, case conceptualization, intervention design and implementation, and evaluation of outcomes" (p. 1). **Corollary 1:** Even well-trained, creative, and flexible clinicians will experience challenges that exceed their clinical competence. **Corollary 2:** Such challenges require supervision that (a) is responsive to therapists' develop-

mental needs and (b) provides specific recommendations to address the needs of families being treated.

2. "Each clinician implementing MST is a hard-working, competent professional who brings unique personal strengths and professional experiences to the treatment process" (p. 2). **Corollary 1:** Supervision takes advantage of each clinician's unique skills in generating treatment plans, in formulating clinician development plans, and in contributing constructive feedback to his or her colleagues—MST group supervision expects clinicians to be active participants in problem solving and not to be passive recipients of supervisor wisdom. **Corollary 2:** Each clinician is doing the best he or she can to achieve sustainable outcomes, therefore each supervisor should not blame the clinician nor the family for failures but should remain solution focused, identifying and addressing barriers to success.

3. "The process of clinical supervision should mirror the process of MST" (p. 1). Supervision conforms to the MST treatment principles and to the MST Analytic Process, and the case conceptualization and intervention plan is a collaborative effort.

4. Ongoing clinical supervision is necessary to monitor adherence to MST and to achieve positive, sustainable outcomes. **Corollary 1:** All clinicians require ongoing supervision because of the natural tendency to drift toward interventions that are overlearned, easy to implement, or emotionally satisfying (i.e., facilitating a client's dependency). Constructive feedback about a clinician's behavior in treatment sessions is needed to support the use of clinical strategies that may be less familiar or comfortable to the clinician. Feedback identifies behaviors that are consistent or inconsistent with MST.

5. "Clinicians, supervisors, and the provider organization that houses the MST program are accountable for outcomes" (p. 2). **Corollary 1:** When families fail to improve in treatment, the clinician and the treatment team do not blame the family, but do identify those *individual* (e.g., parenting deficits, parental fear, or inadequate social supports), *systemic* (e.g., inappropriate school placement), and *treatment-related* (e.g., intervention was ineffective or was implemented without sufficient practice) factors that thwart attainment of the family's treatment goals. **Corollary 2:** Each MST team and corresponding provider organization will do whatever it takes to achieve sustainable outcomes for each family. Thus, MST supervisors and clinicians are always working to enhance their skills.

6. MST supervisors are accountable for the success and development of therapists. **Corollary:** When clinicians fail to achieve outcomes or fail to implement an intervention as prescribed in supervision, the supervisor will not blame the therapist, but will assess the fit of the problem with clinician, supervision, consultation, organizational, and service system factors and will develop an improved plan in collaboration with the therapist.

7. MST supervisors rely heavily on direct observation to determine each clinician's skills, to determine treatment progress, and to monitor clinician progress toward the goals of her or his development plan. **Corollary:** Because it is difficult to retain a participant–observer stance while engaged in the nuances and the complexities of therapy and then to convey that interaction after the fact, work samples are needed to effectively support the therapist's implementation of MST.

Format and Structure of Group Supervision

Frequency and Duration of Group Supervision

Generally, MST supervision is conducted weekly in a small, group format for approximately 2 hours. However, MST supervision is predicated on doing whatever it takes to achieve favorable client outcomes. Supervision can occur several times a day if needed, and supervisors, like MST clinicians, are available 24 hours a day, 7 days a week. As in MST treatment sessions, the objectives of additional supervisory meetings are clearly identified, as are the effective means of meeting those objectives.

Preparation, Case Presentations, and Session Structure

Twenty-four hours prior to supervision, clinicians provide the supervisor with case summaries for each family (see Exhibit 8.2). These detail overarching goals, previous intermediary goals (i.e., weekly steps toward achieving larger goals), and barriers and advances encountered since the last supervision. The clinician must identify factors that may be responsible for problems or advances, must develop new intermediary goals, and must specify empirically supported interventions for the coming week. New intermediary goals logically confront barriers or exploit factors supporting treatment gains.

Prior to supervision, the supervisor reviews the case summaries and

- prioritizes cases based on acuity that need special attention;
- determines if the fit analysis is logical and multidimensional (i.e., includes all pertinent factors across systems contributing to barriers or advances) and can lead directly to an intervention;

EXHIBIT 8.2
Case Summary for Supervision

Family: Therapist: Date:

Child's Age: Start Date:

\# Face-to-Face contacts: \# Phone Contacts:

\# Sessions Cancelled or Missed:

   Weekly Review

1. Overarching MST Goals:

2. Previous Intermediary Goals: Met   Partially Met   Not Met

3. Barriers to Previous Intermediary Goals:

4. Advances in Treatment:

5. How has your assessment of the "fit" between problems and their systemic context changed or expanded?

6. New Intermediary Goals for Next Week:

7. Barriers to New Intermediary Goals:

8. Questions for Supervision and Consultation:

9. Supervision Feedback:

10. Consultation Feedback:

- determines if new intermediary goals are logically connected to identified fit factors; and
- determines if interventions listed in intermediary goals are supported by objective evidence, can be measured, and are consistent with MST principles.

Supervision usually begins with clinicians identifying any clinical emergencies (e.g., youth or caregiver is suicidal, homicidal, or psychotic; youth is at immediate risk of placement; or caregiver wants to drop out of treatment) and any cases that lack progress (e.g., youth continues to test positive for illegal substances). After cases are prioritized, the clinician with the most acute case begins his or her case review. There is no time limit on a case review, though repetition and prolonged story telling are discouraged. Case discussion continues until a clear plan, that has a reasonable chance of success on the basis of the fit analysis, is developed, which typically last between 2 and 10 minutes depending on the clinician's and the family's needs. Thus, a team of three or four clinicians, each serving four families, would review 12 to 15 cases during a 1.5- to 2-hour supervision session.

Using the MST Analytical Process as a guide, case presentations begin by reviewing the clinician's hypotheses and supportive evidence about treatment barriers and advances (i.e., fit assessment). In the case of a substance-abusing adolescent, a clinician might present results of recent drug screens using a graph to link drug-level changes with ecological changes, such as increased parental monitoring. The clinician then presents a plan to address the most proximal factors identified in the fit assessment, and the treatment team offers constructive feedback regarding the assessment and the plan. Feedback ensures that the plan is grounded in a thorough analysis of treatment barriers or advances. Next, behavioral targets are specified, and intermediary goals are developed if needed. The clinician is responsible for knowing how to implement the planned interventions. As a consequence, presentation time might be devoted to enhancing the clinician's skills in providing an evidence-based intervention such as relaxation training or stress inoculation.

The supervisor, with training and support from the MST consultant, ensures supervision time is well spent. When group supervision is going well, most of the time is devoted to active problem solving. Management of group process, of weak presentations, and of clinicians' needs for emotional support, requires the supervisor to balance directive and supportive intervention. Thus, training and consultation strategies focus on the content and the process of supervision. When the process is weak, the supervisor, the therapists, and the consultant assess the fit of the problem, which may include the supervisor's behavior, the therapist's avoidance of issues, or the therapist's skill deficits.

Illustrating the Complexities of Multisystemic Therapy Supervision

Paul is a 35-year-old, White male with a master's degree in social work. He has 10 years experience running inpatient cognitive–behavioral groups for serious emotionally disturbed adolescents and 5 years experience providing individual treatment in a private outpatient clinic. Paul takes considerable pride in his knowledge of cognitive and cognitive–behavioral therapy, and in his provision of family therapy. Although Paul has had a great deal of experience providing cognitive–behavioral therapy, his experience providing community-based clinical services to youths who present serious clinical problems is limited. Likewise, Paul has never been directly accountable for engaging such clients in treatment or for achieving desired clinical outcomes.

Basis and Structure of Individual Supervision

When Is Individual Supervision Appropriate?

Although individual supervision is not the norm in MST (Henggeler & Schoenwald, 1998), it is warranted when the clinician needs to develop specific competencies or skills or when personal barriers to clinical effectiveness need to be addressed. Clinicians are encouraged to request individual supervision when they experience difficulties with a particular family. On the basis of our work with substance-abusing youth (Randall, Henggeler, Cunningham, Rowland, & Swenson, 2001), individual supervision might be indicated when, despite consistent feedback in group supervision, a clinician persists in (a) suggesting that clients are not motivated for treatment, (b) describing clients in judgmental or pejorative language, (c) resisting alternative hypotheses to explain client behavior, (d) describing cases without the requisite precision, (e) relying on clinical stereotypes rather than on hypothesis testing, (f) failing to address treatment barriers, or (g) failing to carry out recommendations from group supervision.

> Paul needed individual supervision to address (a) his use of harsh and critical language to characterize the parents he had difficulty engaging in treatment (e.g., "unmotivated," "not interested in services," "some people just don't want to get better," "she's resistant"), (b) his avoidance of supervision, (c) his failure to carry out supervision recommendations, and (d) his design of interventions that focused exclusively on the child (e.g., anger management).

Structure of Individual Supervision Sessions

Individual supervision begins with a rationale for the session. A fit assessment is conducted to investigate factors proximally related to the problem identified by the supervisor. If a clinician is struggling to conduct a functional analysis of adolescent drug use, which is critical in MST drug treatment, the supervisor might ask the clinician to role-play an analysis with a youth and a caregiver to pinpoint the problem.

> Paul used closed-ended questions with the parent of a substance-abusing youth and did not confront inconsistencies in the parent's responses.

Paul seemed fearful of triggering an angry response from the parent. Using steps for effective problem solving (D'Zurilla & Nezu, 1999), Paul and his supervisor can brainstorm ways of resolving the problem, can select an alternative, and can practice the strategy. In this case, the supervisor and Paul might consider addressing inconsistencies without generating hostility—choosing words, phrases, and scripts that are assertive but that are not pejorative—and assessing results using audio tapes of subsequent sessions.

Clinician Development Plans

A clinician development plan for each clinician is created by the therapist, the MST consultant, and the supervisor. On the basis of the clinician's strengths and needs in providing MST, these plans establish and promote trajectories of therapist growth and skill development. Plans include overarching goals and steps to achieve them in 3 to 6 months. A clinician may be excellent at engaging families in treatment but may be weak in behavioral interventions. His or her goal would be to enhance his or her behavior therapy competencies, and steps to do so might include readings and meetings with the supervisor to review audio taped work or to role-play new skills. MST supervisors rely on observable data and forms to assist with the measurement; forms are available through MSTS. The MST consultant stays abreast of the supervisor's progress in facilitating the clinician's growth and skill development.

Paul's struggles centered around his difficulty with engaging what he called resistant clients. *Resistance* is a term seldom used in the vernacular of MST. It is pejorative, and it suggests the basis for lack of treatment progress resides with the client. Paul's struggle occurs often among therapists working with challenging families.

The fit analysis guiding Paul's development plan is depicted in Figure 8.3. As can be seen in the fit analysis, Paul's difficulty in engaging parents in treatment was primarily the result of his lack of experience and skills with providing community-based clinical services to youth with serious clinical problems and their families. This ultimately led to his negative affect, his victim blaming (i.e., secondary to repeated failures), and his avoidance of both the parent (i.e., via a focus on the child) and supervision (i.e., where he felt negatively judged when his failure to engage the parent became a focus of supervision). His lack of experience and skill in managing severe negative affect and his ruptures in the therapeutic alliance became evident in group supervision. A colleague asked him how he would respond to a mother's refusal to follow his treatment recommendation to set limits with her child. Paul's only intervention was to repeat, "It is critically impor-

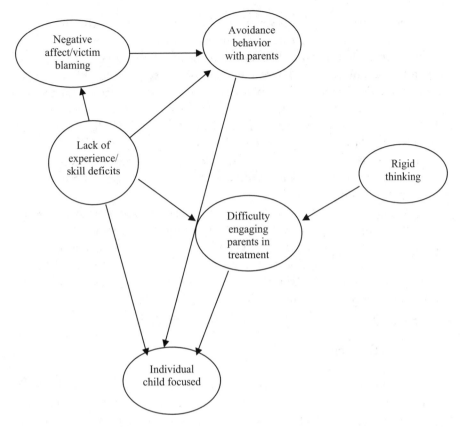

Figure 8.3. Fit assessment of Paul's difficulty with engaging parents in treatment.

tant that your son get limits. He needs structure. He needs you to set limits."
Most MST families have had extensive exposure to social services and have
received lots of similar advice. Paul needs to be aware that such families
can be quite sensitive to the therapist's comments that suggest a parent is
at fault.

Although he struggled with challenging clients, Paul worked hard and
took great pride in his work. He was also very behavioral (i.e., logical and
systematic) in addressing problems and was well versed in teaching clients
cognitive–behavioral techniques, a mainstay of MST.

Paul's strengths and needs were used to inform his development plan
that included strategies to address each factor listed on the fit assessment.
Because of his logical nature, part of his development plan was to operationa-
lize client resistance using language that was less characterological, pejorative, and judgmental and more behavioral. With client resistance redefined
as client refusal of treatment recommendations, Paul was to track instances

of refusal, to observe with his supervisor how his responses either increased or decreased refusal (i.e., in moment-by-moment interactions observed directly or on audiotapes) and to develop specific behaviors and scripts to respond to client refusal. These could be practiced or role-played during supervision. The development plan called for Paul to request immediate supervision whenever he noticed engagement faltering to avoid negative affect that seemed to grow exponentially with each difficult session. The plan also called for Paul's supervisor to require individual supervision whenever Paul's verbalizations were primarily negative, whenever he was unable to reframe parental resistance, or whenever his interventions focused exclusively on the child.

Paul's plan also included the use of thought stopping and the use of cognitive restructuring interventions when parents triggered negative affect. Paul's plan was reviewed monthly and was modified as he progressed. Throughout implementation of the plan, the supervisor normalized Paul's struggles by framing his experiences as reasonable responses for someone who "cares deeply" and by framing his experiences as opportunities to expand his reach to clients with whom many professionals refuse to work.

Supervisor Training

Supervisor training and development continues through the life of a MST program. It focuses on four core competencies of MST supervision: (a) knowledge and skill development, (b) MST group supervision, (c) clinician development, and (e) management of program "Continuous Quality Improvement." Aside from their initial training, each supervisor in collaboration with the MST consultant develops an individualized supervisor development plan to track progress in core competencies of MST supervision.

Supervisors receive instruction in conducting group supervision, providing effective feedback to MST clinicians, and identifying and addressing factors that can influence effective group supervision. MST supervisors receive performance feedback from (a) a review of group supervision tapes, (b) therapist's SAM ratings of supervisor adherence to MST practices, and (c) ratings by the consultant across key MST domains (e.g., promoting clinician adherence to MST principles, promoting the MST Analytic Process, and developing clinician competence). To aid clinician development, MST supervisors receive training in clinician development plans and in providing constructive feedback from audio taped sessions or from field observations. Finally, in the area of continuous quality improvement, supervisors are trained to collect SAM and TAM data, to develop "goals and guidelines" documents that define the MST programs, and to conduct semi-annual program implementation reviews.

COMMON PROBLEMS ENCOUNTERED IN MULTISYSTEMIC THERAPY SUPERVISION

Adoption of any new therapy is a challenge for individuals and organizations (see chaps. 7 and 9, this volume), and starting an MST program is no exception. Several hurdles to effective supervision emerge when clinicians and supervisors learn a new therapy model while delivering the treatment. Among these are negative reactions to change, limitations of the MST supervisor (e.g., lack of clinical, management or teaching skills and being too directive or too nondirective), limitations of the clinician (e.g., wedded to a particular theory or new to cognitive or behavioral interventions), and interaction between supervisor and clinician characteristics. Problems inherent in starting MST programs have been addressed in other publications (Edwards, Schoenwald, Henggeler, & Strother, 2001; Henggeler et al., 1998; Henggeler & Schoenwald, 1998). This chapter focuses on problems encountered in supervision even after the steepest grade in the learning trajectory has been traversed by the supervisor and the clinician.

The most common problems in MST supervision with experienced MST clinicians are (a) knowledge deficits—not knowing how or when to use a certain skill, (b) skill deficits—the absence of relevant behaviors in a clinician's repertoire, and (c) performance deficits—when clinicians have the requisite knowledge and skills but are somehow inhibited in performing these skills. In our recent work with substance-abusing adolescents, functional analysis and contingency management procedures were critical. Yet, we discovered that many clinicians have limited training and experience in fundamental behavioral interventions that are at the core of most evidence-based practices. Skill and performance deficits are expressed in many forms, most commonly in avoidance, negative cognitive sets, hopelessness, and victim blaming.

Avoidance

Because MST services are offered in the home and in the community, clinicians often face negative reactions from their clients, who are considerably less inhibited on their home turf than clients in outpatient offices. Such reactions can generate anxiety or anger in the clinician, who might prevent such unpleasantness by failing to confront or to even keep appointments with some clients. The most common forms of avoidance seen in supervision are failing to carryout recommendations, forgetting specific therapeutic tasks, failing to address treatment barriers, withdrawing from discussions of fit problems or clinical interventions, and, most critically, failing to allow clinical work to be scrutinized. The latter is evident when clinicians have difficulty scheduling field visits or when clinicians make excuses for failing to audiotape—"I forgot to use fresh batteries," "The tape melted," or "The family refused to let me tape." Avoidance perniciously undermines clinician development by preventing exposure to critical learning opportunities with challenging clients and with challenging clinical circumstances.

Negative Cognitive Sets

In the case of negative cognitive sets (Freeman & McCloskey, 2003), the clinician agrees with the supervisory recommendations, only to immediately object—the "Yes, but . . ." scenario. At its extreme, when the supervisor or the team members suggest a course of action, often because the clinician has not generated an effective solution, the clinician consistently refuses the suggestion, disputing the conceptualization of the problem or the suggested strategy.

Hopelessness and Victim Blaming

Just as caregivers can be demoralized from failure to resolve their children's serious problems, even optimistic clinicians, faced with many of the caregivers' problems (e.g., social and financial crises, domestic violence, psychiatric symptoms, partner substance abuse), can feel hopeless. Victim blaming is an insidious professional response to interpersonal ineffectiveness. As Howard (1984) noted, victim blaming is most likely to occur when the client is female (i.e., MST often serves youth in female-headed households); when the clinician cares about the client, as most clinicians do; and when the clinician has little control over what happens (i.e., their best efforts to help have failed).

Because MST clinicians are asked to persevere with populations that many therapists avoid (e.g., conduct disordered, substance abusing delinquents and their families), lack of progress, overwhelming clinical scenarios, and poor coping by clinicians are not surprising. Such challenges are anticipated by the MST quality assurance system, particularly in supervision.

MANAGING COMMON PROBLEMS ENCOUNTERED IN MULTISYSTEMIC THERAPY SUPERVISION

A major factor in the success or the failure of any supervision is the supervisory relationship (see chap. 1, this volume). A poor relationship will not foster adherence to MST. A supervisor, who responds to clinician failure with criticism versus empathy and support, may engender angst and reluctance to disclose clinical difficulties. Supervisor training and consultation are designed to help establish a supportive group supervision process—valued by participants and facilitative of positive outcomes for families. Supervisors must become skilled managers of interactions among participants and between themselves and each clinician. They use three broad strategies to manage supervision problems: (a) collaborating on good clinician development plans, (b) creating a validating supervision environment, and (c) shaping desired clinical behavior.

Collaborating on Clinician Development Plans

When a clinician evinces a problem, part of his or her development plan is to target that problem. During individual supervision, the supervisor and the clinician conduct a fit analysis of the problem. Once the fit factors for the problem are identified, a plan can be developed conjointly by the clinician and the supervisor. If a clinician fails to address a mother's substance abuse, but still wonders why parental monitoring of youth drug use is not effective, an audiotape of the therapist–mother interaction regarding this issue can be reviewed during individual supervision. The tape might reveal the clinician addressed the issue only tangentially, apologized for raising the issue, or provided excessive explanations for discussing the topic. The supervisor might explore what the clinician was thinking and feeling during these interactions and might assess the basis for anxieties that interfere with the intervention (e.g., "The mother might think I am accusing her of being a drunk and might get angry or might fire me"). A clinician could also become anxious when asked to be more assertive during group supervision. Such anxiety can lead to withdrawing from the discussion or to changing the subject. A conjointly developed plan might have two components: (a) strategies to manage the problem during therapy sessions (e.g., diaphragmatic breathing, thought stopping, or exposure) and (b) strategies to help the clinician reduce the problem experienced during group supervision.

Common fit factors for avoidance by clinicians include skill and performance deficits. The conscientious clinician who is trying to do whatever it takes may be reluctant to acknowledge such deficits. Solving such problems typically requires exposure and repetition. Hence, following a detailed functional analysis, the development plan might provide for increased clinician exposure to situations that require the targeted skills or performance, using role-plays, recordings, or field visits with the supervisor or members of the treatment team. At the same time, the development plan might track clinician responses associated with avoidance, and the development plan might be modified based on the results. For example, the clinician might rate his level of anxiety when working with a client who constantly questions his credibility. If the anxiety does not subside following the use of an exposure-based strategy (e.g., role-playing with an extremely hostile client in group supervision), the development plan might be modified to include the use of progressive muscle relaxation.

Creating a Validating Supervision Environment

MST clinicians should ideally look forward to supervision. Supervision is a supportive place that nurtures their growth and their performance for the sake of their clients—a place where clinicians can get help for their most pressing problems encountered in treatment. Empathy and validation are essential in establishing a supervisory alliance within the treatment team. Linehan (1993) described two pertinent types of validation: (a) emphasizing the inherent wisdom in the clinician's emotional, cognitive, and behavioral responses to the challenging clinical context and (b) noting that the clinician has the capacity to better manage difficult clinical circumstances. Through word and deed, the supervisor and the members of the clinical team convey the belief that the clinician's difficulties are understandable (e.g., "Anyone working with this client would feel like you do") and that he or she has the ability and strengths to achieve positive results. Although clinicians often struggle when their clients' difficulties exceed their clinical competencies, such struggles provide the opportunity for clinician development. As one MST team put it, "We don't learn anything new from our successes, but a great deal from our failures." Failure can be framed as *good*, when it promotes therapist growth.

Shaping Desired Clinical Behavior

A premise of MST supervision is that supervisory interventions are more powerful when they are based on observed therapist–family transactions. Supervision that relies on only clinician reports misses important sequences of interaction at the heart of family-based interventions. If the supervisor relied on only the therapist's self-report in working with Paul, the supervisor would get a picture of a parent who was "not really interested" in the welfare of her child. Supervisor effectiveness is enhanced when they observe and reinforce in-session behaviors that lead to client improvements (Kohlenberg & Tsai, 1991). In MST supervision, audio recordings provide an efficient and a valid representation of in-session behavior. Being able to hear how the fine grain of interactions with a caregiver can increase or decrease resistant behavior was critical for Paul. In fact, he was able to identify certain of his words or phrases (e.g., "You should . . .") that invariably increased negative affect from the parent, and he was also able to identify how other words and phrases (e.g., framing parental failure as therapist "poor planning") developed in individual supervision had the opposite effect. Conjoint family sessions with the supervisor and the therapist are reserved for special circumstances (e.g., early in training or when generating solutions for particularly recalcitrant problems).

At the start of group supervision, a worksheet, titled *Catching My Cocounselor Doing Good*, is passed to each clinician. Clinicians are asked to note positive therapeutic interactions heard in their colleagues' tapes. Later, each clinician notes one skill observed from the tape and leads a brief discussion on how and why that skill was beneficial. This exercise recognizes effective clinical behavior, offers practice in focusing on strengths, and sustains a supportive environment that can buffer criticism.

Several other techniques can improve adherence to intervention protocols and can reduce therapist drift. In one approach, clinicians provide a list of therapy sessions conducted since the last supervision and provide the respective audiotapes. The supervisor randomly selects a tape for review. The tape can start at any point in the session, and the supervisor usually limits the review to 15 minutes to ensure that all therapists have an opportunity to receive feedback. In reviewing each tape, the supervisor first asks the clinician what interventions were used during the session and why they were used. The supervisor and the team are free at any time to praise any of the clinician's skills that are consistent with protocol compliance. The supervisor and the team members are also free to ask the therapist about deviations. If good reasons for the deviation are not given, the group brainstorms solutions, and the clinician describes how the solutions could be used in similar situations in the future.

Role-playing is also used extensively during the review of audiotapes to demonstrate appropriate use of an intervention. When a clinician experiences difficulty implementing an intervention according to protocol, the supervisor might first ask if anyone in the group could model the intervention step in which the difficulty occurred. After successful modeling and feedback, the clinician who experienced difficulty should attempt the intervention. The group praises skills that were performed well and offers constructive feedback.

CONCLUSION

As the mental health field grapples with the implementation of evidence-based treatments in real-world practice, the need to develop effective quality-assurance mechanisms is becoming more evident (Schoenwald & Henggeler, 2003). Historically, supervision has varied in its focus from psychodynamic interpretation of clinician transference to staffing of cases to fulfill legal and billing concerns. In contrast, supervision in efficacy trials of psychosocial treatment emphasizes specialized training and fidelity to the treatment model. Treatment developers or principal investigators often serve as the supervisors in such trials. In the real-world deployment of an evidence-based treatment, clinical supervision focuses on the substance and the process of the treatment in the face of difficult interpersonal situations. Supervision in the field ensures that clinicians develop and sustain the knowledge, the skills, and the motivation to implement the treatment. Deployment of a new treatment requires considerable training and support of clinicians and supervisors to achieve positive outcomes. Equally important are procedures to monitor, to measure, and to improve the effectiveness of therapist and supervisor efforts. The MST quality-assurance and improvement system represents such an approach. The MST system surrounds therapists and supervisors with the support and the resources needed to optimize favorable clinical outcomes with very challenging youths and families. Published research has produced evidence of linkages between therapist adherence and youth outcomes (Henggeler et al., 1997; Schoenwald et al., 2000), supervisor adherence and therapist adherence (Henggeler et al., 2002), and consultant adherence with therapist adherence and youth outcomes (Schoenwald, Sheidow, & Letourneau, 2004). In the spirit of quality improvement, additional research on therapeutic, supervisory, and consultation practices and their relationships to one another and to youth outcomes is underway. Supervisors should stay tuned.

REFERENCES

Bronfenbrenner, U. (1979). *The ecology of human development: Experiments by design and nature*. Cambridge, MA: Harvard University Press.

D'Zurilla, T. J., & Nezu, A. M. (1999). *Problem-solving therapy: A social competence approach to clinical intervention*. New York: Springer Publishing Company.

Edwards, D. L., Schoenwald, S. K., Henggeler, S. W., & Strother, K. B. (2001). A multilevel perspective on the implementation of Multisystemic Therapy (MST): Attempting dissemination with fidelity. In G. A. Bernfeld, D. P. Farrington, & A. W. Leschied (Eds.), *Offender rehabilitation in practice: Implementing and evaluating effective programs* (pp. 97–120). London: Wiley.

Freeman, A., & McCloskey, R. D. (2003). Impediments to effective psychotherapy. In R. L. Leahy (Ed.), *Roadblocks in cognitive–behavioral therapy* (pp. 24–48). New York: Guilford Press.

Henggeler, S. W., & Borduin, C. M. (1990). *Family therapy and beyond: A multisystemic approach to treating the behavior problems of children and adolescents*. Pacific Grove, CA: Brooks/Cole.

Henggeler, S. W., & Borduin, C. M. (1992). *Multisystemic Therapy Adherence Scales*. Unpublished instrument, Medical University of South Carolina, Charleston.

Henggeler, S. W., Melton, G. B., Brondino, M. J., Scherer, D. G., & Hanley, J. H. (1997). Multisystemic therapy with violent and chronic juvenile offenders and their families: The role of treatment fidelity in successful dissemination. *Journal of Consulting and Clinical Psychology, 65,* 821–833.

Henggeler, S. W., & Schoenwald, S. K. (1998). *The MST supervisory manual: Promoting quality assurance at the clinical level.* Charleston, SC: MST Services.

Henggeler, S. W., Schoenwald, S. K., Borduin, C. M., Rowland, M. D., & Cunningham, P. B. (1998). *Multisystemic treatment of antisocial behavior in children and adolescents.* New York: Guilford Press.

Henggeler, S. W., Schoenwald, S. K., Liao, J. G., Letourneau, E. J., & Edwards, D. L. (2002). Transporting efficacious treatments to field settings: The link between supervisory practices and therapist fidelity to MST programs. *Journal of Child and Adolescent Psychology, 31,* 155–167.

Henggeler, S. W., Schoenwald, S. K., Rowland, M. D., & Cunningham, P. B. (2002). *Serious emotional disturbance in children and adolescents.* New York: Guilford Press.

Howard, J. (1984). Societal influences of attribution: Blaming some victims more than others. *Journal of Personality and Social Psychology, 47,* 494–505.

Kohlenberg, R. J., & Tsai, M. (1991). Functional analytic psychotherapy: A radical behavioral approach to treatment and integration. *Journal of Psychotherapy Integration, 4,* 175–201.

Linehan, M. M. (1993). *Cognitive–behavioral treatment of borderline personality disorder.* New York: Guilford Press.

National Alliance for the Mentally Ill. (2003, Fall). An update on evidence-based practices in children's mental health. *NAMI Beginnings, 3,* 3–7.

National Institute on Drug Abuse. (1999). *Principles of drug addiction treatment: A research-based guide* (NIH Publication No. 99-4180). Rockville, MD: Author.

Randall, J., Henggeler, S. W., Cunningham, P. B., Rowland, M. D., & Swenson, C. C. (2001). Adapting multisystemic therapy to treat adolescent substance abuse more effectively. *Cognitive and Behavioral Practice, 8,* 359–366.

Schoenwald, S. K. (1998). *Multisystemic therapy consultation manual.* Charleston, SC: MST Services.

Schoenwald, S. K., & Henggeler, S. W. (Eds.). (2003). Current strategies for moving evidence-based interventions into clinical practice [Special issue]. *Cognitive and Behavioral Practice, 10,* 275–323.

Schoenwald, S. K., Henggeler, S. W., Brondino, M. J., & Rowland, M. D. (2000). Multisystemic therapy: Monitoring treatment fidelity. *Family Process, 39,* 83–103.

Schoenwald, S. K., Henggeler, S. W., & Edwards, D. (1998). *MST Supervisor Adherence Measure.* Charleston, SC: MST Institute.

Schoenwald, S. K., Sheidow, A. S., & Letourneau, E. J. (2004). Toward effective quality assurance in evidence-based practice: Links between expert consultation, therapist fidelity, and child outcomes. *Journal of Child and Adolescent Clinical Psychology, 33,* 94–104.

U.S. Public Health Service. (2001). *Youth violence: A report of the Surgeon General.* Washington, DC: Author.

Weisz, J. R. (2004). *Psychotherapy for children and adolescents: Evidence-based treatments and case examples.* Cambridge, England: Cambridge University Press.

Weisz, J. R., Donenberg, G. R., Weiss, B., & Han, S. S. (1995). Bridging the gap between laboratory and clinic in child and adolescent psychotherapy. *Journal of Consulting and Clinical Psychology, 63,* 688–701.

Weisz, J. R., Weiss, B., & Donenberg, G. R. (1992). The lab versus the clinic: Effects of child and adolescent psychotherapy. *American Psychologist, 47,* 1578–1585.

9

TREATING CHILDREN WITH EARLY-ONSET CONDUCT PROBLEMS: KEY INGREDIENTS TO IMPLEMENTING THE INCREDIBLE YEARS PROGRAMS WITH FIDELITY

CAROLYN WEBSTER-STRATTON

Over the past 30 years, hundreds of carefully controlled studies for children and youth have established the value of interventions that can reduce behavior problems and delinquency, can improve children's mental health, and can strengthen family functioning (Weisz & Weiss, 1993). Among research-tested psychotherapies, those based on cognitive–social learning methods may have the most support for their effectiveness (Serketich & Dumas, 1996; Taylor & Biglan, 1998), particularly for treating disruptive behaviors in children, including aggression, oppositional defiant disorder and conduct disorder (Chambless & Hollon, 1998; Dumas, 1989; Kazdin, 2002), and attention-deficit/hyperactivity disorder (ADHD; Barkley, 1996). Together these problems represent the majority of referrals for child mental health services (Snyder, 2001).

Despite such compelling evidence, few empirically supported interventions are widely adopted by clinicians or by teachers in community settings

(Kazdin, Bass, Ayers, & Rodgers, 1991; Weisz, Donenberg, Han, & Weiss, 1995). Early adopters who risk implementing evidence-based interventions often face interpersonal, clinical, or organizational challenges that affect their ability to deliver the intervention with fidelity. A clinical innovator might lack the training or skill to deliver a program, might fail to grasp core treatment principles or processes, or might be unable to adapt protocols to individual client circumstances. The organization may have other priorities and fail to support training and supervision. Diluted treatments may be doomed to failure.

It is essential that sound theory and research support new treatment and that procedures are described clearly and are followed closely. In this chapter, I describe the training, supervisory, and organizational requirements to implement the Incredible Years (IY) Training Series, a multifaceted program developed by Carolyn Webster-Stratton at the University of Washington (Seattle) to prevent and to treat early onset of conduct problems in children. I have identified five key elements to effective program implementation:

1. Standardized treatment materials for clinicians and for clients; using comprehensive manuals; well-articulated protocols; videotapes; and books for parents, teachers, and children.
2. Standardized, quality training for clinicians delivering the intervention.
3. Effective peer support, clinical supervision, and consultation for clinicians.
4. Ongoing, fidelity monitoring, including regular, participant evaluation and certification of clinicians and mentors.
5. Agency or administrative support for clinicians.

This chapter provides detailed information about each of these important steps to program implementation with emphasis on supervision. Before describing them, I briefly sketch the components of the intervention program. Detailed descriptions of the theory behind the program development and the therapy process can be found in other reviews (Webster-Stratton, 1998a; Webster-Stratton & Hancock, 1998; Webster-Stratton & Reid, 2004a).

THE INCREDIBLE YEARS TRAINING SERIES: CONTENT, METHODS, PROCESSES, AND RESEARCH

Delivering the program with fidelity means not only offering all the core content components and required number of sessions but also delivering the program using the recommended therapeutic group process and training methods. In the next section, the core program components will be reviewed as well as recommendations for when additional program supplements may be added to meet the needs of particular families or populations.

The Content and the Use of the Intervention Programs

The core program, entitled BASIC, teaches parents (a) child-directed play and reinforcement skills and (b) specific nonviolent, discipline techniques, including time out, ignoring, logical and natural consequences, and problem-solving strategies. The program starts by focusing on building positive parenting because a strong, positive parent–child relationship is considered to be the foundation for effective discipline. There are preschool and school-age (i.e., up to Grade 4) versions of BASIC, and there are modifications for either a treatment or a prevention focus. There are protocols for a minimum of 12 sessions with video vignettes. However, the program can be extended depending on the group size and the participants' needs. Parents who have neglected their children may need extra sessions on child-directed play to foster more nurturing relationships and may need cognitive and emotional stimulation before learning discipline strategies. Groups using interpreters usually require at least four additional sessions. Parents with extremely difficult children may need three to four extra sessions to develop incentive systems and individual behavior plans. Although protocols suggest time frames for vignettes and for home activities to be completed, the skilled group leader will pace the group according to the participants' learning ability and needs.

There are also additional training program supplements to choose from in order to tailor the program for families with additional goals. A 9- to 12-session ADVANCED program helps parents cope with interpersonal problems and includes training in communication skills, anger management, depression and stress management, problem solving, and ways to give and to get support. For children diagnosed with conduct problems, it is recommended to add the ADVANCED program to the BASIC program, producing a 24- to 26-week protocol. The Supporting Your Child's Education program aids parents in strengthening children's general academic skills and in promoting strong home–school connections. This four-session program can be offered to parents whose children have learning problems or have been diagnosed with ADHD. The Preschool Readiness program is another four-session program that focuses on training parents in social and emotional coaching and in interactive reading skills. This program component can be offered to parents who want to encourage their childrens' emotional regulation, positive peer relationships, and reading readiness. A 22- to 24-week child-training program, the Dinosaur Curriculum, works to ameliorate factors placing children at risk for behavior problems. It teaches emotional literacy, social skills, problem solving, and anger management. It can be offered alone or with the parent program. For children with pervasive, behavior problems at home, at school, and with peers, it is recommended that they participate in the Dinosaur Curriculum, while their parents receive training in their program. Lastly, a teacher training program is available to promote teachers' use of (a) tested management and discipline strategies to decrease classroom aggression and to increase social competence and (b) behavior plans developed in collaboration with parents in training (Webster-Stratton & Reid, 2004b). Our research shows that adding either the Dinosaur Curriculum or the Teacher Training to parent training enhances treatment effects for children with pervasive behavior problems. For the purpose of this chapter, I focus on the BASIC program. Supervision issues for BASIC are applicable to the other IY programs.

Intervention, Behavior-Change Methods, and Processes

Because the extent of children's conduct problems far exceeds existing resources for intervention, IY programs are designed for groups with discussions facilitated by trained group leaders, referred to as clinicians or group leaders in this chapter. The group format fosters mutual support and both normalizes and enriches participants' experiences. Interventions rely on Bandura's (1989) self-efficacy and modeling theory, as well as cognitive–social–learning theory and performance-based methods such as behavioral rehearsal and both live and videotape modeling. Video vignettes depict positive adult–child interactions, effective discipline, and prosocial child behavior. They provide a compelling and a congenial learning format for less verbally oriented families. Video vignettes also promote generalization of parenting skills by portraying models from various cultures, as well as by portraying children of different temperaments and developmental levels.

Research

Positive evaluations of the IY programs resulted in their being recommended as model, blueprints, or evidence-based treatment and prevention programs by several review groups (Chambless & Hollon, 1998; Webster-Stratton et al., 2001). The BASIC programs are supported by seven randomized studies of the treatment version by the developer (Webster-Stratton & Reid, 2003) and by three replications by others (Scott, Spender, Doolan, Jacobs, & Aspland, 2001; Spaccarelli, Cotler, & Penman, 1992; Taylor, Schmidt, Pepler, & Hodgins, 1998). There also have been five studies using BASIC as a prevention program with high risk children; two by the developer (Webster-Stratton, 1998b; Webster-Stratton, Reid, & Hammond, 2001) and three by independent evaluators (Barrera et al., 2002; Gross, Fogg, Webster-Stratton, Garvey, & Grady, 2003; Miller Brotman et al., 2003).

KEY STRATEGIES TO ENHANCE SUCCESSFUL DISSEMINATION AND IMPLEMENTATION

Successful dissemination of the program depends on the successful development of five key strategies focused on quality, standardized training, ongoing technical supervision and consultation, and agency support.

Strategy 1: Standardization of Treatment Materials and Delivery

To ensure fidelity, programs are in an uncomplicated format enabling group leaders to readily learn the required content and skills. Reliance on comprehensive clinician-treatment manuals and on standardized videotapes allows the clinician to focus on facilitating groups, not on memorizing content. Items from the standardized treatment package include books or CDs for the parents, standard weekly home activities, refrigerator magnets and refrigerator notes that summarize key principles, and weekly evaluation forms. Group leaders receive videotape protocols and checklists for each session, a book explaining the program's theory, and a description of the collaborative process for leading groups (Webster-Stratton & Herbert, 1994). A group leaders' manual includes the questions to follow each video vignette, the developer's interpretation of each vignette, and the points for discussion. The manual provides practical guidance on topics ranging from setting up the room for the first session to engaging low-income families to promoting support both within and outside the group (Webster-Stratton & Hancock, 1998).

Strategy 2: Standardized Quality Training Workshops

In addition to detailed materials, standardized training provides clinicians with an introduction to the program content, methods, and group facilitation process. The initial training is offered in a 3-day workshop to small groups of clinicians. Those selected to do the training are certified trainers and mentors who have extensive experience delivering the program and who are exemplary models for demonstrating the therapeutic processes. Videotapes of trainers' actual group sessions allow clinicians to see, and to model, how the trainer works with groups. The trainers also use established performance-based training techniques, including discussion, rehearsal, practice role-playing, brainstorms, values exercises, persuasion techniques, and homework activities. Such variety addresses different learning styles. These techniques parallel those used in the parent program.

A collaborative approach is essential to the treatment process—and to training group leaders. It is empowering, and it triggers less resistance than didactic or prescriptive approaches. Encouraging participants to identify their own goals and barriers increases their confidence and engagement. Collaboration enhances cultural and developmental sensitivity because participants can apply the program's principles to their own experiences. Collaboration reduces dropouts and leads participants to jointly invest in outcomes (Meichenbaum & Turk, 1987; Seligman, 1990).

Clinician training uses all the methods used with parents. Trainers model the collaborative process, asking clinicians to act as parents, to respond to videotapes, and to enter group discussions, role-playing, and values exercises. After the trainer models group-leader strategies, she invites discussion of the therapeutic and the collaborative strategies used in the role-playing. Because role-playing is frequently resisted, the trainer shows how such practice helps leaders understand the insights of parents. Role-playing and live rehearsal are also used to demonstrate skills and to aid understanding in the peer review and in the supervision that follow initial training.

Clinicians-in-training assess the advantages and the disadvantages of all the techniques, identify goals and barriers for delivering the program, and strategize to overcome them. Finally, they evaluate each workshop as in the actual intervention, and they learn how the trainers use evaluations to tailor workshops and to meet participant's needs.

Strategy 3: Peer Support, Clinician Supervision, and Consultation for Clinicians

From this point forward, I use the word *consultant* for the experienced IY trainer or mentor who continues to support the leader's, or the clinician's, work, unless there is a reason to make a distinction between them. After the initial training, group leaders need adequate time to study the materials, to prepare their sessions, and to arrange logistics (e.g., food or day care). Clinicians may be discouraged or demoralized by particular families and their lack of apparent progress. They may also be discouraged by perceived lack of agency support for their implementation of the program. Weekly peer support and clinician consultation are crucial for first-time group leaders.

Consultation and supervision take several forms and may evolve within an agency. For agencies that are implementing the program for the first time, consultants will be offsite but will begin to establish a relationship with the clinicians. It is recommended that clinicians arrange regular telephone consultations with the IY mentor or trainer and use e-mail to ask about doubts or questions. They are also encouraged to submit a videotape of a session, midway through their first group (around Session 5), for further feedback. IY mentors and trainers have been trained to supervise (part of the extensive IY Mentor certification process, which is discussed later in this chapter), have extensive experience with the program, and usually have access to equally experienced colleagues or to the program developer. Such consultants are a vital resource to new IY clinicians. After clinicians have completed one or two groups, about 6 to 9 months after training, it is recommended that they participate in a consultation workshop with IY trainers either onsite or at the IY headquarters in Seattle. In these consultation workshops, group leaders come together to share selected portions of their videotapes. Feedback and supervision regarding videotaped sessions can be a huge asset in helping clinicians gain new ways to handle problems that were particularly difficult for them. Reviews of beginner's tapes frequently reveal difficulties with using the videotapes, with doing role-plays, with adhering to protocols, with tailoring the program to bring families' personal problems to life, or with making strategies developmentally appropriate. Initially, clinicians can be preoccupied with the mechanics of videos, manuals, food, or handout preparation rather than with the therapeutic group process. New leaders tend to be less collaborative and tend to be more prescriptive in their approach. Supervision and the peer-review and support processes are there precisely to help improve their group process skills and their response to individual parent or child issues. In supervision, the clinicians' videotapes will serve as the stimulus to trigger a re-enactment of scenarios faced in the groups. Clinicians practice alternative responses to difficult group situations or questions and gain support from their colleagues. The supervision process is nurturing and caring and is focused on the clinician's strengths, as well as on practicing different strategies. With this kind of warmth from the trainer or mentor, group leaders feel supported and empowered to work successfully with their groups.

Weekly peer support and supervision are recommended for any group leader but are crucial for clinicians running a group for the first time. Peer support is key to continued learning and successful intervention, regardless of a clinician's expertise. Often, group leaders become discouraged when a particular family or child fails to progress. Peer group support and the perspective of the supervisor help the leader to maintain optimism and to find approaches for resistant parents or children. It is recommended that clinicians begin videotaping their groups right away and meet weekly with peers for videotape review and for mutual support. It is the policy of the IY program to train groups of clinicians from the same area or agency, so they can participate in the peer-review process. Individuals are not trained to work without a peer support network. It is also the policy that clinicians from the same agency or locale join the peer-review process immediately after training, even if they do not have an active group at the time.

In many ways, the peer-review process can be considered a variation on group supervision. The process and the advantages of group supervision are detailed in two other chapters (7 and 8) in this volume. When group members share their work and offer constructive support, they not only aid each other in conducting IY groups but also empower themselves as thinkers, self-managers, and evaluators. Even in classic group supervision, it is the practice of supervisors to allow group members to maximize their mutual contribution to the supervisory process, to set their own goals, and to intervene only to guide when the group is unable to carry the process or when core principles are not addressed.

The fact that each member of the peer review group has access to an individual IY consultant who critiques their tapes adds greatly to what the members of the peer-review group can offer each other. Consultants model the style of constructive and supportive feedback they would like to see characterized or interchanged in the peer review groups. Peer-review groups use the IY group process checklists to guide members in critiquing their own and others videotaped sessions. Six areas are rated in the group process checklist: (a) group-process skills (e.g., building rapport, encouraging problem solving, reinforcing parents' ideas, and creating a safe accepting atmosphere), (b) leadership skills (e.g., establishing ground rules; structuring an agenda; highlighting key points; preventing sidetracking; encouraging generalization; balancing affective, cognitive, and behavioral discussion and practice; and reviewing homework), (c) relationship-building skills (e.g., validating and supporting parents' feelings, fostering optimism, normalizing problems, and using a collaborative model), (d) leader's knowledge (e.g., providing accurate rationale for principles, knowing what is developmentally appropriate, and understanding and knowing how to explain cognitive–social–learning theory and principles of behavior change), (e) leader methods (e.g., using videotape modeling and roleplaying, using homework and practice, and engaging in brainstorming sessions to identify barriers), and (f) parents' responses (e.g., engaging in asking questions, in problem solving, and in sharing ideas). This peer-review and self-review processes help clinicians set goals for future sessions. The process of individual goal setting enhances clinician's motivation to adhere to the program content, the methods, and the processes. If the peer process has difficulties, members can send a videotape of their group session to an IY consultant for feedback.

Supervision and consultation may be sought initially at a distance from IY trainers, but it is important for agencies to begin right away to identify candidates to become mentors or internal champions and to build their own training and supervision capacity for the future. Successful supervision when a clinician is first adopting a new, evidence-based intervention requires the trainer or mentor to help clinicians recognize their role as change agents. My experience suggests it is best if the clinicians implementing a new intervention in an agency are eager to do so. Clinicians who decide to implement a new program become innovators in the system. Often called *early adopters*, they are willing to take risks and to try new ideas before they have become well-established interventions in the organization (Rogers, 1995). However, some early adopters are unaware of what it means to be a change agent and do not realize that they must engage in social marketing—being a champion for their new services to families and their professional colleagues—and that they must effectively confront organizational resistance or lack of understanding of their efforts. Consultants need to guide clinicians who assume roles as innovators within their organization.

Strategy 4: Fidelity Monitoring, Including Participant Evaluation and Clinician Certification

Program fidelity—determining if clinicians are adhering to session protocols, key content, and therapeutic process principles—is another aspect of supervision. Many clinicians believe that they can eliminate parts of a mental health intervention or shorten it to be more cost effective. They may even cobble together different programs in a smorgasbord intervention. Training, supervision, and certification help clinicians, and administrators, understand that this approach may dilute or may eliminate the positive effects of the program. Research on children with conduct disorders shows that tested interventions of at least 20 hours in length were more effective than shorter programs. Specific research with the Incredible Years program demonstrates incremental improvement in parent and child behaviors based on the number of sessions attended; parents who attended more than two thirds of the sessions had the most effective outcomes (Baydar, Reid, & Webster-Stratton, 2003). Evidence-based interventions are carefully designed with each session building on a prior session. The recommended number of sessions is considered the minimum sessions needed, and groups may require more depending on their needs and their pace of learning. Supervision helps clinicians know how they can appropriately adapt the program to meet the needs of a particular population. A critical distinction must be made between implementing the core or the foundational elements of the program and stifling clinical flexibility. It is easy for the former to be misconstrued as the latter. In supervision, clinicians are encouraged to discuss their knowledge and experience, so they collaboratively adapt the program to unique, parent goals or to child developmental needs. Clinicians come to understand that the principles that guide the program include being flexible, collaborating with the client in setting the agenda, and having fun, rather than following a precise script to be recited at parents. When clinicians understand this, they realize the program actually encourages the use of their clinical skills and judgment. My experience suggests that clinicians who continue in the program retain the core elements of the intervention while bringing their clinical creativity to bear in the implementation. Supervision helps clinicians balance pursuit of a particular parent's agenda (possibly unrelated to the day's immediate content) in relation to the group process and issues that are relevant for the entire group.

Clinicians ask group participants to complete evaluations of every group session. These weekly evaluations provide feedback on participants' perceptions of the training. They help the clinician to tailor the program to individual learning needs and to become aware of a parent who may be feeling left out, misunderstood, or resistant to an idea presented in the group. From these evaluations clinicians may learn how participants learn best—through modeling or discussion or practice or reading—and then may adapt family home activities accordingly.

A certification or accreditation process allows clinicians to continue their learning process after the initial training and to recognize those who strive to become more competent group leaders. Requirements for certification include the following: adherence to session protocols; parent attendance; positive weekly and final client evaluations for two complete, 12-week, group interventions each lasting a minimum of 12 weeks; two self- and peer-evaluations for each complete program offered using the peer content and the methods checklists; completion of a 3-day authorized training workshop; and satisfactory review of a complete videotape of a group session by a trainer who rates the clinician's adherence to the program content and methods, as well as the clinician's therapeutic skill in the collaborative process. Satisfactory peer review, videotape, parent evaluations, and group attendance indicate mastery of the content and the therapeutic process necessary for certification. Clinicians who become certified can reasonably anticipate achieving effects similar to those achieved in the published outcome studies evaluating the program.

To maintain program fidelity, certified clinicians are encouraged to attend ongoing consultation and technical support workshops every 2 years and to continue participating in peer-review groups within their agency. Client evaluations and completed session protocols are also part of the clinician's accountability to the agency.

Those chosen to become accredited mentors are certified group leaders with exceptional group leadership skills, mastery of the collaborative process, understanding of the research, and desire to support other leaders. They receive further training in supervision and in delivering the core training workshops. Prospective mentors have their group tapes intensively reviewed, participate in supervision and consultation workshops, and colead training workshops with a certified trainer. When mentors complete training and receive positive workshop evaluations and positive mentor supervision evaluations by participants and trainers, they are accredited to offer training workshops and to supervise within their agency or district. Mentors receive consultation, workshops with other mentors, videotape feedback on workshops, further training, and updates regarding the program.

Strategy 5: Ongoing Training and Support for Agencies to Support Clinicians

No program can be faithfully implemented without agency or organizational support for the clinicians and the intervention. The decision to adopt an evidence-based intervention, such as IY, should reflect a consensus among clinicians and administrators that the choice of treatment model best meets their goals, the agency philosophy, and the needs of their clients. In other words, there is a good innovation–agency–clinician values fit. It may be necessary for administrators to re-adjust clinician job descriptions to recognize the clinicians' time commitments to ongoing training, peer support, supervision, recruiting for and carrying out groups. Even though group approaches are more cost effective than individual approaches, administrators may not understand the time needed to call parents weekly, to assure transportation and food are available, to arrange day care, and to prepare materials for the sessions. Sometimes administrators are surprised to find that the initial training does not prepare their clinicians to start groups the following week. It is imperative that administrators understand that learning a new evidence-based intervention will also involve studying the videotapes and training manuals and meeting in peer-support groups to practice with their colleagues. The administrative staff and internal advocates need to assure that there are plans for ongoing consultation and supervision from the outside trainer. The IY trainer collaborates with the organization's internal advocate, provides consultation to clinicians and administrators regarding program implementation, and anticipates possible resistance and difficulties with the intervention. The trainer is in an excellent position to advise the administrators in ways to support clinicians' change efforts. The IY Agency Readiness Questionnaire can help administrators understand what is needed to support the clinician's training, the clinician's needs for logistical support, and the clinician's ongoing consultation and supervision.

It is best if there is an administrative champion, ideally a trained mentor, within the agency who understands the workings of his or her own organization, as well as the requirements of the new program. Research shows that clinicians, who are left to champion a program without an active administrative champion, quickly burn out from the extra work, resent the lack of support, and often leave the agency (Corrigan, 1995). Research indicates that the interpersonal contact provided by the internal advocate is a critical ingredient in adoption of new programs (Backer, Liberman, & Kuehnel, 1986). Administrative champions are often more important to the long-term success of the intervention than to the clinicians.

Administrators may select promising clinicians and persuade them to learn this new intervention. The program will attain a strong reputation if it begins with a few enthusiastic leaders rather than if it begins with a mandate that all clinicians adopt the program. Those who are not risk takers, *late adopters*, will venture into new programs only after respected colleagues are successful (Rogers, 1995). Encouraging clinicians who become certified as group leaders to continue and to become certified as mentors builds the infrastructure of a lasting program. At first, the IY trainers provide direct support to the clinician, as detailed in Strategy 3. However, the goal is to make agencies self-sufficient in their ongoing training and in their support of the program. Administrators can also provide important reinforcement to therapists by recognizing and rewarding those who work to become certified and achieve high quality delivery of the program. Reinforcement, both social and tangible, is important to therapists' ongoing commitment and adherence to this program. Moreover, when administrators promote therapist certification as a way of supporting evidence-based practice, therapists appreciate that they are working toward goals and a philosophy that is highly valued by the organization.

CONCLUSION

Implementing a new evidence-based intervention in an agency is not unlike remodeling a house. The architect (i.e., the program developer or trainer) must work closely with the contractors (i.e., the clinicians and administrators) to explain the blueprints and design features, while the contractors assure that building codes are observed and that workers have the expertise to handle the job. Both the architect and the contractor must be aware of the family's needs and desires, as well as their timeline and budget constraints. As the remodeling continues, there will undoubtedly be changes as the family realizes different needs or as discoveries are made (e.g., workers uncover asbestos or termite damage). This will necessitate a collaborative and a flexible approach with open communication and a common spirit of problem solving. In a similar fashion, the clinicians must be carefully selected and well trained, must be provided with supervision and consultation, must work within a supportive infrastructure, and must be bolstered by quality control of the program delivery. Systematic, regular feedback from the clients (i.e., parents, teachers, and children) and the consultants in the process of collaborative discussion and session evaluations assures that the clinician is implementing the program with sensitivity and with relevance according to the individual family's needs and cultural background and according to the nature of the children's problems.

REFERENCES

Backer, T. E., Liberman, R. P., & Kuehnel, T. G. (1986). Dissemination and adoption of innovative psychosocial interventions. *Journal of Consulting and Clinical Psychology, 54*, 111–118.

Bandura, A. (1989). Regulation of cognitive processes through perceived self-efficacy. *Developmental Psychology, 25*, 729–735.

Barkley, R. A. (1996). Attention-deficit/hyperactivity disorder. In E. J. Mash & R. A. Barkley (Eds.), *Child psychopathology* (pp. 63–112). New York: Guilford Press.

Barrera, M., Biglan, A., Taylor, T. K., Gunn, B., Smolkowski, K., Black, C., et al. (2002). Early elementary school intervention to reduce conduct problems: A randomized trial with Hispanic and nonHispanic children. *Prevention Science, 3*, 83–94.

Baydar, N., Reid, J. B., & Webster-Stratton, C. (2003). Who benefits from school-based preventive parent training programs? The role of mother mental health factors and program engagement. *Child Development, 74*, 1433–1453.

Chambless, D. L., & Hollon, S. D. (1998). Defining empirically supported therapies. *Journal of Consulting and Clinical Psychology, 66*, 7–18.

Corrigan, P. W. (1995). Wanted: Champions of rehabilitation for psychiatric hospitals. *American Psychologist, 50*, 514–521.

Dumas, J. E. (1989). Treating antisocial behavior in children: Child and family approaches. *Clinical Psychology Review, 9*, 197–222.

Gross, D., Fogg, L., Webster-Stratton, C., Garvey, C. W. J., & Grady, J. (2003). Parent training with families of toddlers in day care in low-income urban communities. *Journal of Consulting and Clinical Psychology, 71*, 261–278.

Kazdin, A. E. (2002). Psychosocial treatments for conduct disorder in children and adolescents. In P. E. Nathan & J. M. Gorman (Eds.), *A guide to treatments that work* (pp. 57–85). New York: Oxford University Press.

Kazdin, A. E., Bass, D., Ayers, W. A., & Rodgers, A. (1991). Empirical and clinical focus of child and adolescent psychotherapy research. *Journal of Consulting and Clinical Psychology, 58*, 729–740.

Meichenbaum, D., & Turk, D. (1987). *Facilitating treatment adherence: A practitioner's guidebook*. New York: Plenum Press.

Miller Brotman, L., Klein, R. G., Kamboukos, D., Brown, E. J., Coard, S., & Stout-Sosinsky, L. (2003). Preventive intervention for urban, low-income preschoolers at familial risk for conduct problems: A randomized pilot study. *Journal of Child Psychology and Psychiatry, 32*, 246–257.

Rogers, E. M. (1995). *Diffusion of innovations*. New York: Free Press.

Scott, S., Spender, Q., Doolan, M., Jacobs, B., & Aspland, H. (2001). Multicentre controlled trial of parenting groups for child antisocial behaviour in clinical practice. *British Medical Journal, 323*(28), 1–5.

Seligman, M. (1990). *Learned optimism.* Sydney, Australia: Random House.

Serketich, W. J., & Dumas, J. E. (1996). The effectiveness of behavioral parent training to modify antisocial behavior in children: A meta-analysis. *Behavior Therapy, 27,* 171–186.

Snyder, H. (2001). Child delinquents. In R. Loeber & D. P. Farrington (Eds.), *Risk factors and successful interventions* (pp. 106–146). Thousand Oaks, CA: Sage.

Spaccarelli, S., Cotler, S., & Penman, D. (1992). Problem-solving skills training as a supplement to behavioral parent training. *Cognitive Therapy and Research, 16,* 1–18.

Taylor, T. K., & Biglan, A. (1998). Behavioral family interventions for improving child rearing: A review for clinicians and policy makers. *Clinical Child and Family Psychology Review, 1,* 41–60.

Taylor, T. K., Schmidt, F., Pepler, D., & Hodgins, H. (1998). A comparison of eclectic treatment with Webster-Stratton's parents and children series in a children's mental health center: A randomized controlled trial. *Behavior Therapy, 29,* 221–240.

Webster-Stratton, C. (1998a). Parent training with low-income clients: Promoting parental engagement through a collaborative approach. In J. R. Lutzker (Ed.), *Handbook of child abuse research and treatment* (pp. 183–210). New York: Plenum Press.

Webster-Stratton, C. (1998b). Preventing conduct problems in Head Start children: Strengthening parenting competencies. *Journal of Consulting and Clinical Psychology, 66,* 715–730.

Webster-Stratton, C., & Hancock, L. (1998). Parent training: Content, methods, and processes. In E. Schaefer (Ed.), *Handbook of parent training* (2nd ed., pp. 98–152). New York: Wiley.

Webster-Stratton, C., & Herbert, M. (1994). *Troubled families–problem children: Working with parents: A collaborative process.* Chichester, England: Wiley.

Webster-Stratton, C., Mihàlic, S., Fagan, A., Arnold, D., Taylor, T. K., & Tingley, C. (2001). *Blueprints for violence prevention, Book 11: The Incredible Years: Parent, teacher, and child training series.* Boulder, CO: Center for the Study and Prevention of Violence.

Webster-Stratton, C., & Reid, M. J. (2003). The Incredible Years: Parent, teacher, and child training series: A multifaceted treatment approach for young children with conduct problems. In A. E. Kazdin & J. R. Weisz (Eds.), *Evidence-based psychotherapies for children and adolescents* (pp. 224–240). New York: Guilford Press.

Webster-Stratton, C., & Reid, M. J. (2004a). Strengthening social and emotional competence in young children—The foundation for early school readiness and success: Incredible Years classroom social skills and problem-solving curriculum. *Journal of Infants and Young Children, 17,* 96–113.

Webster-Stratton, C., & Reid, M. J. (2004b). Treating children with early-onset conduct problems: Intervention outcomes for parent, child, and teacher training. *Journal of Clinical Child and Adolescent Psychology, 33,* 105–124.

Webster-Stratton, C., Reid, M. J., & Hammond, M. (2001). Preventing conduct problems, promoting social competence: A parent and teacher training partnership in Head Start. *Journal of Clinical Child Psychology, 30,* 283–302.

Weisz, J. R., Donenberg, G. R., Han, S. S., & Weiss, B. (1995). Bridging the gap between laboratory and clinic in child and adolescent psychotherapy. Special section: Efficacy and effectiveness in studies of child and adolescent psychotherapy. *Journal of Consulting and Clinical Psychology, 63,* 688–701.

Weisz, J. R., & Weiss, B. (1993). *Effects of psychotherapy with children and adolescents.* London: Sage.

10

DIALECTICAL BEHAVIOR THERAPY SUPERVISION AND CONSULTATION WITH SUICIDAL, MULTIPROBLEM YOUTH: THE NUTS AND BOLTS

ALEC L. MILLER AND JENNIFER L. HARTSTEIN

According to a recent national survey, 20% of American high school students seriously considered suicide in the previous year, 15% made a plan, and 8.8% attempted suicide (Grunbaum et al., 2002). Those suicide attempts total nearly one million, with 750,000 requiring medical attention. Sadly, nearly 2,000 American teens take their lives each year. Hundreds of thousands more engage in nonsuicidal self-injurious behaviors (NSIB), such as self-cutting or self-burning. In fact, 15% of a normal high school sample recently surveyed was engaging in NSIB (Muehlenkamp & Gutierrez, 2004).

There are a growing number of teens who have more than one psychiatric disorder and various coexisting life problems (Miller & Glinski, 2000). Although many adolescents face periodic academic, peer, or family problems, one in five teens is seriously challenged by episodes of depression (Birmaher, Ryan, Williamson, Brent, & Kaufman, 1996). Still others are mired in substance abuse, stricken by anxiety, struggling with body image and eating problems, or engaging in violent and illegal activities. These problems often cluster together resulting in multidiagnosed adolescents being referred to treatment to address myriad problems (Miller, Rathus, & Linehan, in press). Several empirically supported treatments exist for single problems or disorders (Kazdin & Weisz, 2003), yet, prior to the development of dialectical behavior therapy (DBT), there was no empirically supported psychosocial treatment for suicidal multiproblem youth.

DBT was originally developed for chronically parasuicidal women diagnosed with borderline personality disorder (BPD; Linehan, 1993a). Since its inception, DBT has been adapted for other populations, including parasuicidal multiproblem youth (Miller & Rathus, 2000). *Parasuicide* is defined as any acute, intentionally self-injurious behavior resulting in physical harm, with or without the intent to die (Linehan, 1993a), and includes any nonsuicidal self-injurious behavior (NSIB); suicide attempts with ambivalent intent; and suicide attempts with clear intent to die. Miller, Rathus, Linehan, Wetzler, and Leigh (1997) adapted DBT for use with parasuicidal adolescents. Because DBT aims at reducing life-threatening behaviors, as well as facilitating treatment engagement and retention, it appears to be a promising therapy for multiproblem adolescents (Rathus & Miller, 2002).

Two of the most common problems associated with treating suicidal multiproblem teens are poor treatment compliance and therapist burnout. These issues are a frequent focus of supervision as consequent problems for the clinician are emotional dysregulation and dismay resulting from the combination of missed or stressful sessions and out-of-session 24-hour availability for repeated suicidal crises, threats, and attempts. Because of the emotional demands of working with these youth (see also chap. 11, this volume), supervision and consultation are considered integral to the DBT treatment model. On the basis of the need to consult to the therapist, in much the same way that the therapist consults to the patient, Linehan (1993a) determined that therapist supervision, the therapist consultation meeting in particular, is a mandatory modality of DBT treatment.

After a brief overview of dialectical behavior therapy, we devote the remainder of this chapter to DBT supervision and consultation used with mental health professionals treating suicidal youth. We will detail the following steps: (a) orienting and commitment, (b) therapist skill acquisition, (c) therapist consultation meeting, (d) individual therapy and telephone consultation supervision, (e) skills group supervision, and (f) adherence to and competence in DBT.

DIALECTICAL BEHAVIOR THERAPY IN A NUTSHELL

Biosocial theory is used to explain the etiology and the maintenance of borderline personality disorder (BPD). According to Linehan (1993a), the central problem for individuals with BPD is pervasive dysregulation of the emotion regulation system. Emotion dysregulation is believed to be the result of a transaction between an individual who is developmentally predisposed to having difficulty regulating emotion and an invalidating environment that intensifies that vulnerability (Linehan, 1993a). Hence, borderline personality symptomatology, including parasuicidal behavior, may result when an adolescent, who is emotionally vulnerable, is placed in an environment that chronically communicates that his or her reactions, feelings, thoughts, or responses are faulty, inaccurate, or otherwise invalid (Miller, 1999). Parasuicidality may serve to regulate affect, as well as to elicit help from an otherwise invalidating environment.

DBT with adolescents consists of 16 weeks of concurrent weekly, individual, and multifamily skills group sessions. A dialectical philosophy provides the theoretical foundation for DBT strategies (Linehan, 1993a). The core dialectic in DBT focuses on the balance between change and acceptance. The therapist must selectively balance problem-oriented change strategies—behavioral analyses, emotional exposure, cognitive restructuring, contingency management, irreverent communication, and consultation to the patient—with acceptance strategies—validation, reciprocal communication, and environmental interventions (Linehan, 1993a; Miller et al., in press).

The therapy specifies a hierarchy of treatment stages and targets. The pretreatment target (i.e., commitment) involves orienting the adolescent and the family to the treatment, establishing agreement on goals, and obtaining a commitment to working toward those goals. Treatment targets subsequently involve the patient's stability, safety, and connection to the therapist. Stage 1 targets include the following: (a) reduce life-threatening behaviors (e.g., suicidal, self-injurious, homicidal, and violent behaviors), (b) decrease therapy-interfering behaviors (e.g., missing sessions, coming late, not completing a diary card, and not collaborating in therapy), (c) decrease quality-of-life-interfering behaviors (e.g., substance abuse, depression, academic problems, and interpersonal problems at home and with peers), and (d) increase behavioral skills. About half of the teens in treatment in our program are on medication (i.e., generally antidepressants and occasionally mood stabilizers), and taking medication is a Stage 1 compliance issue. When Stage 1 goals are generally met, Stage 2 addresses the emotional consequences of past trauma. Stage 3 targets problems in living, such as increasing the adolescent's self-respect and working on other life goals. Finally, Stage 4 addresses one's sense of incompleteness with the goal of increasing one's capacity for joy.

The multimodal nature of the DBT model is necessary to manage myriad problems that swirl in the lives of suicidal teens. Effective treatment is comprehensive and focuses on addressing the highest-order priorities in a systematic manner. Treatment involves five functions that guide the structure of DBT by (1) enhancing the patient's and the family's capabilities, (2) improving motivation to change, (3) ensuring that new capabilities are generalized from the therapy to the patient's everyday life, (4) enhancing the therapist's capabilities and motivation to treat patients effectively, and (5) structuring the environment to support the patients' and the therapist's capabilities (Linehan, 1993a).

Functions 1 through 3 focus on the client; Functions 4 and 5 refer to the treatment team and the therapist. Each function is assigned to different modes of outpatient treatment, with the primary therapist ensuring that the system as a whole is providing each function. The adolescent patient and the family commit to learning new skills, which address parent–child dialectical dilemmas, in a psycho-educational multifamily skills-training group. These skills include emotion regulation, mindfulness, interpersonal effectiveness, distress tolerance, and walking the middle path (Function 1). The teen commits to working in individual therapy to learn new skills, to reduce factors that interfere with the ability to use skills, and to enhance motivation (Function 2) and to ensure that generalization occurs through the use of in vivo interventions, such as phone consultation, or through the use of in vivo therapy interactions when in crisis (Function 3). The therapist, in turn, agrees to provide 16 weeks of treatment, during which he or she participates in a weekly consultation meeting. This meeting provides both technical help and emotional support to the therapist, while helping him or her maintain motivation and while assisting him or her with performing DBT competently (Function 4). The therapist agrees to provide additional environmental interventions when needed, such as collateral family sessions or meetings with other treatment providers or school personnel, to ensure that the patient's condition does not have to get worse for him or her to get additional help (Function 5; Miller, 1999).

ORIENTATION AND COMMITMENT

Before adolescents begin DBT, therapists spend considerable energy trying to engage, orient, and obtain commitment to treatment. In a similar way, before DBT therapists begin their training and application of DBT, supervisors spend considerable time orienting new therapists to the theories on which DBT is predicated. During this phase, they help the therapist balance the potential advantages (e.g., learning an effective, empirically supported treatment and learning behavioral skills that are useful with other patients) and the potential disadvantages (e.g., DBT is time consuming, involving 24-hour crisis availability), before asking new therapists to commit to training. It is imperative that the DBT supervisor clarify the expectations of the new therapists, including attendance at training workshops, length of commitment to their patients and to the treatment team, attendance at supervision (which is usually 1 hour per week for individual supervision and 1.5 hours per week for the consultation group supervision), pager availability, and other agreements. A fully-informed commitment to learning the therapy and a full appreciation of the responsibilities, challenges, and potential rewards of conducting DBT must be made before training is initiated. Commitment is relatively easy to obtain from psychology trainees at our site, because they chose our site specifically for this training opportunity. However, there are trainees from other disciplines and from other sites for whom making a full commitment is more difficult. In this case, all parties acknowledge the degree of commitment obtained and agree to continue discussion with the hope of obtaining full commitment in due time. Just as therapists take a partial commitment from patients, supervisors take a partial commitment from trainees with the intent of broadening and strengthening these commitments over time. One psychodynamically oriented trainee stated the following:

> Initially, I was a complete skeptic. Everything related to behavior therapy seemed shallow and boring to me and somewhat disrespectful of the patient. The truth is, I did not have much knowledge of, or experience in, cognitive–behavior therapies. What I learned this training year was how wrong I was about behavior therapies—in particular, DBT. I learned this through didactics, supervision, consultation team meetings, and primarily through my patients. I tried to follow your advice, and I threw myself into the training experience. All the spoken and unspoken feedback from my patients let me know that this treatment works, and this is what ultimately strengthened my commitment.

THERAPIST SKILL ACQUISITION

DBT is a sophisticated treatment that blends cognitive–behavioral therapy, gestalt, systems, dialectics, and Zen theories. Reading the book and manual alone are insufficient to understanding, implementing, and using the treatment. Therapists initially learn some basic DBT concepts, such as behavioral analysis, learning theory, and cognitive restructuring, through formal didactic training. Graduate students may receive didactic training from their graduate schools or from their practicum sites. We offer an annual 8-week training course at our site that all trainees must attend. The weekly sessions are taught by senior, intensively trained DBT therapists who emphasize the theoretical foundations of DBT, along with the clinical applications.

At other institutions, 1- or 2-day trainings are common. New DBT therapists in nonacademic settings are often sent to receive their didactic trainings from national experts. Ideally, these trainees would attend the intensive 10-day training program or at least a 2-day training. DBT therapists-in-training also learn a considerable amount from the consultation team, where readings are assigned and the last portion of each meeting is devoted to didactic learning.

Learning the actual DBT skills (i.e., mindfulness, emotion regulation, interpersonal effectiveness, distress tolerance, and walking the middle path; Linehan, 1993b), often takes place in the consultation team meeting. New therapists are asked each week to practice a new set of DBT skills by applying them to their own lives. In addition to sharing their homework with the consultation team, each therapist is asked to practice coteaching the skills, as if they were teaching the multifamily skills-training group to teens and to parents. This role-playing and subsequent feedback are extremely useful. We recommend periodic quizzes in the consultation team to ensure that each therapist has overlearned these skills. When new therapists are paged in the middle of the night, they should not have difficulty recalling the specific skills for their suicidal patients. The final and the most effective way to ensure that the DBT skills are learned is to have each trainee colead the skills training group with a senior DBT therapist.

Fruzzetti, Waltz, and Linehan (1997) identified several other therapist skill domains necessary to effectively deliver DBT. First, *radical genuineness* is a form of validation described by Linehan (1993a) in which the therapist treats the patient as an equal in a real relationship. This is an important skill for DBT therapists to use with suicidal adolescents as compared to a more traditional therapeutic relationship that involves more distance, or a one-up stance often observed in a medical model. Radical genuineness may be used by a therapist to irreverently confront a patient by using a tone often spared for family members and close friends: "I think you are making a huge mistake by continuing to pursue that relationship, because every time you do, you resume your drug use and become suicidal." Genuineness also involves warmth and encouragement: "I am so proud of how you handled that situation with your mom. You did great!" Therapists who come from traditional therapy backgrounds often have difficulty shedding their role-bound behaviors. Thus, the supervisor and consultation group leader need to model radical genuineness in these supervisory contexts to enhance the therapist's skills.

Distress-tolerance skills are also critical for therapists working with suicidal multiproblem adolescents. In the face of life-threatening behavior and intense emotions, the therapist needs to learn how to tolerate the patient's distress and how to regulate his or her own emotions without distancing from or punishing patients (Fruzzetti et al., 1997). Like our patients, therapists are required to use mindfulness skills to notice their own distress, so they can use distress-tolerance skills themselves. Some patients are chronically suicidal, and therapists need to learn to tolerate the potential risk of suicide and to still effectively treat the patient, knowing when to accept and to validate the patient's experience and when to push for change.

Finally, as in all therapies, DBT therapists need to learn to nondefensively receive supervisory feedback (Fruzzetti et al., 1997). Because DBT is a complicated treatment to learn and deliver, and because progress is often fairly slow, DBT supervisors and consultation group members are often called on to evaluate progress and suggest alternative ways of intervening. Two important tenets of DBT to which therapists commit in the consultation group are (a) using a dialectical philosophy to treatment and (b) acknowledging that everyone is fallible. The dialectic philosophy reminds us that there may be truth from multiple perspectives. All therapists need to be open to alternative ways of looking at the adolescent, the family, the therapist, and the therapy. These agreements are important to invoke when therapists' emotions interfere with their ability to nondefensively receive feedback.

DIALECTICAL BEHAVIOR THERAPY CONSULTATION TEAM

Linehan (1993a) recognized the need to provide a supervisory forum for the DBT therapist both to promote adherence to the treatment model and to provide support for the frequently emotionally stressed therapist. In fact, DBT colleagues treat the therapist using DBT techniques in the weekly consultation team meeting. The consultation team meeting is comprised of the group and the individual therapists (i.e., as few as two to three therapists) and meets weekly for 60 to 120 minutes. In DBT, the aim is to "enhance client outcomes by anticipating and minimizing (or even preventing) therapist burnout" (Fruzzetti et al., 1997, p. 85). The consultation group is meant to augment therapists' training, effectiveness, and competence, while simultaneously increasing and maintaining their satisfaction and enjoyment in their work. The consultation team members make a number of agreements that are discussed within the team so that a genuine accord can be achieved that helps members adhere to the tenets of DBT and work more effectively with each other. The dialectical agreement and the fallibility agreement were described earlier. For a fuller discussion of the remaining agreements, see Linehan (1993a).

Agenda

The consultation team meeting always begins with a mindfulness exercise to help the members (a) become centered in the moment and (b) practice what they preach. The meeting is organized much like an individual therapy session and begins by setting an agenda (see also chap. 6, this volume). Different teams use variations of an agenda based on the individualized needs of a specific team. On our team, the agenda targets the issues occurring within the therapists' individual and group therapies in a hierarchical order generally prescribed by DBT, which include (a) parasuicidal behavior, (b) therapist burnout, (c) therapy-interfering behavior by both the patient and the therapist, (d) good news, (e) group updates, (f) administrative issues, and (g) didactic learning.

Any patients who have engaged in any parasuicidal behaviors during the past week are discussed first. Given the stress associated with treating parasuicidal youth, the group supervision format affords an opportunity to validate the individual therapist's efforts at coping with his or her patient's parasuicidal behavior. One natural consequence of this behavior on a therapist is the tendency to overreact or underreact by overly pushing the patient toward change or overly accepting the patient's behavior. The consultation team needs to help the therapist observe this behavior and to develop effective and balanced interventions consistent with a DBT framework.

The second agenda item is therapist burnout. Working with multiproblem, suicidal teenagers, who come from chaotic home lives and who frequently need a great deal of encouragement and support to attend sessions, can drain the therapist. The uncertainty of the patient's behaviors and the unpredictable nature of their lives can be difficult for the therapist to manage alone. The consultation group provides a safe, supportive place for the therapist to discuss his or her feelings about the patient and the treatment. At times, the group may have to help the therapist recharge by offering to do pager coverage for a few days or by helping the therapist more clearly identify his or her own personal limits. Targeting therapist burnout is extremely important to ensure the integrity of the therapy. It is imperative to address therapists' burnout before they engage in countertherapeutic behavior (e.g., short sessions, reduced empathy, and an aggressive push to change) or before they suffer effects in their own general functioning (e.g., impaired sleep and appetite, apathy, and hyperarousal). Burnout must be assessed and addressed by the team to avoid patient or therapist dropout or even worse consequences.

The third item on the agenda addresses both patient noncompliance and therapist disengagement. By addressing negative therapist behaviors (e.g., changing appointments, shortening sessions, and repeatedly answering the phone during sessions), the consultation team recognizes that not only patients but also therapists are potentially responsible for interfering in the treatment.

The fourth agenda item is the reporting of good news about a patient or about a member of the consultation team. Good news is anything that relates to the goals of the patient, such as maintaining abstinence from self-harm or drugs and alcohol for a period of time or when in a stressful situation.

Good news may relate to the therapist's goals too, such as recognizing and enforcing personal limits with a demanding patient. It is imperative for the consultation team to take stock of the good news because so much of the group is focused on problems and challenges.

The fifth item on the agenda entails a report from the leaders of both the multifamily skills training group and the graduate group. The group leaders use this time to inform the individual therapists of what skills are being taught to their patients, so specific homework and skills can be reinforced in the individual sessions. It is also an opportunity for the skills trainers to receive support and feedback from the consultation team about managing challenging group members, including teens and parents.

The sixth agenda item involves administrative issues, such as which teens are joining the multifamily group, who is eligible to join the graduate group, or who is ready for discharge. The group typically reserves the last 30 minutes of the session for teaching new material or for watching videotapes of individual or group sessions to enhance therapist's capabilities.

Not surprisingly, disagreements arise on the consultation team. Members learn that it is their own responsibility to skillfully address dissension and to maintain a willingness to address difficult topics openly while supporting one another. In the name of a dialectical worldview in which alternative views are expected, therapists try to appreciate each other's opinions with the ultimate goal of finding a synthesis. For example, one therapist of a 16-year-old female patient expressed concern about the patient's apparent inability to reduce her self-cutting after 15 weeks of treatment. The therapist's opinion, partially informed by a behavioral analysis with the patient, was that the cutting served to justify contact with the therapist between sessions. The therapist wondered whether she needed to increase the frequency of visits to help reduce the self-harm. Another therapist suggested,

> Your patient is supposed to graduate from DBT skills-training, group and individual therapy and to join the graduate group within the next couple of weeks. Is it possible that while she is very connected to you and is afraid to lose you, she also has nothing else going on in her life . . . sadly, her life is DBT. She's been hospitalized three times in the past year, she's gone through outpatient DBT twice, and she's not making progress. Her friends are all in DBT. So, I think she needs to get out of DBT in order to create a life.

The team leader spoke up and raised a potential synthesis to this dilemma:

> Both points are valid. I might suggest telling the patient that she does need to create a life outside of DBT. And, the way to do so is with your help. You might propose to her that if she goes on to the DBT graduate group, she may remain in weekly individual therapy as well,

but under one condition—that she agrees to build a nonDBT life by first stopping her self-harm. You may say to her: "You can't have a nonDBT life if you are cutting yourself every day. So, what might that entail? I would imagine it would entail part-time work, developing friends outside of DBT groups, and so forth." And, I would tell her that if the cutting persisted at the same rate, she may need a higher level of care that would result in losing her primary therapist.

The therapists found the proposed dialectical synthesis helpful, and the group proceeded with the next item on the agenda.

INDIVIDUAL THERAPY CONSULTATION SUPERVISION

In addition to consultation team supervision, all DBT therapists are expected to receive additional individual-therapy supervision and skills-training group supervision. In our program, we pair trainees for weekly, 60- to 90-minute dyadic supervision conducted by an intensively trained DBT therapist. Dyadic supervision allows trainees to learn from each other's cases. The trainee carries one or two DBT patients at a time. Each trainee is expected to videotape or at least to audiotape every session after obtaining signed consent from the adolescent and the parents. Taping sessions allows the supervisor to hear the session as it actually happened, including process and style, such as pauses, tone of voice, and technique. The supervisor typically listens to the beginning of the sessions to ensure that the therapist is properly setting the agenda and addressing the higher target behaviors first. Later in supervision, the trainee often requires help conducting a behavioral analysis of parasuicidal behavior. Tape is invaluable to the supervisor in highlighting what the therapist could have done differently to achieve the goal at hand.

Paralleling an individual therapy session, the DBT supervisor uses a range of DBT strategies with the therapist to help him or her conduct DBT more effectively. The supervisor often uses validation and problem-solving strategies, reciprocal and irreverent communication strategies, case-management strategies, and even dialectical strategies to better help the trainee provide DBT effectively (see Linehan, 1993a). Supervision-interfering behaviors are addressed like therapy-interfering behaviors are addressed in individual therapy—with the use of a behavioral analysis. If the individual therapist regularly forgets to audiotape sessions, behavioral analysis is conducted, commitment is obtained, and solutions are identified. The supervisor and the trainee, like the individual therapist and the patient, must troubleshoot the solutions in an effort to anticipate further obstacles. This is done in a collaborative, noncondescending style that often yields promising results while modeling the treatment for the therapist. Hence, learning is occurring at multiple levels.

TELEPHONE CONSULTATION SUPERVISION

In DBT, patients have access to coaching from their individual therapists around the clock. In a similar way, trainees have access to their supervisors at any time. Patients are encouraged to call their individual therapists to (a) obtain skills coaching before they engage in parasuicidal behavior or other target behaviors, such as drug use or fighting; (b) report good news (e.g., "I was stressed out but listened to music rather than cut myself, like I normally do"); and (c) repair the relationship between the patient and the therapist (e.g., "I was so pissed off by what you said to me that I'm thinking of quitting therapy"). It is mandatory that DBT trainees, who are also unlicensed mental health professionals, call their supervisors after they respond to a page for skills coaching, regardless of the time of day, to report the call, to obtain feedback, and to receive potential coaching of their own.

The following is an anecdote from the second author (Hartstein).

> During my graduate training, I had two very difficult patients, both of whom used the pager for coaching. This meant that I received a great deal of supervision from Alec Miller, as he was my individual supervisor. I still recall the first time I got paged by my patient at 1 o'clock in the morning. My heart began to pound, and my stomach was doing back flips. I had just started doing this treatment. I thought, "I'm not ready to coach someone on how not to harm herself." I returned the phone call and spoke with my patient about what was happening that was causing her distress. We explored options about skills she could use, and she committed to trying them. It was reassuring to know that Alec was there each time to support me. I did not have to feel as though I was handling this difficult patient by myself. Because of my intervention, my patient was able to avoid going to the hospital and was able to stay at home, where we both wanted her to remain as long as it was safe. I imagine that many patients feel the way I did when I called Alec. The belief that you cannot manage the problem on your own decreases when you know that there is someone there to back you up. That safety net helped me to stay sufficiently focused and motivated to continue to help my patient.

Telephone Coaching Call Between Individual Therapist (IT) and Supervisor (S)

The following is an excerpt from a telephone coaching contact occurring at 1:00 a.m.

IT: Jill just paged me for coaching. She got into a big fight with her mother and reported having suicidal thoughts and intense urges to cut. I coached her to use her distress-tolerance skills. She identified listening to music and watching a funny movie as skills she could use to distract herself and to get her through the night. Wow, that was hard identifying which skills she should use when she was so dysregulated, and I guess I was too!

S: Yeah, it's hard doing middle of the night coaching, especially with new patients who do not know the skills well and who are quite dysregulated. How are you doing?

IT: I'm okay. A little anxious, but I mindfully took some deep breaths before I called her, so I would be more present with her.

S: So you used some of your own mindfulness skills. Good thinking. And, I am glad you helped Jill generate some distract skills. How did she respond?

IT: She had a really difficult time coming up with ideas, because she was so dysregulated. She believed that her mother was going to kick her out of the house because of an argument. We had to do some mindful breathing for me to understand her.

S: Okay. You indicated that she was feeling suicidal. Did you assess for a plan and intent? She also has a history of suicide attempts, right?

IT: I did assess for a plan. She said she did not want to kill herself, but she expressed urges to cut herself. She identified her sister as the reason she wants to live. Oh, her sister and her boyfriend, of course.

S: When she said she wanted to cut, what was she going to cut with? Did you ask her to remove the implements? Or did you speak with her mom? I know you obtained a great commitment from Jill, but we want her to remove the items she might use to cut with as well.

IT: No, I didn't think to ask her to get rid of the razor blade.

S: Why don't you give her a call back. Begin with something like, "I was thinking about our conversation, and I realized that I didn't ask you about the razor blade, because I know that is usually what you use to cut with," and go from there. Get a commitment from her to throw the razor blade away down the trash chute or to give it to her mother. What do you think?

IT: Yeah, I agree. I'll call her now to tell her that, and I'll call you back only if she refuses or if another problem arises.

S: Sounds good. Have a good night.

DBT therapists in training must call their supervisors for coaching after they provide telephone coaching to their patients. The supervisory relationship, even on the telephone in the middle of the night, typically parallels the DBT psychotherapy model by validating, by reinforcing, and, at times, by encouraging the therapist to use some skills.

SKILLS GROUP SUPERVISION

It is important that the skills trainers receive supervision from the senior DBT therapist on site. In our setting, the skills trainers videotape their groups and they receive feedback regarding content and style from the senior DBT therapist on site.

Adherence to and Competence in Dialectical Behavior Therapy

As Fruzzetti et al. (1997) pointed out, "the primary target of training, supervision, and consultation in DBT is the competent delivery of DBT" (p. 96). This requires that the therapy closely adhere to the treatment manuals as developed by Linehan (1993a, 1993b) and Miller, Rathus, and Linehan (in press). To meet this target, therapists need to do considerable work. This includes reading the manuals, attending didactic trainings, and regularly attending the individual supervision and the therapist consultation meeting. Equally important is the need for the therapist to strengthen one's own mindfulness, distress tolerance, and nondefensiveness to supervision. Therapists working with suicidal multi-problem adolescents are inevitably prone to emotional dysregulation and to subsequent deviations from this specific treatment approach. Being well versed in DBT and open to supervisory feedback reduces the likelihood of straying, and, if and when it does occur, ensures that drift is easily rectified.

In most nonbehavioral treatment approaches, adherence is rated subjectively by supervisors. In DBT, Linehan has developed a DBT Expert Rating Scale to quantify therapist adherence and competence. Supervisors reliably trained in the scoring of this instrument are able to provide invaluable feedback to ensure therapists are adhering to DBT and are doing so in a competent manner. Therapists who score low on the adherence ratings may find that they are not properly targeting the dysfunctional behaviors, that they are not using dialectical strategies, or that they are not sufficiently validating the patient's valid behaviors. All of these therapy strategies are clearly delineated on the rating form.

CONCLUSION

Working with suicidal multiproblem adolescents induces intense emotions that may cause therapists to deviate from the DBT therapy model. DBT therapists are responsible to acquire numerous new technical skills to be used with their patients, as well as skills to manage their own emotional reactions to their patients' suicidality and emotional dysregulation. As therapists learn DBT more comprehensively and become more spontaneous and fluid, they are better able to integrate and synthesize their own behaviors with those of their patients. Because DBT supervision is part and parcel of the comprehensive treatment approach, it is imperative to integrate interactions that occur in the supervision and the consultation group into a coherent analysis of the entire therapy process (Fruzzetti et al., 1997). Finally, although we acknowledge the challenges of working with suicidal multiproblem adolescents, we also want to highlight the personal and professional rewards of applying the comprehensive DBT model to this patient population. Supervision within the DBT model and with this challenging patient population is a necessity. Working in isolation without supervision would likely result in burnout and potential clinical tragedies, which, we are happy to say, have not happened to us yet.

REFERENCES

Birmaher, B., Ryan, N. D., Williamson, D. E., Brent, D. A., & Kaufman, J. (1996). Childhood and adolescent depression: A review of the past 10 years: Part II. *Journal of American Academy of Child and Adolescent Psychiatry, 35*, 1574–1583.

Fruzzetti, A. E., Waltz, J. A., & Linehan, M. M. (1997). Supervision in DBT. In C. E. Watkins (Ed.), *Handbook of psychotherapy supervision* (pp. 84–100). New York: Guilford Press.

Grunbaum, J. A., Kann, L., Kinchen, S. A., Williams, B., Rosss, J. G., Lowry, R., & Kolbe, L. (2002). Youth risk behavior surveillance—United States, 2001. *MMWR CDC Surveillance Summary, 51*(SS4), 1–64.

Kazdin, A. E., & Weisz, J. R. (2003). *Evidence-based psychotherapies for children and adolescents.* New York: Guildford Press.

Linehan, M. M. (1993a). *Cognitive–behavioral treatment for borderline personality disorder.* New York: Guilford Press.

Linehan, M. M. (1993b). *Skills training manual for treating borderline personality disorder.* New York: Guilford Press.

Miller, A. L. (1999). DBT–A: A new treatment for parasuicidal adolescents. *American Journal of Psychotherapy, 53*, 413–417.

Miller, A. L., & Glinski, J. (2000). Youth suicidal behavior: Assessment and intervention [Special issue]. In P. Kleespies (Ed.), *Empirical approaches to behavioral emergencies. Journal of Clinical Psychology, 56*, 1–22.

Miller, A. L., & Rathus, J. H. (2000). Dialectical behavior therapy: Adaptations and new applications. *Cognitive and Behavioral Practice, 7*, 420–425.

Miller, A. L., Rathus, J. H., & Linehan, M. M. (in press). *Dialectical behavior therapy for suicidal adolescents*. New York: Guilford Press.

Miller, A. L., Rathus, J. H., Linehan, M. M., Wetzler, S., & Leigh, E. (1997). Dialectical behavior therapy adapted for suicidal adolescents. *Journal of Practical Psychiatry and Behavioral Health, 3*, 78–86.

Muehlenkamp, J. J., & Gutierrez, P. M. (2004). An investigation of differences between self-injurious behavior and suicide attempts in a sample of adolescents. *Suicide and Life-Threatening Behavior, 34*, 12–23.

Rathus, J. H., & Miller, A. L. (2002). Dialectical behavior therapy adapted for suicidal adolescents. *Suicide and Life-Threatening Behavior, 32*, 146–157.

11

SUPERVISING THERAPISTS WORKING WITH TRAUMATIZED CHILDREN

KATHLEEN M. CHARD AND JOSEPH E. HANSEL

When trauma confronts a child, the nature of the trauma, the vulnerability and the development of the child, and the response of the caretakers can all shape the impact of the trauma on the child. Research suggests that nearly 25% of children experience a significant trauma by age 16 (Costello, Erkanli, Fairbank, & Angold, 2002). The literature consistently documents their increased risk for a range of psychopathology and impairments including posttraumatic stress disorder (PTSD; Cicchetti & Toth, 1995). Abused children and children exposed to domestic violence are at greater risk of exposing the next generation to violence than those who are not abused or exposed to violence (Ehrensaft et al., 2003). An individual who chooses to help traumatized children requires comprehensive supervision from a qualified supervisor—one who understands trauma, child development, and the interaction of the two; one who fosters an open and productive supervisory relationship; and one who understands the exacting challenge that trauma work presents to any therapist, especially a new therapist working with children.

THE SUPERVISORY RELATIONSHIP

Because trauma work can evoke strong reactions, the supervisor must have a strong, open alliance with the therapist. From the beginning, supervisors must establish the importance of honest communication (Izzard, 2001). Bernard and Goodyear (2004) emphasized that both parties share responsibility for achieving open, direct, and unambiguous communication. Emotions aroused in work with children can be magnified when children have experienced trauma as the result of neglect, abuse, violence, or sadism. Confusion or reactions at odds with the therapists' self-image may lead them to avoid discussing their feelings (Carroll, 1996). These feelings of avoidance often translate into behaviors with supervisees choosing to withhold critical information from supervisors (Nelson & Friedlander, 2001). In what Bernard and Goodyear have called one of the most important studies in the supervision literature, Ladany, Hill, Corbett, and Nutt (1996) reported that supervisee's fail to disclose important material in supervision at a very high rate. Among reasons they give for such failure are that the material is too personal or that the supervisory alliance is poor. Supervisees who feel stressed in supervision, who are unsupported, or who are in struggles with angry supervisors, as described in a study of negative supervision by Nelson and Friedlander (2001), are at a significant disadvantage in working with trauma victims.

Therapists must be able to take their turmoil to a safe place. Creating a safe relationship is the first step in understanding how a supervisee is performing with his or her trauma client. Wells, Trad, and Alves (2003) suggested a relational approach to training supervisors of new trauma therapists. Their approach is not notably different from developmental approaches taken by other writers, such as Friedman and Kaslow (1986) or Stoltenberg, McNeill, and Delworth (1998), although it gives greater attention to issues of self-care. This can build trust in the relationship and acknowledges that the therapist who works with traumatized clients will probably have wrenching concerns to bring into supervision.

Supervisee Development

Skill Development

Therapists develop clinical skills over time. Most novice therapists begin with a bare handful of clinical tools. In their role as teacher (Williams, 1995), supervisors have available a number of manualized treatments for abuse survivors that provide a structured environment for less experienced therapists (e.g., Chard, Weaver, & Resick, 1997; Deblinger, Stauffer, & Steer, 2001). Focused protocols allow the therapist to put more energy into developing the requisite skills for working with clients and to worry less about session content. The manuals include helpful interventions and appropriate homework assignments.

The supervisor overseeing trauma work with children teaches skills that may differ considerably from those required for trauma work with adults. For example, child trauma therapists often use play or art therapy, whereas adult therapists typically rely on verbal expression. Supervisors must be well acquainted with techniques of diagnosis and treatment specific to children to identify and to work with early childhood traumatic experiences (Munson, 2001).

Personal Development

Possessing the requisite intervention skills is but the first step in being able to provide services to trauma survivors. As Wells et al. (2003) emphasized, a capacity for self-care is also critical. Stoltenberg et al. (1998) cited high levels of anxiety, strong need for structure, limited self-awareness, and evaluation apprehension among characteristics of therapists in training. Novice therapists, struggling with their lack of knowledge and their limited sense of being in control and struggling with the emotional affects of working with traumatized individuals, can experience feelings of self-doubt, of incompetence, or of being an imposter in the field of therapy.

Etherington (2000) warned that, "Abuse survivors' experiences of betrayal by the primary caregivers, broken trust, misuse of power, and boundary violations" can create anxious and demanding situations for counselors (p. 377). Etherington alerted supervisors of the following possible situations:

> Under the sway of countertransference a counsellor may report a sense of helplessness, hopelessness, incompetence, and may lose confidence in the power of the relationship. Without this confidence, counsellors might become de-skilled—having a sense that they cannot make up to the client for what they have suffered. Rapid fluctuations in the client's cognitive state may leave counsellors with a sense of confusion and unreality. (p. 378)

Knowing the technique and being able to deliver the technique effectively under stress are very different beasts. Novice therapists can be shaken and can be unsure of how to help the child sitting across the room.

> In supervision with counselors working with the trauma of child sexual abuse we need to . . . ensure a balanced case-load, not too heavily biased with abuse survivors. We need to help counselors explore strategies that they can use to protect themselves when clients need to share graphic details of their abuse. (Etherington, 2000, p. 388)

Trauma work requires supervisor availability and strong support. A supervisor, who is in touch with his or her own struggles as a new therapist and who can share them, may buffer a trainee against discouragement (Izzard, 2001).

ISSUES OF SPECIAL RELEVANCE IN THE TREATMENT OF TRAUMATIZED CHILDREN

Therapeutic Boundaries

It has long been understood that therapists must establish clear guidelines with their clients. Clear, unambiguous boundaries help all parties involved develop accurate expectations for the relationship and provides a margin of safety. The guidance in chapter 10 of this volume for educating suicidal and self-injuring adolescents about expectancies in therapy is equally relevant to work with traumatized teens. Abused children or teens may become aggressive or subtly seductive to determine if they are truly safe with their therapists. In this process, clients may encourage therapists to cross physical or sexual boundaries. Touching a seductive child in an effort to comfort can be easily misread. Abused children may also exploit their victim status to gain sympathy, to gain caring of which they otherwise feel unworthy, or to intensify relationships. They may exaggerate past trauma or lie about new abuse for the same purpose or to create drama and put their therapist in a rescue mode. Even more alarming, they may make false allegations about the therapist to control the therapy relationship or to punish the therapist, who in the child's mind may serve as a surrogate for an abusive parent. Such potential to create havoc clearly requires supervisory vigilance. Crises in the therapy relationship can also intensify or create crises in the supervisory relationship. Supervisors must be aware of and help maintain two sets of boundaries; the first between supervisee and client and the second between supervisee and supervisor (Falender & Shafranske, 2004).

Harper and Steadman (2003) sought to clarify the process of setting and maintaining appropriate boundaries with trauma survivors and to understand why boundary violations occur. They defined boundaries, boundary crossings, boundary violations, and boundary shifts. Their distinctions are helpful, because they allow for a more flexible and human response to the needs of our clients. Observation of boundaries means one's practices respect the individuality of both the therapist and the client and help to create the required safety needed for trauma work. Boundaries are often culturally determined. Direct eye contact with a client might be appropriate in one cultural context but might not be appropriate in another. Boundaries protect both client and therapist from unwanted outcomes. Boundary crossings are instances when a breach has significant potential to cause client harm whether or not harm results. Boundary violations occur when a breach is a reflection of the therapist's agenda and the results are deemed harmful to the client (e.g., a therapist breaks confidentiality in the course of gaining support from a colleague during difficult trauma work). A boundary shift is often a temporary change in the therapeutic relationship (e.g., a therapist becoming more directive during a client's suicidal episode) that is less harmful.

On the basis of two studies, Harper and Steadman (2003) identified themes that can lead therapists to cross boundaries. Some of their findings suggest the supervisory relationship can play a role in boundary violations. Boundary violations may be triggered by being anxious about a client's safety, resenting the supervisor, worrying about the supervisor's feelings, wanting to connect with the supervisor, attempting to balance power with the supervisor, and giving the survivor hope. In addition, supervisors can violate the boundary between themselves and their supervisee by engaging in a more therapeutic relationship or allowing the support required in trauma work to evolve into more of a personal relationship than had been agreed on when the relationship was established (Falender & Shafranske, 2004).

Confidentiality With Children

Isaacs (1999) emphasized that ethical codes support the need for confidentiality and described the benefits of confidentiality to the therapeutic process. However, confidentiality is complicated with children (see chap. 3, this volume). Ethical codes, laws, and school codes can be in conflict, and many practitioners report ambivalence about following them. Isaacs cited a study by Davis and Mickelson (1994) where over 600 school counselors reached only 50% agreement on protecting confidentiality in responding to tested scenarios. They were most likely to break confidentiality in the case of (in descending order) "impending suicide or suicide pact, retaliation for victimization, use of crack cocaine, sexual intercourse with multiple partners when HIV positive, armed robbery, indications of depression, abortion, and marijuana use" (Isaacs, 1999, p. 262). As discussed in chapter 3 of this volume on ethics, some of these situations call for breech of confidentiality, while others are questionable.

Therapists working with traumatized children should not be surprised to find themselves in quandaries regarding confidentiality. If the alleged abuse has not been reported to authorities, it is the therapist's legal and ethical responsibility to report it. Supervisors can role-play with the supervisee how to contact the authorities and how to address the issues with both the child and the caregiver. If the case goes to court, the therapist may be asked to testify. Keeping good records and being sure not to ask leading questions during therapy protects the quality of the therapist's testimony. A supervisor should review the supervisee's notes, and he or she may want to watch videotape of critical sessions. In addition, supervisors should document for their own records when and how certain supervisee behaviors were discussed (e.g., assessment of trauma history, assessment of risk, and risk management planning; Falender & Shafranske, 2004; Falvey, 2002). The potential for the emergence of trauma issues highlights the importance of clarifying the limits of confidentiality when therapy begins.

Compassion Fatigue and Secondary Traumatic Stress

Supervisors working with trauma therapists must be alert to the negative affect of the trauma work on the therapists. This is often referred to as *secondary traumatic stress* (STS) or *compassion fatigue* (CF). Some authors suggest these are the same phenomena (e.g., Stamm, 1999), although others make a distinction between the two. Secondary traumatic stress, also known as *vicarious traumatization*, occurs when therapists are exposed to the traumatic accounts of their clients, resulting in transmission of traumatic stress from the clients to the therapists (Figley & Kleber, 1995; McCann & Pearlman, 1990). Compassion fatigue refers to the cumulative combination of STS and burnout (Figley, 1995). By whatever name, symptoms associated with STS and CF have been found to lower the quantity and the quality of the therapist's interactions with clients.

Supervisors can reduce the risk of STS and CF in their supervisee by normalizing the symptoms of STS and CF as expectable reactions to trauma work. Supervisors must also be sensitive to personal factors, especially a therapist's trauma history that may increase vulnerability to STS and CF. Supervisors can teach strategies for dealing with stress or can encourage their supervisees to attend continuing education trainings related to trauma work at state or national conferences or to attend those sponsored by the American Red Cross. Supervisors can create a supportive environment that preferably includes a group supervision component. Group supervision offers peer support, enables normalizing of emotional reactions to clients, provides opportunities for vicarious learning, and is a source of alternative ideas for dealing with different client situations (Bernard & Goodyear, 2004; Carroll, 1996). Finally, the supervisor can recommend that agencies limit therapists' hours on call or in emergency service work, and can suggest that employees make use of their vacation days and their sick leave when feeling stressed (Meyers & Cornille, 2002). A supervisor concerned that a therapist is having serious difficulty with STS or CF may wish to use an instrument, such as the Florida Secondary Traumatic Stress Scale or the Compassion Fatigue Test—Revised (Stamm, 2002). Overwhelmed therapists can be referred to programs specifically designed to facilitate recovery from STS or CF, such as the Accelerated Program for Compassion Fatigue (Gentry & Baranowsky, 1999).

SUPERVISION AND TREATMENT MODALITIES

When training new therapists supervisors need to attend to the different types of treatments available for working with traumatized children. Group and individual treatment programs can require very different skills and thus different supervision. In addition, with the advent of efficacy-based treatment protocols that have been shown to be effective with children, supervisors are under more pressure to be aware of the various interventions that supervisees may want to effectively learn.

Group Versus Individual Treatment

For many years, therapists have been aware of the benefits of group therapy for normalizing and universalizing the experiences of the client (Yalom, 1995). Traumatized children and teens benefit as well (Cohen, Berliner, & March, 2000). Although therapists should be cautious about doing all the trauma work in groups, as groups can expose members to vicarious trauma, group treatment can be a powerful addition to trauma-based individual treatment (Stamm, 1999). At the same time, supervisees may not understand that individual treatment and group treatment require different approaches. Supervisors who lack this understanding may ineffectively approach group supervision. They may spend little energy on a supervisee's group duties and may focus on the supervisee's individual caseload. A tendency to focus on individual cases, and slight other activities of the supervisee, is also noted in school supervision (see chap. 12, this volume).

Neglect of a supervisee's group work is untenable. Schamess, Streider, and Connors (1997) found that "unsupervised groups are more problematic and fail more than supervised groups" (p. 42). These authors described some of the unique issues of working with traumatized children in groups and stress the need for modality-specific supervision. They argued that skill in supervising a therapist working with individuals does not extend to good supervision of group therapy. Tactics that the individual therapist uses do not readily transfer to group interventions. When faced with a room full of reactive youths, many individual therapists turned group therapists fall back on the familiar and safe. The authors pointed out that much of children's group therapy has become psychoeducational rather than become psychotherapeutic. They wrote, "The marked preference for psychoeducation not only suggest a lack of understanding about psychotherapeutic groups, but also signals significant professional discomfort with the transference enactments and intense affect that characterize therapeutic groups . . ." (p. 411). Therapist's intense emotional reactions to trauma work, described earlier, can be particularly disruptive for group leaders. This fear that adults have when working with traumatized children is captured in the following whimsical observation.

> Generally speaking, adult anxiety is expressed through a need to micromanage children's activities in schools, recreational centers, and community settings. At its source, this anxiety seems to be generated by the unconscious fantasy that children will regress to the kinds of primitive feeling states and id-driven behaviors described by William Golding (1959) in his novel, *Lord of the Flies*. (Schamess, Streider, & Connors, 1997, p. 415)

Making supervisees aware of these potential interfering reactions and helping them avoid them is a crucial task for supervisors. Supervisees who are overly apprehensive about group reactions can be reminded that, "Traumatized children regularly participate in groups at home, school, and play . . . And, although they may not flourish in group interactions, their carefully constructed (albeit maladaptive) defenses almost always prevent decompensation" (Schamess et al., 1997, p. 406). Although the eventual goal of therapy may be to change maladaptive defenses, those defenses paradoxically provide a buffer against the emotions of group interaction. Supervisors, who can reassure supervisees that their youthful clients are not the hot-house flowers they assume them to be, can allay the supervisees' anxieties related to groups.

Empirically Supported Treatments

The push in mental health to demonstrate effective treatments and to provide accountability puts pressure on supervisors and therapists to master empirically supported treatments (ESTs), especially when hoping to obtain funding from insurance companies. Edgeworth and Clark (2000) reviewed a number of controlled treatment studies for abused children. Formats included various family therapies, concurrent therapies for parents and children, and separate group and individual therapies for children; the latter format is more common for sexually abused children. Most treatments had positive effects. The authors concluded that the types of changes were related to the study design and that combining intervention strategies probably had a synergistic effect. Edgeworth and Clark also listed a number of manuals and measures used in abuse treatment. A recent review of cognitive–behavioral therapy (CBT) approaches for youth with PTSD (Feeney, Foa, Treadwell, & March, 2004) found growing evidence for the effectiveness of CBT approaches. Feeney et al. (2004) warned that many youth may present with more complex symptoms than PTSD, especially sexually abused children, and that programs designed for single-incident trauma may not be effective for more sustained trauma. They also noted the likely importance of family intervention in addressing certain types of trauma, such a sexual abuse.

Supervisors need to take care in adopting new, empirically supported treatments. Henggeler, Schoenwald, Liao, Letourneau, and Edwards (2002) questioned how effectively treatments may be transferred from the settings where they originate to clinical practice (see also chaps. 7 and 9, this volume). Henggeler et al. (2002) noted the intense attention to treatment fidelity and the use of manuals and clinical supervision in university research settings, while "skill development in community settings often follows the 'train and hope' approach (e.g., 1- to 2-day workshops with minimal follow-through) and clinical supervision typically focuses on administrative requirements and providing practitioners with social support" (p. 155).

Henggeler et al. (2002) also reported that some supervisory behaviors, such as focusing on mechanics or on building therapist competence, were negatively related to some desired outcomes. The supervisor's level of expertise in the therapy being used was positively related to the therapeutic relationship. The authors noted that evidence that the therapy was not going well could evoke more supervisory emphasis on mechanics and on building therapist competence, but the data does not provide a real explanation for their paradoxical findings. It is clear that supervisors must not only know what treatments are probably effective, but must also collaborate with the supervisee to evaluate whether a given treatment is working with a particular client.

SPECIAL SUPERVISION ISSUES IN WORKING WITH TRAUMA

Although direct care of the child is the most important issue that must be attended to when working with traumatized children, there are other issues that can affect the work that the therapist does with the child. For example, the way the trauma is manifested, suicidal intent, high risk behaviors, and policy implications can all impact therapeutic change.

Trauma Manifests Itself in Many Forms

Different types of child abuse can elicit different psychological reactions, thus supervisors should be aware of the range of client responses to abuse. Although the most common psychiatric disorder associated with child abuse is posttraumatic stress disorder, the comorbidity with other disorders is very high, especially with depressive, anxiety, and adjustment disorders.

There is also significant evidence to support the appearance of dissociative and bipolar disorders in children who have been abused (Kendall-Tackett, Williams, & Finkelhor, 1993; Munson, 2001).

Issues of Youth Suicide

The specter of child suicide hangs over the heads of therapists working with traumatized children. One of the most unnerving situations for a therapist is when a client considers or engages in suicidal–parasuicidal behaviors. Because the frequency of such behaviors is high among individuals who are trauma survivors, therapists working with this population should be prepared to handle suicide risks, threats, and attempts. Chapter 10 of this volume is devoted to the issue of suicidal and parasuicidal behavior in teens.

A child's serious, self-inflicted injury or actual suicide can be devastating for a therapist. King (2003) discussed how supervisors and agencies can address instances of child suicide. King cited Horwath's (1995) lessons learned from her interviews of care providers who worked with children who were killed during abuse or who committed suicide. Horwath observed that all staff are affected and that the subject can become taboo. Staff can be better prepared for such tragedies. Debriefing should be offered and training should involve a discussion of the emotions involved with such incidents. There is recognition that providers at centers where suicidal children are seen should be trained to manage incidents of child suicide. Supervisors are often the intermediary between the agency policy–training and the therapist. They may encourage preventive training to foster professional resilience and to avoid a negative chain of events in a crisis (Rutter, 1987). Supportive supervision can help prevent therapist outcomes such as a loss of skill or the departure of an otherwise effective therapist from the profession.

Risky Interventions

Therapists are often called on to intervene in school settings after a trauma. These therapists and others who undertake trauma work have come together to form an association and to develop trauma intervention guidelines (see *Practice Guidelines for the International Society for Traumatic Stress Studies*; Foa, Keane, & Friedman, 2000). One activity that bears scrutiny is peer-counseling groups at schools. Lewis and Lewis (1996) examined the structure, the supervision, and the effectiveness of peer programs in the schools to prevent suicide. They found that many schools (31%) have peer-helping programs that are not supervised by a professional counselor. The "no-counselor, supervisor groups" had the highest rates of suicide (i.e., at least one suicide at the school), followed by the "no program schools," and then finally followed by the "counselor supervised programs." Such findings highlight the risk of well intentioned, but poorly supervised, trauma interventions. Even more frightening, Lewis and Lewis suggested that some programs might disinhibit rather than prevent suicide and noted that two students committed suicide while serving as peer helpers. These findings suggest great caution should accompany the use of peer counseling.

Issues in Crisis Counseling

Another area that warrants discussion is crisis, or critical incident, counseling. Not every child needing trauma therapy will be an established client. Often, therapists will be one of the first professionals to work with children who survive terrible events, such as natural disasters, accidents, parental violence or suicide, school violence or, more recently, exposure to terrorism. Yule (2001) discussed the need to have effective individuals working with children who recently survived disasters or survived accidents where their lives were threatened. He also expressed concern that poor intervention can slow recovery or can make a trauma situation worse. Lorvin (1999) described considerations when working with children who have recently experienced parental suicide. He suggested helping the child regain a sense of safety, helping the child re-establish a sense of trust and self-esteem, and later helping the child overcome hopelessness and restore strengths. More recently, systemized treatments have been developed to address trauma in the schools (Stein et al., 2003) and organizations, such as the Center for Safe Schools (http://www.center-school.org/), have been created to offer technical assistance and Web links to resources for addressing a wide range of crises in the schools.

Issues of Agency Policy

Agency policies shape how clinicians approach trauma and how they are prepared for work with trauma survivors. A recent survey (Hanson, Hesselbrock, Tworkowski, & Swan, 2002) explored a number of agencies' policies concerning trauma work and found that agencies rarely screen clients for trauma histories. Only one agency had a written trauma policy. The majority of agencies did not offer trauma-specific treatments nor refer outside the agency for such services. Only 10% of the agencies reported routine trauma-related supervision or case conferences. Fifty-eight percent of the clinicians surveyed indicated they had received no trauma-related supervision and 61% of them had no continuing education in trauma work. Although this data is representative of a limited number of agencies, the findings suggest that supervisors may need to be proactive in forging agency policy that can support trauma work. Given the percentage of children who experience trauma, trauma work can be expected in any child-serving practice. Supervisors can help to craft a policy that mandates group and individual supervision time for all therapists working with trauma clients. For example, recognizing the need for support, Linehan (1993) required a consultation group for all therapists conducting dialectical behavioral therapy with self-harming clients.

CONCLUSION

As the mental health field has become more aware of the impact of abuse on clients, it has also acknowledged the need for more advanced supervision for therapists working with these clients. Because no training program can provide specialized training for the many types of clients that a therapist may see, it falls on the shoulders of the supervisors to ensure that supervisees behave ethically and effectively, while also attending to their own self-care.

REFERENCES

Bernard, J. M., & Goodyear, R. K. (2004). *Fundamentals of clinical supervision* (3rd ed.). Boston: Allyn & Bacon.

Carroll, M. (1996). *Counseling supervision: Theory, skills, and practice.* London: Cassell.

Chard, K. M., Weaver, T. L., & Resick, P. A. (1997). Adapting cognitive processing therapy for child sexual-abuse survivors. *Cognitive and Behavioral Practice, 4,* 31–52.

Cicchetti, D., & Toth, S. L. (1995). A developmental psycopathology perspective on child abuse and neglect. *Journal of the American Academy of Child and Adolescent Psychiatry, 34,* 541–565.

Cohen, J. A., Berliner, L., & March, J. S. (2000). Treatment of children and adolescents. In E. B. Foa, T. M. Keane, & M. J. Friedman (Eds.), *Effective treatments of PTSD* (pp. 330–332). New York: Guilford Press.

Costello, J. E., Erkanli, A., Fairbank, J. A., & Angold, A. (2002). The prevalence of potentially traumatic events in childhood and adolescence. *Journal of Traumatic Stress, 13,* 99–112.

Davis, J. I., & Mickelson, D. J. (1994). School counselors: Are you aware of ethical and legal aspects of counseling? *The School Counselor, 42,* 5–12.

Deblinger, E., Stauffer, L. B., & Steer, R. A. (2001). Comparative efficacies of supportive and cognitive–behavioral group therapies for young children who have been sexually abused and their nonoffending mothers. *Child Maltreatment, 6,* 332–343.

Edgeworth, J., & Clark, A. (2000). Child abuse. In A. Clark (Ed.), *What works for children and adolescents? A critical review of psychological interventions with children, adolescents and their families* (pp. 17–48). London: Routledge.

Ehrensaft, M. K., Cohen, P., Brown, J., Smailes E., Chen, H., & Johnson, J. G. (2003). Intergenerational transmission of partner violence: A 20-year prospective study. *Journal of Consulting and Clinical Psychology, 71,* 741–753.

Etherington, K. (2000). Supervising counselors who work with survivors of childhood sexual abuse. *Counseling Psychology Quarterly, 13,* 377–389.

Falender, C. A., & Shafranske, E. P. (2004). *Clinical supervision: A competency-based approach.* Washington DC: American Psychological Association.

Falvey, J. E. (2002). *Managing clinical supervision: Ethical practice and legal risk management.* Pacific Grove, CA: Brooks/Cole.

Feeney, N. C., Foa, E. B., Treadwell, K. R. H., & March, J. (2004). Posttraumatic stress disorder in youth: A critical review of the cognitive–behavioral treatment outcome literature. *Professional Psychology Research and Practice, 35,* 466–476.

Figley, C. R. (1995). *Compassion fatigue: Coping with secondary traumatic stress disorder in those who treat the traumatized.* New York: Brunner/Mazel.

Figley, C. R., & Kleber, R. J. (1995). Beyond the "victim": Secondary traumatic stress. In R. J. Kleber, C. R. Figley, & B. P. R. Gersons (Eds.), *Beyond trauma: Cultural and societal dynamics* (pp. 75–98). New York: Plenum Press.

Foa, E. B., Keane, T. M., & Friedman, M. J. (Eds). (2000). *Effective treatments of PTSD.* New York: Guilford Press.

Friedman, D., & Kaslow, N. J. (1986). The development of professional identity in psychotherapists: Six stages in the supervision process. *Clinical Supervisor, 4,* 29–49.

Gentry, J. E., & Baranowsky, A. B. (1999). *Treatment manual for accelerated recovery from compassion fatigue.* Toronto, Ontario, Canada: Psych Ink Resources.

Hanson, T. C., Hesselbrock, M., Tworkowski, S. M., & Swan, S. (2002). The prevalence and management of trauma in the public domain: An agency and clinician perspective. *The Journal of Behavioral Health Services and Research, 29,* 365–380.

Harper, K., & Steadman, J. (2003). Therapeutic boundary issues in working with childhood sexual-abuse survivors. *American Journal of Psychotherapy, 57,* 64–79.

Henggeler, S. W., Schoenwald, S. K., Liao, J. G., Letourneau, E. J., & Edwards, D. L. (2002). Transporting efficacious treatments to field settings: The link between supervisory practices and therapist fidelity in MST programs. *Journal of Clinical Child Psychology, 31,* 155–167.

Horwath, J. (1995). The impact of fatal child abuse cases on staff: Lessons for trainers and managers. *Child Abuse Review, 4,* 351–355.

Isaacs, M. L. (1999). School counselors and confidentiality: Factors affecting professional choices. *Professional School Counseling, 2,* 258–266.

Izzard, S. (2001). The responsibility of the supervisor supervising trainees. In S. Wheeler & D. King (Eds.), *Supervising counsellors: Issues of responsibility* (pp. 75–92). London: Sage.

Kendall-Tackett, K. A., Williams, L. M., & Finkelhor, D. (1993). Impact of sexual abuse in children: A review and synthesis of recent empirical studies. *Psychological Bulletin, 113,* 164–180.

King, S. (2003). Managing the aftermath of serious case reviews. *Child Abuse Review, 12,* 261–269.

Ladany, N., Hill, C. E., Corbett, M. M., & Nutt, E. A. (1996). Nature, extent, and importance of what psychotherapy trainees do not disclose to their supervisors. *Journal of Counseling Psychology, 43,* 10–24.

Lewis, M. W., & Lewis, A. C. (1996). Peer helping programs: Helper role, supervisor training, and suicidal behavior. *Journal of Counseling and Development, 74,* 307–313.

Linehan, M. (1993). *Cognitive–behavioral treatment of borderline personality disorder.* New York: Guilford Press.

Lorvin, M. (1999). Parental murder and suicide: Posttraumatic stress disorder in children. *Journal of Child and Adolescent Psychiatric Nursing, 12,* 110–117.

McCann, I. L., & Pearlman, L. A. (1990). Vicarious traumatization: A framework for understanding the psychological effects of working with victims. *Journal of Traumatic Stress, 3,* 131–149.

Meyers, T. W., & Cornille, T. A. (2002). The trauma of working with traumatized children. In C. R. Figley (Ed.), *Treating compassion fatigue* (pp. 39–56). New York: Brunner-Routledge.

Munson, C. E. (2001). *Assessment, diagnosis and treatment of the traumatized child.* Binghamton, NY: Haworth Press.

Nelson, M. L., & Friedlander, M. L. (2001). A close look at conflictual supervisory relationships: A trainee perspective. *Journal of Counseling Psychology, 48,* 384–395.

Rutter, M. (1987). Psychosocial resilience and protective mechanisms. *American Journal of Orthopsychiatry, 57,* 316–331.

Schamess, G., Streider, F. H., & Connors, K. M. (1997). Supervision and staff training for children's group psychotherapy: General principles and applications with cumulatively traumatized, inner-city children. *International Journal of Group Psychotherapy, 47,* 399–425.

Stamm, B. H. (1999). *Secondary traumatic stress: Self-care issues for clinicians, researchers, and educators* (2nd ed.). Baltimore: Sidran Foundation & Press.

Stamm, B. H. (2002). Measuring compassion satisfaction as well as fatigue: Developmental history of the Compassion Fatigue and Satisfaction Test. In C. R. Figley (Ed.), *Treating compassion fatigue* (pp. 107–119). New York: Brunner/Mazel.

Stein, B. D., Jaycox, L. H., Kataoka, S. H., Wong, M., Tu, W., Elliott, M. N., et al. (2003, February 5). Mental health intervention for schoolchildren exposed to violence: A randomized, controlled trial. *Journal of the American Medical Association, 290,* 603–611.

Stoltenberg, C. D., McNeill, B., & Delworth, U. (1998). *IDM supervision: An integrated developmental model of supervising counselors and therapists.* San Francisco: Jossey-Bass.

Wells, M., Trad, A., & Alves, M. (2003). Training beginning supervisors working with new trauma therapists: A relational model of supervision. *Journal of College Student Psychotherapy, 17*(3), 19–39.

Williams, A. (1995). *Visual and active supervision: Roles, focus, techniques.* New York: Norton.

Yalom, I. (1995). *The theory and practice of group psychotherapy.* New York: Basic Books.

Yule, W. (2001). When disaster strikes—the need to be "wise before the event": Crisis intervention with children. *Advances in Mind–Body Medicine, 17,* 191–196.

12

SUPERVISION IN SCHOOL MENTAL HEALTH

SHARON H. STEPHAN, ELEANOR T. DAVIS,
PATRICIA CALLAN BURKE, AND MARK D. WEIST

Recent decades witnessed a significant movement in child and adolescent mental health toward the implementation of school-based services (Weist, 1997). Recognizing that schools alone cannot address student emotional and behavioral problems and that many, if not most, youth in need of services fail to access school and community services, many community agencies (e.g., mental health centers and health departments) partnered with schools to improve access to and quality of mental health care for youth (Kutash & Rivera, 1996; Weist, Myers, Hastings, Ghuman, & Han, 1999). We call this collaborative effort to develop a full array of school-based, mental health services *expanded school mental health* (ESMH). Although many local efforts may be less ambitious than those described as ESMH, the lessons of ESMH apply to most school-based, mental health services. Schools usually have their own staff, including school counselors,

Supported by cooperative agreement U93 MC 00174 from the Office of Adolescent Health, Maternal, and Child Health Bureau (Title V, Social Security Act), Health Resources and Services Administration, with cofunding by the Center for Mental Health Services, Substance Abuse, and Mental Health Services Administration.

school social workers, and school psychologists that provide limited mental health services. Therefore, ESMH programs augment existing programs (Pavola, Carey, & Cobb, 1996; Waxman, Weist, & Benson, 1999). An augmentation strategy means ESMH staff that come from outside the school often conduct a delicate dance to fill gaps and to advance programs without stepping on the turf of school staff. The choreography of this dance is one factor that makes supervision in ESMH unique. To avoid missteps in this chapter, *school* is used as an adjective for staff employed by the schools, and ESMH or school-based will be used for clinicians entering schools as part of a community collaborative. This chapter reviews the challenges of supervising mental health services in schools, suggests guiding principles, and offers examples from the growing quality-improvement literature as it applies to supervision in the schools.

BACKGROUND

Over the past 2 decades, the mental health needs of school children and the problem of accessing services for them have led to increased federal, state, and local support for services in the schools (Weist, Evans, & Lever, 2003). This trend is reinforced by data suggesting that ESMH programs reach many minority youth and students with less obvious problems such as depression and anxiety—children who often fail to receive services in traditional sites (Weist et al., 1999). Evaluation data also document the effectiveness of ESMH programs in improving a number of emotional, behavioral, and academic outcomes in students (Armbruster & Lichtman, 1999; Nabors & Reynolds, 2000).

Supervisors in ESMH programs have available a growing literature on quality assessment and improvement (QAI) in school mental health services. This literature includes (a) reviews on the background, present challenges, and critical issues in the field (Adelman et al., 1999; Evans, 1999; Flaherty, Weist, & Warner, 1996); (b) reviews and conceptual articles focused on QAI (Ambrose, Weist, Schaeffer, Nabors, & Hill, 2002; Nabors, Reynolds, & Weist, 2000; Weist, Nabors, Myers, & Armbruster, 2000); (c) articles on interdisciplinary collaboration and effective practice in the schools (Pavola et al., 1996; Rosenblum, DiCecco, Taylor, & Adelman, 1995; Waxman et al., 1999); and (d) outcome evaluations of school mental health programs (Armbruster & Lichtman, 1999; Jennings, Pearson, & Harris, 2000; Nabors & Reynolds, 2000).

The Center for School Mental Health Analysis and Action (CSMHA), one of two centers federally funded in 1995 to advance school mental health in the United States, has been a leader in recent efforts to investigate and to establish standards for the QAI process. Staff at CSMHA conceived a set of 10 empirically supported principles reflecting best practice in school mental health programs. Based on criteria for health and mental health care for children developed by the National Assembly on School-Based Health Care and the Child and Adolescent Service System Program, these principles serve as a foundation for research on services in schools. For each principle, CSMHA staff developed corresponding indicators that allow ESMH programs to assess their status and to develop plans to improve their practice. Key indicators of quality ESMH programs include easy access to services, stakeholder involvement, evidence-based practice, well-trained staff, and appropriate, effective supervision.

A central CSMHA principle of best practice in ESMH states that staff members are held to high ethical standards; are committed to children, adolescents, and families; and display an energetic, flexible, responsive, and proactive style in delivering services. Two indicators that correspond to this principle specifically address school mental health supervision—(a) Do you generally feel well trained and well supervised to handle the unique demands of school-based practice? and (b) Do you feel supported by your supervisor and other management staff? In developing and using these indicators, CSMHA staff carefully studied supervision in school settings. The authors' experience with supervisory issues was also forged in the University of Maryland School Mental Health Program (SMHP), a well supported and effective ESMH program that works collaboratively with CSMHA. Established in 1989 in four schools, the SMHP now operates in 30 elementary, middle, and high schools in Baltimore. Staff at the SMHP includes social workers; clinical, school, and counseling psychologists; licensed professional counselors; and child and adolescent psychiatrists, as well as trainees in these disciplines from the premasters to postdoctoral levels. This chapter reflects the fruits of our hands on efforts in the SMHP.

ADDRESSING THE DEMANDS OF CLINICAL TRAINING AND SUPERVISION IN EXPANDED SCHOOL MENTAL HEALTH

Unlike professionals specifically trained to work in schools (e.g., school social workers or counselors), clinically trained ESMH professionals who enter the schools encounter a new system and culture (see Sarason, 1982, for a thoughtful guide to this culture). New ESMH clinicians must learn to work with limited space and materials. They must learn a significant body of laws and regulations pertaining to special education. They must learn to creatively match services to funding sources. The literature on the supervision of school counselors, including school-employed psychologists and social workers, can inform the process of ESMH training and supervision. The first author also participated in recent surveys of ESMH clinicians to gain a perspective on their work, on models of service delivery, and on supervisory and training needs (Turner, Marcantonio, & Stephan, 2003; Stephan, Davis, & Callan, 2004). This will also inform the discussions which follow.

Integrating Mental Health Clinicians Into the School

Integrating oneself into the school setting is critical for the acceptance of services provided by ESMH clinicians. Each system and each school will present their own challenges, and the ESMH professional will need guides and informants. It is hoped that the supervisor knows the school well enough to guide the supervisee in establishing alliances and in avoiding minefields. If, however, the supervisor has no prior exposure to a school, it is recommended that he or she make a visit to the school or conduct on-site supervision, accompany the clinician to meetings with the principal or school staff, and become familiar with the school's characteristics (e.g., demographics, performance, and neighborhood). To facilitate school integration, training and supervision should address each of the following dimensions: (a) establishing rapport with school staff; (b) assessing school needs and planning services; (c) informing staff of the programs and services offered through ESMH; (d) involvement on school teams or committees; and (e) establishing services that fit existing school programs, services, and staff.

Establishing Rapport With School Staff

New school mental health clinicians promote integration by developing rapport with teachers, administrators, school-employed mental health workers, and other school staff (Tashman, Waxman, Nabors, & Weist, 1998). As described in chapter 7 of this volume, a collaborative spirit and positive relationships may be more critical than one's services in establishing a new program. Supervisors might suggest avenues to facilitate rapport, such as joining teachers for lunch, participating in staff's social activities, attending school events (e.g., performances, ball games), or simply engaging staff and students in the halls.

Assessing School Needs and Planning Services

In collaboration with school staff, clinicians should conduct a broad assessment of school needs to match services to staff, student, and family concerns and to avoid duplication of resources (Weist et al., 2000). An initial assessment creates an excellent venue for collaboration and for learning from school personnel. Expectancies can be clarified regarding the services and the role of the ESMH clinician. School expectancies (e.g., "We'll have someone to straighten out the disruptive children") may be quite different from clinician expectancies (e.g., "This will be a great place to provide preventive services"). In approaching needs assessment, supervisors can help clinicians consider the scope, the formality, the timing, the language, and the content of the assessment in light of the school's culture. Needs assessment and resource mapping can occur in forums or in focus groups with students, families, and teachers and may include brief surveys on pressing problems in the school and on recommendations to address them. Examples of pressing problems that ESMH staff might be asked to address include, teacher–student conflict, school climate issues (e.g., safety, harassment, and respect), and bullying. Strategic analysis and planning sessions with school mental health staff can identify gaps in services and highlight ineffective versus effective approaches. A good needs assessment will augment the services of school staff and address the priorities of all stakeholders.

Informing Staff of the Programs and Services Offered Through Expanded School Mental Health

Working within the framework established in the assessment, ESMH clinicians must educate school staff, formally or informally, about their work. Given the stigma sometimes associated with mental health services, clinicians should be alert to dispel any myths about their purpose and function. They should describe their services in straightforward, jargon-free, and user-friendly language. Supervisors should encourage clinicians to engage school personnel in ongoing dialogue. They can also assist clinicians in defining their roles and responsibilities to school staff. For example, the ESMH clinician will consult with faculty on effective discipline, but will not be a disciplinarian; or the clinician may assist a teacher in finding resources when he comes to her with a family problem, but may not offer him services. As one clinician in Stephan et al.'s (2004) focus group indicated, "Supervisors help remind us what our role is as a clinician and help us to have boundaries."

Involvement on School Teams or Committees

A strategic step in integrating oneself into the school is to participate with school staff in groups, such as a child study team, a crisis intervention team, or a school climate committee, that facilitate the mission, the morale, or the future of the school. Supervisors should encourage clinicians to collaborate with school staff when they think they can contribute to school improvement efforts (Stephan et al., 2004).

Establishing Services That Fit Existing School Programs, Services, and Staff

Because ESMH clinicians augment existing services, they must avoid the turf of current providers (Pavola et al., 1996; Waxman et al., 1999).

One school social worker may work with parents to help children who are lagging academically, while another may conduct groups for children with low self-esteem. A school psychologist, backlogged with special education evaluations, may have struggled to carve out a niche to counsel a group of potential dropouts. Supervisors should emphasize the need for ESMH clinicians to be aware of the roles and the expertise claimed by existing staff and the vital need for collaborative relationships. Collaboration requires a mutual respect and a refusal of any group to accept situations that compromise the other (e.g., accepting the offer of an office from a principal that displaces a school counselor twice a week). Staff turnover, budget adjustments, and political maneuverings all influence the climate of a school. Periodic assessments of that climate are relevant to supervision. A changing environment necessitates sensitivity to organizational issues and flexibility from ESMH clinicians.

Because school integration is a continuous process, it should be consistently addressed in supervision. In Stephan et al.'s (2004) study, clinicians reported that supervisors helped with introductions to school administrators in understanding a school's mental health needs, in developing priorities, in improving time management, and in defining boundaries.

Understanding the Community

Clinicians report that a supervisor's knowledge of a school's surrounding community helps establish meaningful services to youth and families (Stephan et al., 2004). Is it a multiethnic community? Are there tensions between student groups? Do these tensions spill over to staff? What is the history of the community's relationship with the school or with mental health services? Such information is crucial in developing programs appropriate to the community's culture and context (Weist et al., 2000). Turner et al. (2003) also noted that a supervisor's awareness of community resources is critical given a new clinician's limited time, experience, and training. The experienced supervisor can assist the clinician in referring youth and families to appropriate resources, such as legal, housing, or recreational services.

Ensuring Adequate School Resources

Scarce resources and competing demands for space may require supervisors to advocate for a suitable treatment environment (Turner et al., 2003). Clinicians often joke that they are lucky to get the janitor's closet to see students. They may have to carry charts from room to room, meet students in the library, or negotiate with school staff to access a telephone. Consider the following vignette:

A newly hired postdoctoral fellow, on her first day in the school, discovered that her office space was reassigned, and she now had a shared cubby with no phone and no locked file. Wisely, she approached her supervisor with her dismay, rather than confronting school administrators early in her tenure and at a hectic time in the school year. Until the matter could be resolved, the supervisor advised her in this situation to refrain from seeing students in the cubicle setting, because their privacy could not be ensured, and advised her instead to use her time becoming acquainted with teaching staff, conducting classroom observations of students on her caseload, and attending school meetings. Acting as her advocate, the supervisor visited the principal, who had contracted for services and offered the fellow a private space, a phone line, and a secure space for files. The on-site meeting allowed the principal to grasp the necessity of adequate resources and to correct the situation.

Understanding Education Policies and Regulations

In a focus group, ESMH clinicians emphasized the need for supervisors to have a working knowledge of education policy and of relevant federal, state, and local initiatives (Stephan et al., 2004). Any supervisor of mental health services for children should have a working knowledge of special education laws and regulations, but such knowledge is essential in supervising school-based clinicians. The No Child Left Behind Act of 2001 (P.L. 107-110) and the President's New Freedom Commission on Mental Health (2003), both have implications for providing mental health services in schools. Laws and regulations are often the basis of advocacy in the schools. When an ESMH clinician presents a need to advocate for a child, the supervisor can help her balance the needs of the child and the need to maintain an effective alliance with the school. With regard to special education, most regions have independent advocacy groups to which families can be referred.

Different Grade Levels Pose Different Challenges

Presenting problems, resources and staffing differ at different grade levels. Weist et al. (2000), for example, found that school administrators rated substance abuse and behavioral problems as worsening from elementary to high school. Internalizing problems, such as anxiety and depression, were considered most serious in high school. These findings suggest ways in which administrators' expectancies can facilitate or can hinder school programs. Although the data of Weist et al. suggested school administrators were less attuned to internalizing issues in younger children, the transition from elementary to middle school can be very stressful for shy and fearful children. Supervisor's understanding of the interface between child development, childrens' problems, and school expectancies can guide ESMH clinicians in developing effective, prevention programs.

School-Based Clinicians Confront a Range of Presenting Problems

Referrals to school-based clinicians vary greatly in complexity. Clinicians often express concern about the abundance of referrals and the severity of presenting issues given their time constraints and their scope of training (Stephan et al., 2004). When treatment needs are beyond a clinician's expertise or exceed time and program constraints (e.g., regular individual therapy or intensive daily contact), supervisors must support clinicians in making informed adjustments or outside referrals. Supervisors can assist in the development of a referral protocol and can identify potential referral sources. Some school districts have alternative programs for youth with special needs (e.g., hard of hearing or aggressive youth). These youth often require specialized services and, therefore, require ESMH clinicians, and supervisors, with special expertise.

Walking Alone on the Service Continuum

School-based clinicians, who are often the only mental health providers in the school, may feel a need to provide a full continuum of care. Although school mental health programs often seek to establish a continuum, including universal prevention activities, targeted interventions, and direct treatment, supervisors lead clinicians in managing service demands while maintaining quality and avoiding burnout. Consider the following vignette:

> When a seasoned, social worker attended a recent group supervision meeting, she worried that she was being pulled in too many directions to be effective in any of her pursuits. She had been asked to lead a universal mental health promotion program, to offer mental health presentations in several classrooms, to serve on three school committees, and to run several prevention groups with the health and guidance staff—all while meeting her billing requirements for individual and family therapy with more serious clinical cases. She was extending her hours at the school and was clearly stressed.
>
> Her supervisor and colleagues discussed strategies to alleviate her stress, while maintaining quality care. They suggested she meet with other health and mental health providers in the school to coordinate their efforts, to ensure youth in need were served, and to avoid service duplication. One colleague shared a strategy of arriving 30 minutes prior to the start of the school day to organize paperwork, outline a schedule, and plan for flexibility in the event of no shows or crises. The supervisor also suggested that the clinician resist her inclination

to continue seeing students and families until quitting time and that the clinician allow herself 30 minutes to wrap up paperwork, session notes, and other details. Finally, the group discussed boundaries and limit setting, encouraging the clinician to prioritize her work without feeling compelled to save the world, or, in this case, to save the school.

Preparing School-Based Clinicians to Offer Crisis Intervention

Family tragedies, the death of a child, and the suicide of a classmate, all require a mental health response in the schools. On a broader scale, natural disasters, outbreaks of school violence, and terrorism call for crisis intervention. Supervisors should help ESMH clinicians collaborate with school personnel in the development of plans for both expected and unexpected crises in the schools (see also chap. 11 of this volume regarding supervision of trauma therapy).

Matching Services to Funding

Sustained funding is an ongoing struggle for ESMH programs. Often they rely on blended funding from multiple sources. Supervisors should be aware of the contracts, the grants, and the other support available to the program. Then they can assist clinicians in aligning their services with funding sources and can assure that clinicians meet requirements dictated by funding agencies, such as working with a certain number of students each week (Stephan et al., 2004).

SUPERVISORY SUPPORT OF SCHOOL MENTAL HEALTH CLINICIANS

Given the unique demands of ESMH, it is critical to ensure that clinicians feel adequately supported in their roles. Comprehensive training to prepare clinicians for school settings and for informed clinical supervision is key to meaningful support. Supervision should also encourage the use of empirically supported therapies—a strategy illuminated in chapter 7 of this volume.

On-Site Versus Off-Site Supervision

School mental health supervisors are often located off-site, unlike the traditional settings where supervisors and supervisees operate in the same clinical setting. They may practice in a clinic, a program office, or a different school and may supervise clinicians in multiple sites. In rural areas, schools may hire master's-level professionals, who require supervision by state regulation and who can find supervisors only outside their community. The benefits of on-site supervision are so sufficient that we encourage at least some supervision to occur in the supervisee's school. Most ESMH clinicians interviewed by Turner et al. (2003) indicated that their ideal supervision arrangement would be school based. These clinicians noted that on-site supervision, whether or not the supervisor actually worked on site, provided a sense that the supervisor understood the intensity and the volume of their caseloads. On-site supervision also promoted the supervisor's understanding of the school's policies, staff, climate, and organization.

Supervisors Match Supervision to the Demands of School Practice

Supervision should encompass the diverse activities of counselors in the schools. Kahn (1999) noted that clinical supervision traditionally emphasized one-on-one counseling and frequently failed to incorporate other facets of school-based service, including group counseling, consultation, coordination, and prevention. Roberts and Borders (1994) surveyed school counselors and found that their preferences for supervision were often inconsistent with what they received. Although most of their time was devoted to counseling students, many received supervision from school principals who emphasized administrative and program issues rather than emphasizing counseling skills. The ESMH clinicians surveyed by Stephan et al. (2004) reported the opposite experience—supervisors tended to emphasize clinical case review and to shortchange school-specific or program concerns.

Offering Structured, Consistent Supervision

School mental health clinicians consider consistency and structure to be critical elements of supervision (Stephan et al., 2004). Working in school environments that were often chaotic, clinicians wanted regular supervisory support. Supervisors who demonstrated reliability and respect for the supervision process were highly valued. This same sentiment is reflected in a list of practices to avoid from the supervision literature:

> Showing up late for supervisory sessions or ending them early, canceling supervision or scheduled meetings times, receiving and accepting telephone calls or other interruptions during supervision, seeming preoccupied, writing clinical notes and looking at other materials during supervision, and in any way demonstrating a lack of investment in supervision and in the supervisee. (Barnett, Youngstrom, & Smook, 2001, pp. 219–220)

Offering Supervision Throughout Professional Development

Supervisors must be mindful of the different needs of supervisees based on their training and experience. For example, Roberts (2001) noted that school-based interns and trainees require significant help to build the confidence and self-sufficiency demanded by a school environment. Matthes (1992) claimed that school-based trainees were often expected to assume the same responsibilities as experienced clinicians and were confronted with sink-or-swim situations. He argued that such situations were disrespectful to the trainee and were potentially dangerous to the students being served. Such situations clearly call for supervisory intervention to protect all parties. More advanced school mental health clinicians require less daily management and confidence-building than those who are not as advanced, but they benefit from supportive supervision to promote clinical skills, to decrease isolation, and to encourage self-care to prevent burnout (Stephan et al., 2004). Although provision of supervision is standard for students and trainees, it is not necessarily provided for practicing school mental health clinicians, particularly those who are licensed (Page, Pietrzak, & Sutton, 2001). Despite this tendency, ESMH clinicians interviewed by Stephan et al. emphasized the value of supervision throughout their school careers. Although they noted that the nature of supervision might change over the course of one's professional development, they said the need for supervisory support endures. Other supervisory interests expressed by the ESMH clinicians included supplementing individual supervision with peer or group supervision and training in specific techniques and interventions relevant to school mental health throughout the supervisory process. This reflects openness to the introduction of empirically supported interventions.

Supervisor Training

Although supervision is a critical component of quality in school mental health programs, few supervisors receive prior training in supervision. In a national survey of school psychologists, Ross and Goh (1993) found only 11.2% of supervisors had actually received graduate coursework or training in supervision prior to supervising clinicians. Holloway and Neufeldt (1995) reported similar findings, and suggested that the lack of supervisor training may reflect "a holdover" from traditional models that assumed a trained therapist was a good supervisor. Expanded school mental health programs, therefore, should consider engaging supervisors in a training process encompassing both general guidelines for successful supervision and approaches specific to work in the schools.

CONCLUSION

The future growth and improvement of ESMH programs hinges on services that are valued, that demonstrate high quality, and that lead to results desired by school and community members. Effective supervision is critical to effective ESMH, yet our review found limited literature on school-based supervision. Supervision of school services is a priority research and training need. Although the school mental health field is developing rapidly, estimates indicate that most schools still provide little mental health care for youth. Funding for comprehensive programs, such as ESMH, remains tenuous. In this environment, supports for programs and for program staff are often minimal or nonexistent. Supervision, if funded through school mental health contracts, is normally funded at nominal levels (e.g., 1 hour per week). Although this may meet minimal standards, it probably falls short of what school clinicians need and can be a barrier to important practices, such as on-site supervision by off-site supervisors. Significant advocacy is needed to improve the support and infrastructure for ESMH programs. High among the needed improvements is intensive, quality supervision to implement a range of strong, empirically supported interventions for the stressed children in our schools.

REFERENCES

Adelman, H. S., Taylor, L., Weist, M. D., Adelsheim, S., Freeman, B., Kapp, L., et al. (1999). Mental health in schools: A federal initiative. *Children's Services: Social Policy, Research, and Practice, 2*, 95–115.

Ambrose, M. G., Weist, M. D., Schaeffer, C., Nabors, L. A., & Hill, S. (2002). Evaluation and quality improvement in school mental health. In H. S. Ghuman, M. D. Weist, & R. M. Sarles (Eds.), *Providing mental health services to youth where they are: School and community-based approaches.* New York: Taylor & Francis.

Armbruster, P., & Lichtman, J. (1999). Are school-based mental health services effective? Evidence from 36 inner-city schools. *Community Mental Health Journal, 35*, 493–504.

Barnett, J. E., Youngstrom, J. K., & Smook, R. G. (2001). Clinical supervision, teaching, and mentoring: Personal perspectives and guiding principles. *The Clinical Supervisor, 20*, 217–230.

Evans, S. W. (1999). Mental health services in schools: Utilization, effectiveness, and consent. *Clinical Psychology Review, 19*, 165–178.

Flaherty, L. T., Weist, M. D., & Warner, B. S. (1996). School-based mental health services in the United States: History, current models, and needs. *Community Mental Health Journal, 32*, 341–352.

Holloway, E. L., & Neufeldt, S. A. (1995). Supervision: Its contributions to treatment efficacy. *Journal of Consulting and Clinical Psychology, 63,* 207–213.

Jennings, J., Pearson, G., & Harris, M. (2000). Implementing and maintaining school-based mental health services in a large urban school district. *Journal of School Health, 70,* 201–296.

Kahn, B. (1999). Priorities and practices in field supervision of school counseling students. *Professional School Counseling, 3,* 128–132.

Kutash, K., & Rivera, V. R. (1996). *What works in children's mental health services? Uncovering answers to critical questions.* Baltimore: Brookes Publishing.

Matthes, W. A. (1992). Induction of counselors into the profession. *The School Counselor, 39,* 245–250.

Nabors, L. A., & Reynolds, M. W. (2000). Program evaluation activities: Outcomes related to treatment for adolescents receiving school-based mental health services. *Children's Services: Social Policy, Research, and Practice, 3,* 175–189.

Nabors, L. A., Reynolds, M. W., & Weist, M. D. (2000). Qualitative evaluation of a high school mental health program. *Journal of Youth and Adolescence, 29,* 1–14.

Page, B. J., Pietrzak, D. R., & Sutton, J. M. (2001). National survey of school counselor supervision. *Counselor Education and Supervision, 41,* 142–150.

Pavola, J. C., Carey, K., & Cobb, C. (1996). Interdisciplinary school practice: Implications of the service integration movement for psychologists. *Professional Psychology: Research and Practice, 27,* 34–40.

President's New Freedom Commission on Mental Health. (2003). *President's New Freedom Commission on Mental Health, achieving the promise: Transforming mental health care in America.* Rockville, MD: Author.

Roberts, E. B., & Borders, L. D. (1994). Supervision of school counselors: Administrative, program, and counseling. *School Counselor, 41,* 149–157.

Roberts, W. B. (2001). Site supervisors of professional school-counseling interns: Suggested guidelines. *Professional School Counseling, 4,* 208–216.

Rosenblum, L., DiCecco, M. B., Taylor, L., & Adelman, H. S. (1995). Upgrading school support programs through collaboration: Resource coordinating teams. *Social Work Education, 17,* 117–124.

Ross, R., & Goh, D. (1993). Participating in supervision in school psychology: A national survey of practices and training. *School Psychology Review, 22,* 63–80.

Sarason, S. B. (1982). *The culture of the school and the problem of change* (2nd ed.). Boston: Allyn & Bacon.

Stephan, S. H., Davis, E., & Callan, P. (2004). [Focus group responses of University of Maryland School Mental Health Program clinicians.] Unpublished raw data.

Tashman, N. A., Waxman, R. P., Nabors, L. A., & Weist, M. D. (1998). The PREPARE approach to training clinicians in school mental health programs. *Journal of School Health, 68,* 162–164.

Turner, E., Marcantonio, C., & Stephan, S. H. (2003, October). *Supervision in school mental health*. Poster presented at the 8th annual conference on Advancing School-Based Mental Health, Portland, OR.

Waxman, R. P., Weist, M. D., & Benson, D. M. (1999). Toward collaboration in the growing education–mental health interface. *Clinical Psychology Review, 19*, 239–253.

Weist, M. D. (1997). Expanded school mental health services: A national movement in progress. *Advances in Clinical Child Psychology, 19*, 319–352.

Weist, M. D., Evans, S. W., & Lever, N. A. (2003). Advancing mental health practice and research in schools. In M. D. Weist, S. W. Evans, & N. A. Lever (Eds.), *Handbook of school mental health: Advancing practice and research* (pp. 1–8). New York: Kluwer Academic/Plenum Publishers.

Weist, M. D., Myers, C. P., Danforth, J., McNeil, D. W., Ollendick, T. H., & Hawkins, R. (2000). Expanded school mental health services: Assessing needs related to school level and geography. *Community Mental Health Journal, 36*, 259–273.

Weist, M. D., Myers, C. P., Hastings, E., Ghuman, H., & Han, Y. (1999). Psychosocial functioning of youth receiving mental health services in the schools vs. community mental health centers. *Community Mental Health Journal, 35*, 69–81.

Weist, M. D., Nabors, L. A., Myers, C. P., & Armbruster, P. (2000). Evaluation of expanded school mental health programs. *Community Mental Health Journal, 36*, 395–412.

INDEX

Abused children, 193. *See also* Child
    abuse
    confidentiality when dealing with,
        197–198
    ethics in reporting cases involving,
        197–198
    and seduction, 196
    and therapeutic alliances, 19
    underserved treatment of, 36
Abuse survivors, 195
Accelerated Program for Compassion
    Fatigue, 199
Accountability
    and MST supervision, 146
    and multisystemic therapy, 145
    in supervisory relationship, 53–57
Acculturation, 78
Achenbach's dimensional measures, 36
A-C-T model of limit setting, 100–101
Adaptation, 128
ADHD. *See* Attention-deficit/
    hyperactivity disorder
Adlerian play therapy, 90–91, 98
Adolescent drug use, 139–140
Adult psychotherapy, 17
Adult talk therapy, 95
ADVANCED program, 163
Advocacy, 24, 67–68
Agencies, 20–21
    for Incredible Years Training Series
        support, 171–172
    policies affecting therapists working
        with traumatized children,
        203–204
Agenda setting, 111, 113, 119
American Academy of Child and Adoles-
    cent Psychiatry, 40
American Psychiatric Association, 66
American Psychological Association
    (APA)
    and dual roles of treatment provider,
        66
    Law and Mental Health Professionals,
        58n1

Anxiety disorders, of children, 125.
        See also Coping Cat program
APA. *See* American Psychological
        Association
ASPPB. *See* Association of State and
        Provincial Psychology Boards
Association of Play Therapy, 91
Association of State and Provincial
        Psychology Boards (ASPPB)
    and first supervisory settings, 20
    and supervisor–supervisee skill gap,
        13–14
Attention-deficit/hyperactivity disorder
        (ADHD), 44, 163
Audiotaping sessions
    avoidance in, 153–154
    in MST supervision, 156–157
Avoidance
    in audiotaping sessions, 153–154
    fit factors for, 155
    in multisystemic therapy supervision,
        153–154
Axline, Virginia, 91

Baerger's treatment of risk, 61n2
BASIC program, 163–165
Behavioral rehearsal, 164
Behavior-change methods, 164
Behaviorists, 39
Behavior therapy. *See also specific
        types, e.g.:* Dialectal behavior
        therapy
Bickman, L., 40
Bioethics, 52
Borderline personality disorder (BPD),
        178–179
Boundaries, 22–23, 196–197
Boundary crossing, 197
Boundary shift, 197
Boundary violations, 197
BPD (borderline personality disorder),
        178–179
Burnout, therapist. *See* Therapist burnout

Dialectical behavioral therapy (DBT)
supervision, 180–190
with individual therapy consultation
supervision, 186–187
skills group supervision for, 189
with telephone consultation
supervision, 187–189
and therapist skill acquisition,
181–183
therapy consultation team for,
183–186
Dinosaur Curriculum, 163–164
Discrimination model, 21
Distress-tolerance skills, 182–183
Division of Clinical Psychology (APA),
40
Domestic violence
children exposed to, 193
ethics when dealing with, 60
DSM–IV–TR. *See Diagnostic and Statistical
Manual of Mental Disorders*
Dual relationships, 63–64

Early adopters, 169
Early-onset conduct problems, 161
Eclectic-based orientations, 130
Ecology, social, 139
Ecosystemic play therapy, 91
Education policies, 215
Efficacy studies, 144
Electronic networks, 14
Emotional arousal, 119
Emotional awareness, 25
Emotion dysregulation, 179
Empirically supported treatments (ESTs),
44
for diagnosis and treatment analysis,
40–41
and efficacy, 144
manualized, 123
for therapists working with trauma-
tized children, 200–201
Enlarging the meaning, 97–98
ESMH. *See* Expanded school mental
health
EST. *See* Empirically supported
treatments
Esteem-building, 96–97
Ethical base, 54–55
Ethics, 51–68

for accountability in supervisory
relationship, 53–57
advocacy in, 24
in child abuse/neglect/domestic
violence situations, 60
and client record confidentiality,
59–60
of clinical and forensic role
entanglement, 66
of confidentiality, 197
in dual relationships, 63–64
in evaluating incompetent and
impaired professionals, 66–67
and high-risk behaviors of clients,
61–62
in identifying criminality and
exploitation, 67
and informed consent, 58–59
lapses of, by child clinicians, 53
and legal problems, 57–67
professional board regulations for,
52–53
and professional development, 24
in reporting abused children cases,
197–198
with suicidal clients, 60–61
supervision techniques for
monitoring, 56–57
in termination of clinical
relationships, 64–66
and treatment confidentiality, 60
in wrap-around treatment
approaches, 62–63
Ethnic diversity, of supervisees, 73
Evaluation
as a function of supervision, 25
of incompetent and impaired
professionals, 66–67
self-evaluation, 25
of supervisees, 26–27
of supervisors, 27–28
of supervisory process, 26–27
of therapeutic process, 25
Evidence-based treatments, 40, 44.
See also specific types, e.g.:
Incredible Years Training
Series
applicability, 124
in community settings, 123
inexperience in implementing, 162
intervention length for, 169

Expanded school mental health (ESMH),
209–220
clinical training/supervision demands
of, 211–217
and community understanding, 214
in different grade levels, 215–216
and education policies/regulation, 215
and integrating mental health
clinicians into school, 212–214
and referrals to school-based
clinicians, 216
school resources for, 214–215
services vs. funding for, 217
supervisory support of, 217–219
Exploitation, identifying, 67

Family therapists, 39
Family therapy, 9
FEAR (Coping Cat program), 125–126
Feedback
in dialectal behavior therapy, 183
and multisystemic therapy
supervision, 145, 152
to supervisee during cognitive
therapy, 113–114
Feeling reflection, 96
Fidelity monitoring, 169–171
Filial therapy, 91, 101–103
Fit (term), 139
Fit analysis, 150, 155
Fit circle, 139–140
Fit factors, 155
Florida Secondary Traumatic Stress
Scale, 198
Focus on child, 94
Forensic roles, 66
Freud, Anna, 90
Friedberg, R. D., 114
Funding, for child psychotherapy, 38–39

Gender concerns, 16
Genuineness, radical, 182
Gert, B., 54
Gestalt play therapy, 98
Good intentions, 52
Grade levels (schoolchildren), 215–216
Group process checklist, 168
Group supervision, 16, 29
in CAADC, 128

example, 150, 151
and group process checklist, 168
managing, 154–155
for MST, 146–148
and multisystemic therapy
supervision, 146–148
for skills in DBT, 189
Group therapy
for parasuicidal adolescents, 184
peer-counseling groups, 202–203
supervisee in, 16
for traumatized children, 199–200,
202–203
unsupervised, 199
Guerney, Bernard, 102
Guerney, Louise, 102
Guided discovery, 109, 110

Haley, J., 39
Hallucinatory whitening, 80
Hansel, Joe, 61n2
Health Insurance Portability and
Accountability Act (HIPAA), 59
Helms, Janet E., 75
High-risk behaviors (children), 61–62
Holloway's systems approach to
supervision (SAS), 9, 10
Homework assignments, for supervisees,
116

IDM (individual development model) of
supervision, 15–16
Illusion of color blindness, 80
Incredible Years (IY) Training Series,
162–173
agency/organizational support for,
171–172
and behavior-change methods, 164
clinician supervision for, 166–169
clinician training in, 166
consultation for, 166–169
content of, 163–164
fidelity monitoring of, 169–171
group process checklist in, 168
intervention length for, 169
IY Agency Readiness Questionnaire,
171
IY Mentor certification, 167
peer-review in, 168

Incredible Years (IY) Training Series, *continued*
    peer support for, 167–168
    quality training workshops standard-
      ization for, 165–166
    recommendations for use of, 164
    for research, 164–165
    self-review in, 168
    standardized treatment package for,
      165
    strategies for, 165–172
    treatment materials/delivery standard-
      ization for, 165
Individual development model (IDM) of
    supervision, 15–16
Individualized treatment, 199–200
Individual supervision, 149
    and fit analysis, 155
    in multisystemic therapy supervision,
      149–150
    structure of, 149–150
Individual therapy consultation
    supervision, 186–187
Informed consent, 58–59
In-session behaviors, 156–157
Institutional/community setting, 19–21
Instruction, 27–28
Interdisciplinary training, 20–21
Interpretation, 43
Intervention, in filial therapy, 102
IY. *See* Incredible Years Training Series
IY Agency Readiness Questionnaire,
    171
IY Mentor certification, 167

Joint custody, 58
Jungian play therapy, 90, 98

Kanner, Leo, 17
Kazdin, A. E., 39
Kendall, P. C., 125–126
Klein, Melanie, 90

Laboratory research, 40–42
Landredth, G., 102
Late adopters, 172
Law and Mental Health Professionals, 58n1
Learning culture, 20

Legal problems, 57–67
Limit setting, 22, 99–102
    A-C-T model of, 100–101
    in filial therapy, 102
    in play therapy, 99–101

Manualized cognitive–behavioral therapy,
    125. *See also* Coping Cat program
Manualized empirically supported
    treatments, 123
Manualized treatments, 126–127
Manuals, 124–125
Marketing, social, 169
McClure, J. M., 114
Medical University of South Carolina,
    142
Medications, psychotropic, 37
Mental health system
    laws of, 58n1
    practices hurtful to children, 24
Mentors, 170
Modeling
    for ethical behavior, 24
    as a function of supervision, 28
Monitoring, 25
Moral rules, 54
MST. *See* Multisystemic therapy
MST Analytical Process, 141–142, 148
MST do-loop, 141
MSTS (Multisystemic Therapy Services,
    LLC), 142
Multicultural Counseling Knowledge and
    Awareness Scale, 75
Multicultural Environment Inventory—
    Revised, 76
Multicultural Supervision Inventory—
    Supervisors Version, 75
Multisystemic therapy (MST), 137–142,
    157–158
    and accountability, 145
    agency support of, 20
    clinicians implementing, 145
    conceptual basis for, 139–140
    drug treatment, 149–150
    MST Analytical Process, 141–142,
      148
    MST do-loop, 141
    and Multisystemic Therapy Services,
      LLC, 142
    principles, 140–142

Weekly consultations, 143
Weisz, John, 4
Whom-to-treat decision, 44
Work Group on Clinical Child
    Psychology (APA), 40–41
Wrap-around treatment approaches,
    ethics in, 62–63

Youth Anxiety and Depression Study
    (YADS), 125

CAADC cases vs., 130, 131
    supervision model at, for Coping
        Cat program, 128–132
    training model at, for Coping Cat
        program, 129
Youth suicide. *See* Suicide

Zero to Three: National Center for
    Infants, Toddlers, and Families,
    36

ABOUT THE EDITOR

T. Kerby Neill, PhD, completed a liberal arts degree in the Great Books program at the University of Notre Dame. He became interested in psychology during a 3 ½-year shipboard stint as a naval officer. In 1968, he finished a doctoral program in clinical psychology at Catholic University in Washington, DC, and began a 2-year postdoctoral fellowship in child psychology at the Menninger Foundation. After working for 4 years as director of an inner-city children's program for Yale University Medical School, Dr. Neill and his family moved to Lexington, Kentucky, where, over 22 years, he revived an interdisciplinary child guidance clinic for the Bluegrass Regional Mental Health and Mental Retardation Board, for which he developed an internship rotation approved by the American Psychological Association. He became a recognized child advocate and a leader in improving Kentucky's system of care for children with severe emotional problems.

Since 1995, Dr. Neill has served as a consultant to mental health programs, worked for 2 years as a volunteer in Guatemala, and closed his full-time career in the Department of Psychiatry at the University of Kentucky where he remains a voluntary faculty member. He continues to be an advocate and to consult part time, and he volunteers in a free mental health clinic for Lexington's Latino families. He has published numerous articles and two book chapters prior to editing this book. He has provided clinical supervision over a span of 35 years and offers advanced workshops on clinical supervision. Joyfully married for over 40 years, Dr. Neill relishes time with his wife, children, and grandchildren.

618.9289
N413

LINCOLN CHRISTIAN COLLEGE AND SEMINARY

3 4711 00186 6286